Ghostly
Past,
Capitalist
Presence

Man with giant ghost: from Ashutosh Mukhopadhyay's *Bhut Petni*

Ghostly Past, Capitalist Presence

A Social History of Fear in Colonial Bengal

Tithi Bhattacharya

Duke University Press Durham and London 2024

© 2024 DUKE UNIVERSITY PRESS
All rights reserved
Designed by Matthew Tauch
Typeset in MeropeBasic by Westchester Publishing Services

Library of Congress Cataloging-in-Publication Data
Names: Bhattacharya, Tithi, author.
Title: Ghostly past, capitalist presence : a social history of fear in colonial Bengal / Tithi Bhattacharya.
Description: Durham : Duke University Press, 2024. | Includes bibliographical references and index.
Identifiers: LCCN 2023046407 (print)
LCCN 2023046408 (ebook)
ISBN 9781478030713 (paperback)
ISBN 9781478026464 (hardcover)
ISBN 9781478059691 (ebook)
Subjects: LCSH: Religion and science—India—Bengal—History— 19th century. | Ghosts—India—Bengal—History. | Ghost stories, Bengali— History and criticism. | Bengal (India)—History—19th century. | Bengal (India)—Civilization—19th century. | Bengal (India)—Colonial influence. | India—History—British occupation, 1765–1947. | BISAC: HISTORY / Asia / South / India | RELIGION / Hinduism / General
Classification: LCC DS485.B44 B488 2024 (print) | LCC DS485.B44 (ebook) | DDC 954/.1403—dc23/eng/20240322
LC record available at https://lccn.loc.gov/2023046407
LC ebook record available at https://lccn.loc.gov/2023046408

Cover art: Man with giant ghost, from Ashutosh Mukhopadhyay's *Bhut Petni*.

Contents

A Note on Conventions · vii
Acknowledgments · ix

Introduction. Uncanny Histories: Ghosts, Fear, and Reason in Colonial Bengal · 1

ONE   "Undisciplined, Playful and Yet *Bhadra*": Old Ghosts and Their Advocates in an Age of Enlightenment · 22

TWO   The New Spirits · 55

THREE   Deadly Spaces: Haunted Homes and Haunting Histories · 82

FOUR   Enacting Ghosts: New Spirits, New Rituals · 97

FIVE   National Ghosts, Ghostly Nations · 130

Conclusion. Thinking about Ends and Beginnings · 155

Notes · 159
Bibliography · 187
Index · 203

A Note on Conventions

For the spelling of Bengali names, simplicity has been my central consideration. I have mostly avoided diacritical marks and retained some customary English renditions: Tagore, not Thakur. Notable Indian figures have been referred to by their first names but indexed under their last names, as is common in South Asian scholarship.

Acknowledgments

I started thinking about writing a book about Bengali ghosts more than a decade ago, but somehow the time was never right to give these Beings the attention they deserved. In the interregnum, many monsters appeared on the political scene, and I abandoned my ghosts to write a few books on feminism and Marxist theory. But I remained haunted.

I came back to the project while visiting a sugar plantation in the Caribbean, full of its own ghosts crying out for historical voice. That is a story for another day. However, since this book has been brewing for years, I have accumulated more debts than I can repay or even catalog.

A history of ghosts is, as I discovered, as difficult to write as it is rewarding. The difficulty was in its not having any predecessors in the field, even though, as a field, nineteenth-century Bengali history is one of the most oversubscribed. This challenge, however, enclosed its own reward. It allowed me to create my own archive as I worked and brought me in contact with some of the most generous scholars, friends, and comrades, whose contribution to shaping this project is as important as my own. The work of academic scholarship is so often performed in seclusion. It is the contribution of colleagues and comrades that help situate that work in the wider field and give it the context and bearing it needs.

I first discussed my ghosts with Sumit Sarkar and Tanika Sarkar, and both, in their characteristic fashion, gave me the indulgence I needed to begin this very odd project. Mandakranta Bose and Tirthankar Bose welcomed me as a family member when I was struggling to define the project on a postdoc at the University of British Columbia. My friend for many decades, Prachi Deshpande, was one of the first people to host my ghosts when I gave a talk at Berkeley on her invitation. Judith Misrahi-Barak at the University of Paul Valery brought many of us ghost hunters together at her conference, Postcolonial Ghosts. There, in the stunning city of Montpellier, I first tested my argument about spectral spatiality. It was about the same time that Rangan Chakraborty, then in charge of the Sunday section of the Bengali daily, *Anandabazar Patrika*, asked me to write about my research for the paper. I am very grateful to Rangan da, as that Bangla piece really was the kernel of this book. Rebekah Sheldon at Indiana University shares my interest in ghosts and goblins but does a much better job of articulating their connection to the modern; she gave me the opportunity to present my work to a group of brilliant co-thinkers whose rich comments and contributions helped me enormously.

I thought I was misreading my email when Amitav Ghosh agreed to read a copy of this manuscript. His excitement and encouragement for this book are more a testament to his generosity than to my competence. I will never be able to write such history-haunted novels, so I satisfied myself by writing a history about haunting.

Over the years I received several grants from Purdue University to make trips to the archives; without those, this book would have taken even longer than it did. My colleagues in the History Department at Purdue, Whitney Walton and Susan Curtis in particular, let me impose my many ideas and written drafts on them. Whitney and Susan are mentors that every woman faculty deserves; they remain intellectual godmothers to many projects, including my ghosts. My research assistant, Xuening Kong, was invaluable in locating typos and providing stimulating conversations about Chinese ghosts. Matthew Sayers, whose book *Feeding the Dead* was an important contribution to the field, turned out in person to be a wonderful interlocutor, with scholarly impulses both generous and generative.

David McNally's work on capitalism's monstrosity was such a delight and inspiration for this book. David is a comrade who shares his time and ideas enthusiastically with anyone wanting to understand capitalism. We are all lucky that he fights the system with the same vigor.

As a Marxist feminist I am naturally suspicious of families, but Pablo, Eliza, and Levi defy all misgivings and drown me in both memories and joy while making me greedy for more.

Gareth Dale became a cheerleader of my ghosts from the moment I took the book off the back burner. In a similar vein, Indranil Roychowdhury provided a home for me in Kolkata in the warmest, and most capacious, sense of the word. When I told my editor at Duke, Courtney Berger, that the book was about real ghosts rather than metaphorical ones, she said, "All the better." That's when I knew that both my Beings and I had found a home at Duke. My thanks go to the entire team at Duke and to my very careful copyeditor, Erin Davis.

Bill was away for some of the book's writing. I am grateful he came back.

The book, among other things, explores why and how precolonial ghosts were exiled out of the domain of fear (and into humor/children's literature) and their place usurped by the modern gothic. I ask why occultism and spiritualism among the Bhadralok intelligentsia emerged as "accepted" modes of reflecting on the afterlife and try to make sense of how such practices were imbricated in an ambient, but ever present, Hindu revivalism.

But why ghosts? One way to answer that question is to ask, "Why not?" After all, these Beings who dominated precolonial lifeworlds and provided meaning to them deserve the attention of the modern historian. But there is another reason. Since 1992 (the year of the destruction of the Babri Masjid by the far right), as scholars and citizens, we have all been trying to make sense of the rise of Hindutva. A lot of historical analysis of this "rise" has involved tracing its roots to nineteenth-century nationalism and the nation-state. While that kind of scholarship is important, I understand it to be akin to looking at the main avenues of social change. In this book I am interested in the alleyways, the by-lanes along which this change accreted. The exile and defanging of premodern ghosts and the crowning of the modern gothic as the *sole* mode of articulating fear were processes that helped compose a new lifeworld of the Hinduized nation. The ghostly world was a contested one. I study the contestations in order to better understand the consequences.

Which is why this book is for Shayari, the mightiest of Beings and the inheritor of the world we build.

Introduction

Uncanny Histories: Ghosts, Fear, and Reason in Colonial Bengal

The Tagore family of Jorasanko remains perhaps the most legendary family of nineteenth- and twentieth-century Calcutta.[1] Almost every member of this vast and uniquely talented household has been repeatedly commemorated and acknowledged in print and history. Dwarkanath Tagore, the nineteenth-century entrepreneur, was recognized and admired not only in Bengal but also by contemporary European royalty. His son, Debendranath Tagore, a leading figure in the reform movements of the nineteenth century, has gone down in history as Maharshi or the saint. Debendranath's youngest son, Rabindranath Tagore, Nobel laureate, reformer, and nationalist, needs no introduction. In addition to these more famous representatives, the Tagore family brimmed with writers, reformers, and iconoclasts. I, however, want to talk about those neglected members of the Tagore household who were duly honored by the Tagores themselves but have been sadly neglected by the present-day critic. This is perhaps because they were not living members of the family. I refer here to the ghosts who resided in the various trees and darkened, unsupervised corners of the Jorasanko house.

Rabindranath Tagore's account of his childhood, *Chelebela* (1940), begins with the bittersweet story of the Brahmadaitya's flight. This saintly Brahman ghost resided peaceably in a nut tree in the western part of the Jorasanko mansion. He would often stretch his legs between the tree and

FIGURE I.1 · Brahman ghost: from Parashuram's "Bhushundir Mathe"

the third-floor terrace and observe the everyday life of humanity with appropriate philosophical disdain.² He was not the only nonliving member of the Tagore family, for several other Beings similarly coexisted at Jorasanko alongside the living. There was, for instance, the greedy *shankhchunni* (a variety of female ghost), who could never pass up a good smelly fish. In the dark underground rooms where drinking water was stored lived other Beings famous for their huge ears, oppositely turned ankles, and gaping maws. All these Beings "people" the young Rabindranath's memoirs as concretely and as poignantly as his close relatives. In a city where electricity was yet to arrive, and trams were still pulled by horses, the Brahmadaitya and his comrades were not yet part of an unbelievable "fantastic" but, just like their human counterparts, were very much equal citizens of everyday reality.

Rabindranath's autobiography consequently is not structured in the manner of a supernatural narrative wherein he is leading his readers into the hesitant domain between faith and rationality. It is rather a realist account of the Calcutta of his childhood, still shaded by the greenery of ancient trees and quiet ponds, yet unharmed by the harsh light of the modern. The particular analogy of light and darkness is actually carried to an exquisite conclusion when Rabindranath recounts the circumstances that forced the domestic Brahmadaitya to finally leave. Eventually all the ponds of this older Calcutta, writes Rabindranath, were filled up, and they carried away with them the green veil of a rural dream. Electric lights blazed away the darkness. "The nut tree," he continues, "still stands, but even though it is still convenient to spread one's legs, the Brahmadaitya can no longer be found. There is more light now, both inside and outside."

Rabinandranath Tagore's account is an excellent entry point for our discussion of the uncanny in nineteenth-century Bengal, as it highlights some of the major themes that this book seeks to examine. Our starting point is the note of nostalgic regret in Rabindranath's narrative when he laments the flight of the Brahmadaitya. The ghost here is clearly tied up with a childhood world of safety, stable assurances, and simple beliefs. His disappearance likewise is contrasted with an adult world of rationality, urbanity, and a complex existence. While the implication for this sharp divide between the modern moment and romantic nostalgia for the premodern is consequential for the general argument of this book, let me begin here with something that primarily drew me to this project on the colonial uncanny.

First, a word about the concept itself. I want to retain here the original Freudian formulation of the "uncanny" as Freud famously defined it in his 1919 essay. For Freud, the uncanny, or *unheimlich* (the unhomely) was not the polar opposite of the *heimlich* (home/homely), but "that species of the frightening which leads back to that long known to us, once very familiar."[3] The uncanny returns us to what we tried to obscure, occult, or, to use Freud's language, repress. This makes the uncanny, as Homi Bhabha has insisted, a paradigmatic colonial and post-colonial condition, where "the uncanny forces of race, sexuality, violence, cultural and even climatic differences . . . emerge in the colonial discourse as the split and mixed texts of hybridity."[4] When we meet our premodern and modern ghosts we will note a sharp contrast between them, a contrast that I argue is because this modern sense of uncanny does not exist for our premodern ghostly Beings. Instead, they follow a different trajectory of fear and dread.

Consider the portrayal of the Brahmadaitya in Rabindranath's narrative and how it is carried out in remarkably realist terms, without resorting to the standard accoutrements of uncertainty and terror, the more common constituents in the portrayal of the fictional supernatural. Not only is the Brahmadaitya regarded without fear, but he is also remembered with feelings bordering on kinship. The reader is not left with an uncertainty about the existence of ghosts, the common emotional precondition of a modern ghost story, but a more fundamental uncertainty. We are left undecided on whether to celebrate the disappearance of the ghost and his verdant world of secure beliefs. In other words, the reader, along with the Tagores' pet Brahmadaitya, is left uncertain and resentful at the single most important element of nineteenth-century ideology: enlightenment rationality. The flight of the Brahmadaitya thus draws a line in the sand. For the child Rabindranath, he takes away with him an older world of companionable Beings and leaves behind a harshly lit and rootless modern or—to insert such affective modes into established circuits of intellectual debate—the Brahmadaitya abandons the young Rabindranath to a Weberian world of disenchantment. His departure can be regarded as an ideological marker, where the old certainties end and a new era begins.

This book is about the history and consequences of the flight of the Brahmadaitya. It maps, among other things, *how* the premodern ghosts were fundamentally different from their modern counterparts in their portrayal, emotional history, and social context; *why* they were displaced; and *in what ways* their departure was a symptom of a wider ideological calcification of national and religious identities. A warning is perhaps necessary here: I try, in this book, to write a *social history of fear*, thus making it a book about "real" ghosts, not metaphorical or Derridean ones. Race and empire predicated on capitalist development are crucial scaffolds to the story I tell here, for they help explain why and how the precolonial ghosts were exiled out of the domain of fear (and into humor/children's literature) and their place usurped by the modern gothic. I look at the rise of occultism and Spiritualism among the Bhadralok intelligentsia as "accepted" modes of reflecting on the afterlife and how such practices were imbricated in an ambient, but ever present, Hindu revivalism.

Old Ghosts for New

In 1879, Peary Chand Mittra, novelist, reformer, businessman, and leading intellectual, wrote that "for the last sixteen years," he had been "associated with spirits who are not away from me for a moment" and that he was "talking with them as I talk to those who are in flesh." Peary Chand first published this and other similar essays on Spiritualism in European journals such as the *London Spiritualist* and eventually compiled them into a book, *Spiritual Stray Leaves*, in 1879. "I am anxious," he wrote, "that spiritualism be solemnly thought of."[5] Peary Chand was a pioneer, but in a burgeoning field. From the mid-nineteenth century, the great and good of Calcutta were heavily involved in a wave of Spiritualism, broadly understood. Planchettes and séance sessions became a regular part of the social milieu of intellectuals, nationalists, and theologians alike. Societies such as the Calcutta Theosophical Society (1882) and the Calcutta Psychical Society (1904) sought to employ modern empirical methods to understand death and the afterlife. "Belief" and "faith," which were previously understood to be resolved issues, part of one's religion, suddenly became unstable categories needing new methods of embedding, namely, scientific proof. Consider this exchange with the older Rabindranath and his protégée, the poet Maitreyi Debi. When asked by Rabindranath to read some essays in Theosophist journals, Maitreyi declined, saying she did not "believe"—*biśbāsa*—in such things. Rabindranath was anything but pleased:

> Ah, here's your problem. Yes, while there is no proof (pramāna) to aid belief, there is no disproof (apramāna) either, is there? That which is equally true or untrue, how can I think of it only as untrue? You have all become great scientists these days. You disbelieve all that cannot be *systematically proved* [English in original]. How many things have proof in this world? There might be things in this world that are yet to be proved, or that can be proved. They may lie beyond human knowledge. They were *meant* [English in original] to be occulted, sometimes they reveal themselves to special individuals, but do not leave behind crude signs of proof.[6]

Gyan Prakash's history of science, in which he identifies the emergence of science in this period as a new arbiter of forms of knowledge (or science's transformation into modern Science, if you will), is a critical interlocutor for my argument. Science's role, Prakash shows, was not to wield "despotic power" but to negotiate between and authorize incommensurable knowledges. Prakash replaces a simplistic model of liberal modernization where Science and its attendant practices are imagined as bulldozing into oblivion what they deemed as un-Science or anti-Science. It is certainly true that the British and Western-educated Bengali elite alike campaigned vigorously against superstition. But what is significant about Prakash's argument about Science as *arbiter*, rather than despotic, is that it draws attention to processes by which Science emerged as the authorial power to legitimize *all* knowledge worlds. In other words, it became the framing device through which all phenomena were filtered and thereby judged. In his polemic with Maitreyi Debi, Rabindranath does not actually denounce Science but extends its authorial power. For him phenomena that lacked "systematic proof" were not that which could be deemed unscientific but were phenomena merely waiting for Science to develop adequate explanatory tools to understand them. This is precisely the framework that the Bengali Bhadralok developed about practices involving death and the afterlife, such as séances and planchettes. Occultism and/or Spiritualism, terms used interchangeably, were always referred to as Science. Questions of the existence of the soul or what happens to the soul after death, were sought to be resettled through the language of Science. Peary Chand Mittra noted occultism and Spiritualism as "two sciences" that both "evolved by the will-force" and "engaged the attention" of ancient Hindu scholars. This will-force was "the subtle body, or *linga sarira* . . . which lives after the natural body dies." But it was no longer enough to evoke the ancient sages to "prove" the workings of this subtle body, so Peary Chand tells us that the soul was "composed of subtle particles, rudiments, or atoms" perceptible to "beings of a superior order."[7]

One key project of this book is to explore these new ideas about the afterlife that emerged in contrast to the old ghosts, such as Rabindranath's Brahmadaitya, and ask how far such ideas reframed new relationships among Science, Superstition/Magic, and Religion. I note these categories in capital letters, for while the borders between them were certainly renegotiated in this period, I aim to show that the categories themselves were coproduced under the sign of the modern.

The literary corollary to what I call Scientific Spirituality was the appearance of unique ghost stories in the Bengali press loosely modeled on the Victorian Gothic form. Both these developments, those in the literary world and in the practical world of spiritual explorations, marked a sharp contrast from older, precolonial forms of thought about ghosts and the spirit world. The older ghosts were denizens of a multifaith, heterodox world where fear of them was a realist one, as real as the fear of wild animals. Like the natural world of wild beasts, there were several typologies of ghosts; some lived in the Sheora tree, some liked the wild marshes, while still others liked to possess newborn infants. The stories featuring such Beings, always oral, were never about the death that birthed them but rather about their lives. In these tales, ghosts married other ghosts, held elaborate feasts, gave birth to babies, and even died. In the vivid descriptions of their lives, these ghosts were stunningly different from the gothic specter whose entry into fiction was anchored in modern morality, in textual rigidity, and in a clear set of gendered expectations.

Here I want to signpost another key feature of my argument: I make a critical distinction between modern and premodern ghosts. Scholars of ghosts and the gothic most often operate with the discursive frames of "revival" or "remanent" when it comes to ghosts, historians favoring the former frame, anthropologists the latter. For instance, in his history of memory-making about the First World War, Jay Winter sees the growth of European

Spiritualism following the war as an "avalanche of the 'unmodern.'"[8] Ghost sightings by returning soldiers, and their participation in séances and related activities, are understood by Winter as "traditional, even archaic" forms arising from the deadly conflict.[9] In contrast, Heonik Kwon, in his powerful anthropological study of ghosts that appeared to the Vietnamese following the American war, similarly does not distinguish between the old folk ghosts and the new war ghosts, but sees the latter as the continued legacy of the former in a new, tragic context of imperialism and injustice.[10] Both these disciplinary traditions take "ghosts" as a category to be stable across time. This book departs radically from both traditions and makes a case to treat both fear and the expressions of fear as deeply historical categories. Going even further, I challenge the notion that the term ghost (bhut, *pret*) can be applied to both modern and premodern Beings. I use the term "Being" in a manner similar to the way Marshall Sahlins employs the terms "metapersons" or "metahumans." In his final scholarly work, Sahlins leads us through a rich survey of the scholarship on immanentist and transcendentalist cultures, underscoring that for most of human history we lived in an immanentist universe where the "familiar distinction between the 'spiritual' and the 'material' . . . [was] not pertinent." In such a society a "cosmic host of beings and forces comprise an all-round substrate" of all human endeavor, including but not limited to, work, political authority, and social reproduction. Sahlins reminds us, pace Levy-Bruhl, that here "nothing is undertaken without having recourse to enchantment."[11] Transcendentalist societies, in sharp contrast, transported all divinity to a "transcendental 'other world' of its own reality, leaving the earth alone to humans."[12] The presence of enchantment in modernity is the survival, according to Sahlins, of the immanent in our transcendental world. While not agreeing with the "survival" trope for modern enchantment, in this book I understand the premodern ghosts to be Beings in this "metahuman" sense, and in chapter 1, I make a case for why they must be seen as distinct in their species-being from modern ghosts.

Relatedly, for reasons that we later examine in detail, the coming of capitalist modernity to the ghost world meant a new *incorporation* of Beings. Stripped of their individual particularities, each Being was classified under the general rubric of a ghost or bhut. Vastly different genealogies containing historically specific origin stories were clubbed together in classic Linnaean fashion. The powerful Hudum Deo[13] who could summon rains in North Bengal, the headless Kandha Kata[14] who was immune to the exorcist's spells, the beautiful and formidable *shankhchunni* who longed for a family life with children (and would take yours)—creatures who had their specific histories as separate Beings—began to be cataloged by the colonial administrator and Bhadralok ethnologist alike as part of a single genus: bhut. Once captured in this manner, concrete attributes were abstracted and generalized. "The "ordinary bhūt," the civil servant turned amateur folklorist William Crooke wrote, belonged to "the Kshatriya, warrior, Vaisya, trader, or sūdra, menial classes," but the "Brahman Bhūt known as Brahm or Brahmadaitya [was] a different variety." Even though Crooke "cataloged" creatures that varied widely in their manners, ferocity, and utility, he was unhesitant in giving them common features:

> Ordinary bhūts are as tall as palmyra trees, generally thin and very black. They usually abide in trees, except those which the Brahm frequents. At night and especially at midnight they wander about the fields and frighten travellers. Like the Jinn, they prefer dirty places to those which are clean, so when a man attempts to get a Bhut into his power he makes the experiment in some dirty, retired place, and offers only half-cooked food, so that the creature may not have time to gobble it up and perchance rend the adventurer. They do not enter the temples of the great gods, but lurk in the vicinity in the hope of getting a share of the offerings. . . . They are usually stark naked and are fond of women, whom they occasionally abduct.[15]

These multiple Beings were soon evacuated from the realm of fear into the realm of ethnography or children's literature, with the immaturity of women, children, and the lower classes offering the common thread. Their rehabilitation in children's literature deserves a separate analysis of its own, which I do not attempt in this book. What I discuss instead is why the presence of these Beings in this literary genre did not signify fear, but its opposite: that fear had been drained from them and that they were now sufficiently sanitized to meet Bhadralok children. How and why did these Beings get disarmed? In 1842, seventeen-year-old Michael Madhusudan Dutta won a gold medal at Hindu College for his essay on female education in which, with due severity, he chastised women for being "unable to give up their belief in the existence of ghosts, notwithstanding the strong remonstrances of Reason, and the evidence of Science because the impressions left on the mind by the idle tales heard or recited in the nursery could not be effaced."[16] Belief in premodern ghosts became the marker for unreason, and by the end of the nineteenth century you could catch a *petni* or a *mamdo* only in an ethnographer's notebook, or they would lurk, powerless, in children's tales, thoroughly defanged by Bhadralok derision. As S. Mukerji noted in the preface to his popular collection *Indian Ghost Stories* (1914), he had heard such stories primarily from two kinds of sources, from "my nurse . . . my father's coachman, Abdullah, who used to be my constant companion . . . [and] from my friends who are Judges and Magistrates and other responsible servants of Government, and in two cases from Judges of Indian High Courts." But Mukerji was clear that a "story told by a nurse or a coachman should certainly not be reproduced in this book. In this book, there are a few of those stories only which are true to the best of the author's knowledge and belief."[17]

I develop my argument about the old and new ghosts in three connected ways.

First, I outline the conceptual framework that sustained narratives of the "supernatural" before the advent of modernity. I argue that premodern ghosts force us to critically examine the very notion of the supernatural and reveal its very modern genesis. Robert Segal has observed something similar in Edward Tylor's argument about "primitive" spiritualism, whereby, for the indigenous tribes under study, spiritual ideas were intensely material, as society lacked any sense of immateriality.[18] Lucien Febvre has gone even further, arguing that there existed no vocabulary for "unbelief" in sixteenth-century France.[19] Ghosts and similar Beings of premodernity gesture toward a fluid and commodious notion of the *natural*—where the natural and the human world do not have sharp conceptual divisions, and consequently the boundaries of the natural world are capacious enough to contain both the living and the dead.

Second, I locate the historical tensions that perforated this earlier framework from the nineteenth century onward, particularly with the spread and generalization of English education. I note that the older ghosts do not simply disappear with the coming of more enlightened times but acquire specific locations within a new cartography of beliefs. I argue that this mapping was a process by which a heterogeneous mental world of belief—teeming with Beings from multiple faith-worlds—was striated into two strictly separate classificatory categories of Religion and Superstition/Magic. This harsh striation of belief was, I contend, necessary for processes of class formation, and ultimately, for one particular class to craft its own view of the future nation.

Third, and finally, I try to situate the discourse of the modern uncanny within contemporary colonial society, where the dividing line between reason and un-reason was anything but simple or stable. Following from scholars such as E. J. Clery, I look at the development of the modern uncanny as being anchored to the development of capitalism as a specific ensemble of social relations. I propose that the fundamental inscrutability of capitalism as a system dictates certain specific forms for the spectral world and, simultaneously, that the nesting of capital in the colonial world created important fractures in the previous understanding of the natural world and transposed new categorization of the nature/culture divide onto this society. Consequently, the "new" spirits that emerged from this process were not only different from their premodern counterparts but, unlike their premodern brethren, were also endowed with a higher mission regarding class and nation formation.

Accordingly, chapters 1 and 2 trace the differences between the old ghosts and the new spirits. Since the phenomenon of haunting presumes spatiality—there can be no ghosts without a space for them to haunt—chapter 3 tries to understand why changes in notions of space actually ran parallel to and influenced changed perceptions of haunting. If the first three chapters involve a range of literary sources, chapters 4 and 5 are more the "history" chapters. In them I try to write a history of practices, in the original *histoire des mentalités* sense. As all good folktales will tell you, it is hard to capture specters, and even harder to capture them through archival sources. I therefore do not so much "capture" them as sense their presence in changing funeral rites, laws, and the steady encroachment of machinery in everyday life.

In chapter 4 I develop a more granular analysis of the relationship between practices of spirituality and capitalism's insistence on certain modes of being, but here I want to say a few words about the system's own occult potential. Even though Marx employed multiple images of monstrosity and demonic powers to describe the system, most theorists have noted such imagery as rhetorical flourishes. David McNally is a rare exception who has given us a stirring account of why such images befit capitalism as a system, as capitalism was "both a modern horror-story and a mystery tale, each inexplicable outside the language of monstrosity."[20] McNally's argument draws on Marx's concept of abstract labor, the form of labor that is the motor of capital accumulation. The conceptual parameters of this process are important to the overall argument of this book, so let me introduce here a few key themes.

Marx shows us how capitalism homogenizes all forms of concrete labor, such that all uniquely varied acts of labor are converted to their quantitative form alone, thus making all labors exchangeable with each other because of their undifferentiated state. McNally's work adds a crucial commentary to this process of abstraction. He argues that to become abstract labor, the concrete labor of human beings goes through a "process of *real abstraction*," wherein unique labor is "effectively *disembodied*, detached" from the worker performing it. As "identical and interchangeable units of homogenous labor power," the skills and bodies of workers are then "dissected, fragmented, cut up into separable pieces subjected to the direction of an alien force, represented by a legion of supervisors, and embedded in rhythms and processes of work that are increasingly dictated by automatic programmes and systems of machinery."[21] Thus, when Marx writes how capitalism "mutilates the worker" or rails against capital's "demonic powers," he is describing a real process of monstrosity that the system encodes. Based on this understanding, McNally, like Michael Taussig before him, offers a powerful analysis of modern witchcraft tales, zombie attacks—especially from the global south—and shows how, against capital's "occult process" of exploitation, these stories ought to be read as the resistance chronicles of ordinary human beings.[22] The stories *make visible* the violence inherent in accumulation, a violence that capital hides— occults—behind ideologies of "equal exchange" and "honest day's work." In this light, we can see why the occult and certain forms of magic, far from being carryovers from the past, actually *belong* to modernity.[23] Scholarship on the place of magic in modernity, however, varies greatly, and it is important to pick out some of the threads of scholarly dispute and agreement.

Enchantment, Disenchantment, Reenchantment

If we take Rabinandanath Tagore's lament about the departing Brahmadaitya literally, then the world of nineteenth-century Bengal might appear to us as the world did to early anthropologists like James Frazer and Edward Tylor, among the first to present reason as a propulsive tool of social evolution driving human progress through the grid of

It is certainly true that both the colonial administrator and the Westerneducated Bengali elite subscribed to such an epistemic grid.[24] If, for the former, all Indians were mired in, or at least susceptible to, magic and superstition, for the latter, such a view was inflected by caste, class, and gender, making the lower classes, Muslims, Dalits, and women the repositories of such harmful ideas.[25] Comments by Rashbihari Bose on the legends and ballads of Bhagalpur for the journal of the Asiatic Society of Bengal exemplifies the contemporary Bhadralok approach to such matters. Bose found no evidence of "demon worship" in Bengal or in most of Bihar, but where such backward practices existed, it was undoubtedly "owing to the close vicinity of the Kols," an indigenous group.[26] Premodern ghosts, then, fared badly. Children's textbooks were sanitized of "superstition" by editing out all supernatural content, even stories about speaking animals. Ramananda Chatterji, cofounder with Brahmo reformer Shibnath Shastri of the first children's journal *Mukul*, campaigned explicitly against ghosts in children's literature. Writing with some ferocity in *Probasi*, Ramananda urged authors to exclude tales, and even illustrations, of fearful ghosts from "all books and journals."[27]

The question for us is not whether this framework existed—it did—but what to make of it. For example, it is obvious that ghosts did not belong to Science, but did they belong to Superstition/Magic, or Religion? How were the boundaries for each drawn in a colonial society? Were such boundaries stable? Most importantly, who drew the boundaries?

There is an abundance of scholarly literature on the relationship between these three, always heavily contested, categories. Tylor's *Religion in Primitive Culture* (1871) and Frazer's *The Golden Bough* (1890) are some early reflections on their distinctions, intimacies, and outright oppositions. While Tylor and Frazer followed the rigid modernization shown in the grid above, later anthropologists introduced a more generous reading. Bronislaw Malinowski's *Magic, Science and Religion* (1925) remapped Science as belonging to the "profane" domain and "Magic and Religion" as belonging to the "sacred." In one fell swoop, the three categories were thus moved from an evolutionary schema to a coeval one, a move that both enriched and complicated their relationship. Both Emile Durkheim in *The Elementary Forms of Religious Life* (1912) and his close associate Marcel Mauss, in *A General Theory of Magic* (1902), further blurred the boundaries by proposing Magic as an early iteration of Science, thereby establishing a historical continuity between the domains/categories. The Bhadralok occultists we will meet in this book could almost be called Durkheimian in their approach, for all believed that what passed as "occult" in their time would be proven to be hard "Science" by a later age. What is of critical interest to us here is *why* these explanatory models coexisted. How did the Bhadralok intellectual subscribe to the Frazerian model when it came to women and lower castes, all the while blurring the domains of science, religion, and superstition when it came to certain kinds of occult knowledge and practice? Our task then is to understand not just which rules and tools of inquiry were employed by the Bengali occultist but how that inquiry was organized to generate new norms of inclusion and exclusion.

Let us go back to Rabindranath's regret at the rapid disenchantment of his world and situate that regret considering these multiple explanatory models that coexisted for his contemporaries. Rabindranath was reflecting on the Brahmadaitya in 1940, but we can trace a similar note of nostalgia in European writers as they confronted their own modern moment. Consider the Scot Robert Fergusson's comments as he traveled through northern Scotland in the 1880s. He found "civilization" to have "crept in upon all fairy strongholds and disenchanted the many fair scenes in which they were wont to hold their court." In a near echo of Rabinandranath Tagore, Fergusson concluded that "the light of science has shone upon every green mound and dispossessed it of its fairy inhabitants."[28] John Aubrey is even closer to Rabindranath when, as far back as the 1680s, he observed that the "divine art of Printing and Gunpowder have frightened away Robin-good-fellow and the Fayries."[29] Two critical questions confront us as we untangle these echoed sentiments across space and time. Does the modern moment, no matter when and where it is perceived to have arrived, always come equipped with a decline in magic? And relatedly, if the first proposition holds, then can we craft a definition of the modern through its exile of ghosts and spirits?

Max Weber's central thesis about modernity is predicated on answering the first question in the affirmative, but with an added twist. In his classic work on Protestantism, Weber postulated that the Protestant Reformation was shaped, even engendered, by the values and impulses of a new economic order that would go on to mark a profound transformation in human history—namely, capitalism. Capitalism required new modes of behavior for acting on the world, and Protestantism created the religious motivation for such behavior. Protestant emphasis on good works in the here and now as a way of glorifying god was combined with delayed gratification as a sign of piety in personal conduct. Such values legitimated the new order's accumulation drive and its corollary requirements such as investment of profits rather than their direct, immediate consumption, as was the norm in precapitalist economies. It is not a coincidence that Science emerged in the same period as a distinct discipline with clear boundaries and new institutions, such as the Royal Society (established in London in 1645), to promote it. Robert Merton supplemented Weber's original argument in his remarkably astute account of the relationships among Science, capitalism, and the Reformation:

> The positive estimation by Protestants of a hardly disguised utilitarianism, of intramundane interests, of a thoroughgoing empiricism, of the right and even duty of *libre examen*, and of the explicit individual questioning of authority were congenial to the very same values found in modern science. And perhaps above all in the significance of the active ascetic drive which necessitated the study of Nature that it might be controlled. Hence, these two fields [Protestantism and Science] were well integrated

and, in essentials, mutually supporting, not only in seventeenth-century England but also in other times and places.[30]

"In other times and places" is an important part of Merton's argument, and it allows us to place Rabindranath and John Aubrey within the same frame despite their belonging to different time lines and histories, so let us pause here for a moment to reflect on it.

Both Aubrey and Rabindranath are commenting on the moment of their own confrontation with the modern. The uncanny similarity of their comments should urge us to evaluate their encounters experientially rather than calendrically, as the former allows us to assess the two moments as coeval while the latter puts Europe "ahead" of its "backward" colonies. This is a bold claim and deserves disaggregation into its three main component parts. First, following scholars such as Reinhart Koselleck and Johannes Fabian, I understand the modern temporality to be singularly unique. Second, I believe focusing on the calendrical moment when a society confronts modernity sanitizes the processes of its arrival. Third, unless we anchor the modern moment (for any society) into a conception of capitalism as an *uneven and combined* political-economic form, we fall back on racist tropes of modernization theory.

To begin with temporality: in his classic study, Reinhart Koselleck assesses modernity as different from all previous forms of historical periodization and time-reckoning. Unlike previous epochal measures (such as religious or dynastic), modernity was characterized by a form of periodization that was entirely temporal. The newness of the "new time" was predicated on a double understanding of the future: a simultaneous emptying out and an extension. Freedom from Christianity's eschatological fear of an imminent end of the world coupled with new discoveries in science allowed Europe, for the first time, to imagine a future that did not end. Limitlessness, in turn, made the future abstract and empty, drained as it was of all spatio-historical specificity. It was during the period of the European Enlightenment, propelled by the social forces of the Industrial and French Revolutions, that time acquired it final qualitative attributes, qualities that could embed themselves only because time had by then shed all its specificity and had been abstracted into a generalized emptiness. Koselleck urges us to bear in mind that it is also during this period that the concepts of "progress," "development," "crisis," and "Zeitgeist" all gained temporal determinations that they never had before. Modernity, then, from its inception, was a very specific sort of time-consciousness, one that emptied time of its historic specificity (time of gods, time of kings) and that, once drained, this new time could be loaded with qualitative categories and become the vehicle of History.[31] Johannes Fabian's work on the relationship between temporality and colonialism remains the most thoroughgoing investigation of this new spatio-temporal epistemology. Fabian both follows and adds to Koselleck's argument of stripping time of specificity in order to create the time of an immanent History. In a close study of evolutionary science, Fabian shows how the new time had to be first "naturalized" in order for it to become a "variable independent of the events it marked." This in turn allowed Cartesian Science "to plot a multitude of *uneventful* data over neutral time . . . separated from events meaningful to mankind."[32] But Fabian also takes Koselleck's argument a step further with his discussion of two conceptual developments of the nineteenth century that inserted a new sense of spatiality to time: "1. Time [was conceptualized as] immanent to, hence coextensive with, the world . . . or nature . . . ; 2. Relationships between parts of the world . . . in the widest sense of both natural and sociocultural entities . . . [could now] be understood as temporal relations."[33]

Fabian is suggesting that, since the Enlightenment, time was used in European bourgeois discourse as a tool for "distancing and separat[ing]" different part of the world, giving the European colonizer a place "ahead" of everyone else on a linear timeline. Further, this "aheadness" itself was invested with specific qualitative and historical characteristics—all of which, lo and behold, could be found in Europe alone. What made "the savage significant to the evolutionist's Time" was that "he [lived] in another Time."[34]

The postcolonialist scholar shares (and in some cases predates) Fabian's disquiet about modern temporality. Thanks to this work, we can no longer think about broad claims, such as those of "universalism" or "modernization" attending European intellectual projects from the sixteenth century, without also thinking about these projects' imbrications with colonial violence.[35] Demonstrating that modern institutions and modern practices in the non-Western world have evolved in ways that are radically different from recognized Western equivalents, this scholarship has argued that, since the forms of non-Western modernity were so crucially different from the Western models, they ought to be recognized not as affiliates or derivatives of the Western model but that we consider the possibility of alternative or multiple modernities, such that the modern form as articulated in Europe does not serve as our only template of diagnosing modernity.[36] Attractive and empowering as this argument maybe, it leaves us wanting in two analytical respects: (1) Without a substantive definition of modernity, how are we to recognize its alternative? In other words, if the alternative form is different in every respect from its European counterpart, then what about it makes it "modern"? And, relatedly, (2) If we are to nominate a particular social institution or practice of the colonial world as "modern" in an alternative sense, then what ultimately are our registers for doing so?

It is clear from their writing that the colonial intelligentsia in Bengal understood there to be a modular modern; the point for them was to then mix, alter, and amend that modern to fit their own context. The Bengali occultist could thus on the one hand condemn older, folk ghosts as "superstition," while writing scholarly essays on the scienticity of séances. We should probe this assemblage model of colonial modernity, as it leaves important questions unanswered: Why are only certain elements "borrowed" from the categorical "West" and mixed with the equally categorical "East" and not others? What is the *logic* of "mixing" of the various heterogeneous elements? Most important, what elements constituted the assumed modular modern?

These questions should allow us to circle back to capitalism as an immensely transformative but historically specific socioeconomic order, which I see as the staging ground, the determining context, for the modern. But here, rather than ask the more popular question, "Which modern?" we should ask the question, "Which capitalism?" For while modernity, as an ontological category, has been given permission by many postcolonial scholars to be *infinitely variable*, capitalism in this scholarship is often seen as *prohibitively singular*. Capitalism is too often associated with a very limited number of identifiers, most of which, ironically, sound similar to standard modernization rhetoric.

There is of course some truth to the singularity of capitalism that manifests with an inexorable logic, irrespective of geography. Some necessary conditions of the system remain stable across space and time—the violent separation of humans from their means of subsistence; the domination of abstract labor over the concrete; and the generalization of commodity exchange through a world market where all products, no matter their use, origin, and method of production, are exchanged against their abstract equivalent—that is, money. But rather than simply see these as features, they are best seen as *outcomes* of capitalist implantation. Seeing them as outcomes or results allows us to, first, appreciate the stunningly diverse and intensely adaptable means employed by capital to get to these outcomes in different societies and, second, explain why all capitalist societies will display certain commonalities but such core features will be layered with multiple histories and practices attentive to the specific historical development of each society. As the economist Anwar Shaikh recently put it, "Capitalism's sheath mutates constantly but its core remains the same."[37]

This processual understanding of capitalism thus allows us to both hold on to its "iron laws," as the universal, and simultaneously acknowledge the infinite variations on the application and consequences of those laws to different societies, or the particular. Dipesh Chakrabarty's evocative concept of History 1 and 2 is one highly stimulating method of conceiving this relationship between the two categories. In *Provincializing Europe*, Chakrabarty seeks to demonstrate how universal concepts of modernity, History 1, despite their accidental origin in Europe and their being imposed on the colonial world through imperial violence, encounter in these worlds History 2, or "pre-existing concepts, categories, institutions and practices through which they [such concepts] get translated and configured differently."[38] Partha Chatterjee is even more explicit in outlining capitalism's procedure of establishing a universal grammar for multiple, particular societies and their interactions within and without: "If there is one great moment that turns the provincial thought of Europe to universal philosophy, the parochial history of Europe to universal history, it is the moment of capital—capital that is global in its territorial reach and universal in its conceptual domain. It is the narrative of capital that can turn the violence of mercantile trade, war, genocide, conquest and colonialism into a story of universal progress, development, modernization, and freedom."[39]

Throughout this book we will see this shadow play between the universal and the particular. We will see why certain forms of spectrality become "universal" and acceptable across multiple colonial societies by their Western-educated elites, while other kinds become disreputable or are banished outright.

This entanglement of the universal and the particular, mediated as it is through the logic of capital accumulation, is absent from what can be called the theory of the "secular decline of magic." Keith Thomas's classic study, for example, firmly dating the "distinction between religion and magic" to the sixteenth century, declares the triumph of the former over the latter. Like Weber and Merton before him, Thomas tells an absolutist story of the secular decline of "magic" caused by the amalgamative effects of Protestantism, the scientific revolution, and the rise of capitalism. Like Weber and Merton, Thomas is not wrong. But he is also not right. Scholars have pointed to three distinct ways in which his assessment fails to satisfy. First, as Hildred Geertz has identified, Thomas makes a category error, for "it is not the 'decline' of . . . magic that cries out for explanation, but the emergence and rise of the label 'magic.'"[40] Second, E. P. Thompson rightly takes Thomas to task for visibilizing the views of a minority, that of intellectuals and scientists, and ignoring popular instance of magic, or "movement[s] of counter enlightenment."[41] Third, there are scholars who disprove the "decline" thesis by cataloguing the various ways in which "magic" survived the sixteenth-century moment of rupture and continues to flourish in the present day: my personal favorites are Spanish iPhone apps for exorcism,[42] Vietnamese ghost-gods who accept offerings of Coke and Pepsi,[43] and stories of demonic underwear from Ghana.[44]

While useful, these evaluations of the decline thesis do not consider the ways in which the decline thesis is also correct, not least in the sense that it forms the hegemonic common sense of modernity, in all its spatiotemporal expressions. Criticism of the decline thesis sometimes sees it as a case of scholarly misrecognition, one that fails to account for all the multiple examples of coexistence of magic, reason, and religion. But what the decline thesis notes is a *tendency* in modernity to police the borders between Science, Magic, and Religion according to a new set of norms and to attempt to redefine the remit of each. This tendency is the defining score of modernity and is indifferent to geographical location.

But it is not the validation or refutation of the decline thesis that ought to be our critical lens for analyzing modernity's approach to ghosts, but a conception of capitalism as structurally *uneven and combined*.[45] Such a lens makes it possible to explain why instantiations of the modern vary according to geographical location—as capital enters different societies at different moments and with different intensities—but nonetheless carry certain traces of commonality.[46] John Aubrey and Rabindranath can mourn their common loss, but separately, across the wilderness of the modern.

Sacred Spirits

Undoubtedly the reevaluation of death and the afterlife in colonial Bengal was itself a cultural response to a wider set of changes whereby new social processes such as rural to urban migration and generalized Western education were altering the fabric of everyday life. The new "scientific" understanding of ghosts and spirits, however, was not simply different from older orally transmitted ghost stories. The new ghosts embodied a highly particularized notion of the afterlife, one that sought to combine a version of high Brahmanic Hinduism with modern science. From the 1850s onward, older "traditional" ghosts and demons were considered to be the products of feminine and/or peasant superstition and hence argued into nonexistence by a Western-educated middle class that was deeply invested in more "modern" forms of spirituality such as séances and spirit photography. The marginalization of older ghosts and demons becomes particularly significant when we find that these scientific investigations of the middle class into the realm of the supernatural were conducted within an exclusivist framework of Brahmanic Hinduism.

A series of journals published from the mid-nineteenth century onward provide unique insight into this discursive connection between hierarchical Hinduism and the new science of spirituality. The mission statement of *Aloukik Rahasya* (1908) for example stated that the journal was founded to reinvigorate interest and belief in "traditional" high Hindu thought (*sanātana dharma*) through the medium of "scientific Occult." The editor of *Aloukik Rahasya*, Kshirod Prasad Bidyabinod, a renowned chemistry professor at the University of Calcutta, was one of several Western-educated and "scientifically" trained individuals of the period who sought to use the new sciences of Europe to reanimate the old hierarchies of Hinduism. These journals, while celebrating Hindu Science, simultaneously led a vigorous campaign against indigenous ghosts and older supernatural practices that the authors argued were the product of female and lower class "superstition."

The new and indigenously developed "Science" of spirituality merits critical attention, as it constituted a new convergence of rationality and faith. Existing literature on the Indian spiritualist movement focuses almost exclusively on its institutional aspect by considering groups such as the Theosophical Society as a site for the development of radical anticolonial nationalism.[47] There is, however, a salient lacuna in historical research when it comes to discerning the *appeal* of Spiritualism as a new characterization of "science" and faith in the Indian colonial context.

Scholars of Bengal have expressed surprise at the remarkable revival of a hardened and restrictive Hinduism from the 1850s in the region.[48] An older oral world of supernatural practices embodied in a repertoire of spells, spirit-possessions, charms, and local deities was replaced by a textual and orthodox version of Hinduism, which eventually recast itself as the consciousness of the fledgling nation. This book expands on this existent scholarship on religious revivalism but departs from it in one significant way. My main contention is that, in order to understand the habitation of religion under modernity, we need to approach the problem not through the highway of religious orthodoxies but the backroads of the more diffuse category of the supernatural—through public rituals and acts of "faith" and "superstition."

The ghost worlds of the nineteenth century suggest that the relationship between older and newer supernatural practice is of consequence because this relationship brings together discourses that have been insufficiently considered in the same frame of reference. In the context of the colonial world, more thought needs to be given to the construction of the modern "public sphere," which, even while claiming irreligiosity in its juridical scaffolding, can display a surfeit of religiosity in its civic practices. The nation-states' preoccupation with past-ness and modern disciplinary history has been the focus of much recent scholarship.[49] But what this scholarship lacks is an adequate understanding of the more insidious process by which previous conceptions of "religion," due to its perceived location in modernity's past, enter the modern public sphere through the more dangerous categories of cultural memory and civic rituals. The emergent discourse on "Scientific Spiritualism" cannot simply be seen as proof of the resilience of Hinduism. Instead, this book indicates the complex interaction among categories of faith, nation formation, and historical consciousness whereby the very outlines of what is perceived to be "religion" can be altered under modernity.

The substitution of vernacular heterodoxies of faith by elitist Hindu homogeneity cannot be adequately understood if we approach such a process from the elite perspective. Instead of this top-down methodology, my project examines the problem from "below," that is, through a study of older Indigenous magic and supernatural practices. This methodology demonstrates how the exorcism of older ghosts from the modern public sphere was intended to have a series of complex consequences ranging from the gendering of belief to the anchoring of a specific version of Hinduism as the voice of the new nation.

The constitutive sources for this project can be indexed along similar methodological lines. On the one hand, I look at vernacular ghost stories, personal accounts, and various manuals on magic such as texts describing Indic and Islamicate practices of catarchic astrology and astral magic. These texts are then balanced and contrasted with more official ones, such as government records outlining official mortuary policies, proceedings of the several spiritual societies, and the journals that sought to harden popular opinion on "superstition."

While Science remained for the Bengali elite a marker of modernity and nationhood, my project examines how the same elite redrew the borders of what was deemed to be scientific in order to suit their specific historic needs. This book is thus an intervention in larger disciplinary concerns about the relationships among religious studies, the history of science, and social history. The invocation of modern Science to marginalize older ghosts into the realm of the "feminine" and "superstition" outlines for us several congruent historical processes that are impossible to understand through the lens of a single discipline. The Bengali elite was trying to construct a new Science of spirituality that was commensurate with both continuous forms of thought, such as Hinduism, and discontinuous historical phenomena, such as the increasing elaborations of modern state forms and modern institutional grids.

Recent world events indicate that religious identity has clearly moved from being the cultural unconscious of modernity to one of its more violent markers. In other words, the location of religion in the public sphere is now so entrenched that policymakers tend to use "modern" categories to acknowledge its stability, such as "political" Islam and Hindu "fundamentalism." This book, while tracing this process of imbrication between faith and modernity, shows that the ability to anticipate and analyze faith does not necessarily depend on a study of textual orthodoxies but, rather, on popular civic practices that arrogate the right to speak for "religion." The ghosts in this book show us that history "has many cunning passages, contrived corridors" through which dominant ideas take shape. And once we grasp this, "After such knowledge, what forgiveness?"[50]

ONE

"Undisciplined, Playful and Yet *Bhadra*"

Old Ghosts and Their Advocates in an Age of Enlightenment

Now that the book is finished, I know that this was not a hallucination, a sort of professional malady, but the confirmation of something I already suspected—folktales (fiabe) are real.—ITALO CALVINO, *Italian Folktales*

The bhut was a member of the family in rural Bengal. . . . I was young and visiting my grandfather in our village when a neighbor came to see him. After chatting for a while, the gentleman remarked, "a petni is really irritating (tyakto) us." The method of this irritation was that whenever fish was fried in the kitchen, the petni would appear and in her nasal voice beg for fish. The funny thing was that no one listening was surprised by this neighbor's story. Everyone assumed it to be very natural: bhuts loved fried fish, so of course they would irritate and demand their share.—HUMAYUN AHMED, *Amar Priyo Bhuter Galpo*

In the spring 1857, as Calcutta prepared for the impending threat of an uprising,[1] the noted intellectual Rajendralal Mitra (1822–91) published an excellent study of ghosts, titled "Bhoutik Byapar" or "Ghostly Matters," in his journal, the *Bibidartha Sangraha*. Rajendralal's career as a man of letters was stellar, even for his times, which had produced a multitude of such men.

He had a law degree and was fluent in several languages including Hindi, Sanskrit, Persian, Urdu, and of course his native Bengali. An enthusiastic and well-respected participant in the educational and cultural projects of the times, Rajendralal was also active politically, having served for several years as the president of the British Indian Association, the precursor to the Indian National Congress.[2] He was, by modern standards, a highly unusual source of intelligence about ghosts and their activities. And in this regard Rajendralal does not disappoint us. The short essay is a wonderful tongue-in-cheek comment on ghosts in particular, and belief in the supernatural in general. It is of interest not only for its dry wit about the so-called irrationalities of life but also for its effective disordering of the usual categories of rationality and faith in political terms. A colorful "historical" account of ghosts is employed by Rajendralal to make an inimitable argument about nationalism and British colonial rule.

It is perfectly clear, Rajendralal informs us at the outset, how ghosts come into being. Accidental or untimely death gives birth to a ghost, and this rule is valid for all ghosts internationally. But, despite their universalism, ghosts do have certain particularities. They are, for instance, partial to women and children. According to Rajendralal, in all nations of the world ghosts are never far from the hearts and minds of this chosen demographic. He then provides us with a list of activities that we can reasonably expect of ghosts: "They are by nature undisciplined, playful and yet bhadra [polite]. Their activities include throwing a few stones in the dark, making some needless noises, opening closed doors without any apparent purpose, manifesting in horrible forms, and sometimes possessing the simpleminded young wife of the family; besides the above they are not known to harm humans in any particular way. However, they are likely to carry out their own form of justice if they are wronged."[3]

Doubtless Rajendralal's ghosts fall into the same category as Rabindranath's domestic Brahmadaitya in their near-genial relationship to the human world. Their spectrality is almost mitigated by their traceable predictability: we are made aware of their functions and hence their limitations. Most importantly, we feel the uncomfortable imminence of their nature to our own, captured intensely in Rajendralal's deliberate use of the word *bhadra*.

The word carries a history of its own, too elaborate to reproduce here. Suffice to say that it is a very specific designation meant for a distinct social group in colonial Bengal, the Bhadralok, whose social identity was to a large extent predicated on caste, class, and English education and concomitant perceptions of Enlightenment rationality, making them close historical relatives of the Victorian gentleman.⁴ The inclusion of ghosts by Rajendralal within the hallowed circle of *bhadra*-hood explicitly establishes their kinship to the social world of mortals. This insidious feeling of kinship is not to be taken lightly, and we will have occasion to refer to this aspect later in detail. But, for now, let us continue with Rajendralal's account.

The people of India, Rajendralal explains, were by far weaker than Europeans and were characteristically less skilled in the industrial arts. It follows then that the Indian ghost would be inferior to the European ghost; the two were indeed as comparable as a mature adult was to a child. Rajendralal's brand of unnerving irony persists as he continues with his catalogue of differences between the Indian and European ghost. Europeans, he informs us, did not bother with spells or potions but used sheer intellectual force and cunning to control the spirit world and bend it to their will. This is clear from how the spirit world responded to these geographical regions. Having recounted several incidents of supernatural occurrence in Europe and North America, Rajendralal ruefully declares, "Our native ghost-practitioner works very hard to get a ghost to make a little noise on a thatched roof; this brings him fame. The English dealer in spirits regards this activity as mere trifling; he can make his ghosts create fabulous sounds from any number of household instruments."⁵

This remarkably sharp witticism from one of the leading intellectuals of Bengal turns a central colonial assumption on its head: that of India as the land of eternal religion and belief and Europe as the land of secular rationality. It was this idea of the unchanging "Orient" that, more than any other, formed the foundational presumption of nineteenth-century European scholarship on India. Scholarship since the 1980s has adequately explored the roots of this intellectual tradition and determined its underlying political function.⁶ What we have in Rajendralal's essay is an unusual refutation of this discourse from a contemporary figure. Without detracting from his light tone, Rajendralal documents various instances of the supernatural in Europe and North America and consciously builds up a narrative of what can only be regarded as international gullibility. True to the empiricist tradition of his times, nowhere does Rajendralal explicitly state his own position regarding these events, letting the description of the accounts speak for themselves. The narrative strategy serves him well, for the impassive presentation of non-Indian occult manifestations blatantly ridicules the assumptions of "rationality" by Europeans.

In his final remarks, Rajendralal admits that his readership may not be inclined to believe in the events that he had narrated. In this he does not blame them, as the ghost practitioners had surpassed even the "Grape-shot drinkers of Bagbazar" (an obvious intoxicant) in their distortion of reality. But the journal, Rajendralal insisted, was committed to discussing "all national and international issues: fabulous or moral, instructive or edifying," and hence the discussion about ghosts. The essay, he concludes, was not intended to "test the faith of the readers; if they choose not to believe in these happenings, we shall not be mortally offended."[7] At this point, given the subtle anticolonial slant to the essay, it seems remiss not to discuss briefly the intended readership of such a piece.

The journal *Bibidartha Sangraha* (1851) was published by the Vernacular Literature Society as part of its mission to develop and enlarge the sphere of Bengali literary endeavors. The journal published critical studies on leading subjects such as archaeology, history, the life sciences, art, and literature. Printed at the Baptist Mission Press, it was noted for its beautiful printing and illustrations. Although publication, under the two editors Rajendralal Mitra (1851–59) and Kaliprasanna Singha (1861), remained somewhat irregular, the year in which the essay on ghosts was published saw a full cycle of nine issues of the periodical.[8] According to the reports of the Vernacular Society, 39,600 copies of *Bibidartha Sangraha* had been printed by 1857, giving the journal an average print run of 1,100 per issue.[9] This number may appear modest if we do not take into account two important qualifiers that determined readership in the nineteenth century.

First, literacy rates remained considerably low and corresponded to class/caste and gender privileges throughout the colonial period. It must be remembered that, even as late as 1901, the total number of literate people in the province, according to census reports, was only 210,253.41.[10] It can be safely assumed that more than half of this number consisted of people who had the most basic literacy skills, thus undoubtedly excluding them as potential consumers of a journal such as the one under discussion. Second, a contradictory social practice actually undermined the statistical import of recorded literacy figures. Books were not simply read by the literate; they were also widely listened to by those excluded from the select ambit of literacy. Several contemporary observers insist on listening as a regular mode of consumption of the written word.[11] About the *Bibidartha Sangraha*, specifically, Rajendralal Mitra, as editor, reported to the Vernacular Literature Society in 1859 that the journal continued to "claim a wide circle of readers in the Mofussil [districts outside of Calcutta] for whose improvement and entertainment it . . . [was] especially designed."[12] Moreover, in 1857, to boost and diversify sales, the society had also adopted the novel strategy of employing a female hawker, who had free access to the women's quarters in the homes of the educated gentry. The society went as far as to say that they felt "much encouraged" by the success of this approach.[13]

The number of actual printed copies of the journal can therefore give us only a very elementary understanding of the actual scope and extent of readership. Rajendralal's essay on ghosts may have been read by a numerically small section of society, but it can be assumed to have distilled ideas and opinions that went far beyond such specific numbers. More importantly, the essay was both catering to and representing what was perceived to be the select circle of the *bhadra*: those twice blessed by class, caste, and Western education. There is an easy assumption of unity of opinion and cultural experience that runs like a secret language throughout the text. It makes stating the author's position redundant in the faith-versus-rationality debate: the author and his readership are kindred souls who share in this gentle irony about the supernatural. But let us remind ourselves of Rajendralal's curious use of the word *bhadra* regarding the ghosts themselves. Although it is part of this ironic discourse, the word actually overflows with cultural insinuations about affinity—and rightly so, for the ghosts of the nineteenth century, in perception and representation, often unsettlingly dissolved the distinction between the world of the dead and that of the living.

"Traditional" Ghosts and "Authentic" Roots

Who were these "traditional" ghosts that Rajendralal was ready to include in the hallowed circle of the *bhadra* or cultural gentility? Some clues to their distinguishing characteristics are provided for us in his essay. Let us remind ourselves of what he saw as essential attributes of ghosts: indiscipline and playfulness but with a touch of innate politeness. Their deeds, we noted, were making disembodied noises, appearing in fearsome forms, and possession, usually of the young and the female of the human species. On a more disturbing note, Rajendralal cautioned us about their predilection for purveying "their own form of justice."[14]

Rajendralal's description might serve as a basis for exploring the lineage of what I call the "traditional" or premodern ghosts. His sketch is demonstrably not fabricated by him for the sake of literary effect, for there exists a remarkable uniformity in the descriptive pedigree for a precolonial ghost.

In 1874, the native Christian missionary and scholar Reverend Lal Behari Day (1824–92) published a detailed ethnographic novel about rural Bengal titled *Govinda Samanta or the History of a Bengal Raiyat*. Later in this section we shall have occasion to discuss this unique text in detail. Here, let me reproduce, in its entirety, the exceptional genealogy that Day presented for traditional ghosts:

> Of Bengali ghosts, that is the spirits of Bengali men and women, there is a great variety; but there are five classes that generally make their appearance. . . . The first and most honorable class of ghosts are those which pass by the name of *Brahmadaitya*, or the spirit of departed Brahmans. . . . Unlike other ghosts, they do not eat all sorts of food, but only those which are considered religiously clean. . . . They are for the most part inoffensive, never doing harm to benighted travellers. Another class of ghosts, and they are by far the most numerous class, are simply called *Bhutas*, that is spirits. They are the spirits of departed Kshatriyas, Vaishyas, and Sudras. . . . The *Bhutas* are all male ghosts. There are two classes of female ghosts, called *Petnis* and *Sankhchunnis*. *Petnis* are terribly dirty. . . . They are [also] very lascivious, trying to waylay benighted passengers for the gratification of their lusts. . . . *Sankhchunnis*, or *Sankhachurnis*, so called in the opinion of some demonologists, because they put on clothes as white as *sankha* (conch-shells), . . . they are not so filthy as *Petnis*, but equally dangerous. Another class of ghosts are the *Skandhakata*, so called from the circumstance that their heads have been cut off from above their shoulders. These headless ghosts are probably the most terrible of the whole set, as they have never been known to spare any human being. . . . Muhmedan ghosts, usually called *Mamdos* . . . are regarded as infinitely more mischievous than Hindu ghosts.[15]

Day here produces for us a testimony of folk belief in which both ghosts and their behavior are carefully mapped to steer clear of them. It is noteworthy how Rajendralal's essay and Day's account both underscore the safeness of these Beings, "inoffensive" and "harmless" are terms that are repeated as descriptions.

If Day provided a format for model behavior for traditional ghosts, during the same period, Ashutosh Mukhopadhyay published an entire collection of ghost stories, *Bhut Petni*, which catalogued the pursuits of such creatures.[16] This collection of established fables about traditional ghosts proved to be immensely successful. Originally intended for children, the book was approved by the director of public instructions as a suitable book for school awards and libraries in 1939, and it earned several "gold and silver medals and First-Class Certificates" from various exhibitions and nationalist enterprises. It had not lost its popularity even by the 1950s, its impressive twelfth edition being published in 1955.[17]

There are nineteen stories in the collection, each in its way fulfilling a requirement for what we may regard as standard behavior for premodern ghosts. Of the nineteen tales, only one has a prince as its protagonist; the rest consistently have as heroes and central characters various members of the lower classes. The word that describes almost all human characters is *garib*, or poor. The poor laugh, suffer, love, often cheat, and connive to better their lot. Sometimes they win and do end up marrying the fabled princess, but often they do not. But, even as they lose in life, they are never patronized or belittled in the narrative mode, thereby conclusively betraying the social origin of these tales. But before we investigate the various features of the premodern ghouls, it is important to ask the questions, where did Ashutosh Mukhopadhyay come by these stories and how and why did he document them.

The shock of the uprising of 1857 acted as a catalyst for colonial policy to study and catalog "popular" Indian literature. For the first time it became painfully clear that the rulers were unaware of what a large cross-section of their subjects were thinking. It is hence not coincidental that there was an unprecedented growth in researching and tracing folk beliefs, stories, and practices from the middle of the nineteenth century.[18] From tracking down textual sources of the upper caste/classes of the high Orientalist era, colonial focus shifted decisively to an ethnological survey of the oral culture of the masses as an entry point into their mental world. This imperial anthropological impulse was further systematized in 1878 with the establishment of the Folk-Lore Society in London. Not unlike most epistemic quests under colonialism, ethnographic queries too were never very far from the practicalities of rule, and several leading officials of the colonial administration — Richard C. Temple, William Crooke, George Grierson — were also keen folklorists. They maintained regular contact with the Society in London and published frequently in the society's journals. Administrative publications and formal government documents also began to include significant amounts of folkloric material from this period. The Muslim nobility had conclusively "proved" their disloyalty in 1857 and, despite their temporary vows of allegiance to the Raj, distant rumblings of discontent could be heard even from the English-educated Hindu Bhadralok in Bengal. The upper classes that had once held the promise of a stable bulwark for empire had seemingly turned seditious overnight. The turn to mass culture by the British was hence a display of both caution and hope.

Folk belief, however, held a different kind of promise for the Bhadralok of Calcutta. By the middle of the century, dreams of prosperity under a benevolent government had begun to fade for the Bhadralok gentry. Growing evidence of British racism was combined with an increasing awareness that the Bengalis had been systematically pushed out of all areas of capital accumulation.[19] Thus, despite fervent vows of loyalty by the Calcutta gentry during the uprising, hopes of improvement under the British had begun to sour for the new generation of the educated upper classes. The initial representation of this disillusionment was in depicting the present as disarticulated and immoral.[20] But this strong binary polarization of time into a congenial past (*sekal*) and an apocalyptic present (*ekal*) was eventually resolved discursively through a new mode of historicization. From the 1870s onward there was a renewed effort on the part of the upper-class Bhadralok to "recover" an authentic Bengali tradition, that which had apparently survived uncontaminated by British influence, in particular, and modernity in general. Rural Bengal came under renewed focus of the Bhadralok ethnologist and historian, both as embodiment of an unsullied past and deliverance for a national future.[21]

The publication of Lal Behari Day's *Govinda Samanta*, in 1874, marks an important beginning for the above trend. Day was a graduate of the missionary Alexander Duff's General Assembly's Institution and, while there, had converted to Christianity under Duff's tutelage. He had already established his ethnologist credentials by publishing several essays on indigenous festivals, sports, and religious practices in the various issues of his journal, the *Bengal Magazine*. However, his novel *Govinda Samanta*, steeped in "ethnographic realism," far surpassed his previous publications and created a veritable sensation in colonial Calcutta.[22] On the year of its publication it received the best book award in both Bengali and English for illustrating so vividly the social and domestic life of the rural masses. The bulk of the material for the novel was genuine ethnographic data collected by Day from the southern district of Burdwan in Bengal between the years 1850 and 1873. Within four short years, a second edition of the book appeared, with three additional chapters and under the new and more explicit title, *Bengal Peasant Life* (1878). After the first spate of revisions the book saw steady sales in the next decade, with a new edition each in 1879, 1880, 1884, 1888, 1892, 1906, 1908, and 1909.

Day's novel, however, despite its uniqueness, should be seen as an expression of what was becoming a pervasive trend to recover an authentic and indigenous national heritage. Two years prior to the publication of *Govinda Samanta*, Bhadralok enthusiasts had started the *Hindu Mela*, Hindu Fair, to exhibit national "traditions." The annual fair, a great success in its early years, was designed to revive traditional songs, dances, sports, and methods of storytelling as proof of a non-anglicized Bengali heritage. In 1883, when Day followed the success of *Govinda Samanta* with a classic collection of Bengali folktales, *Folk Tales of Bengal* (1883), an academic justification for such projects had already been formulated by none other than the young Rabindranath in the Tagore family journal, *Bharati*. Citing nursery rhymes and "tales told by the maids" as the inspired roots of his creativity, Rabindranath innovatively secured rural Bengal to the historical project of the new nation. The Bangiya Sahita Parishat, founded in 1893 by him and other like-minded intellectuals, institutionally consolidated what had been until then emotional and disparate searches for cultural roots. We look more closely at the Spiritualist-historical roots of the Bangiya Sahita Parishat in chapter 5, but for now it is enough to state that the organization aimed to inquire into the ethnology and folklore of Bengal and, from 1894, began to publish the journal *Sahitya Parishat Patrika*. This journal became home to innumerable essays on folklore and ethnographic literature from the leading intellectuals of the age.

The past of Bengal—preserved, according to the Bhadralok, only in the timeless culture of the peasants—finally became useful as the stimulating model for the future.

But, far from being timeless, the ghosts that we follow in this chapter seem like Gramscian scholars. They follow Gramsci's insights on folklore as a vital aspect of "common sense," or what he theorized as "spontaneous philosophy"— the philosophy accessible to and elaborated by ordinary people to make sense of the world. We leave behind the national-teleological frame insisted on by the Bhadralok and meet the ghosts with Gramsci. For only then will we be able to discern the ways in which this subaltern common sense, as posited by Gramsci, was "in opposition (also for the most part implicit, mechanical and objective) to 'official' conceptions of the world (or in a broader sense, the conceptions of the cultured parts of historically determinate societies . . .)." The ghosts we meet will illuminate for us the lifeworld of rural, precolonial Bengal, not elaborated, as Gramsci reminds us, in "systematic and politically organized and centralized" ways, but often "adulterated and mutilated"; we will nevertheless find in these stories, "surviving evidence" of that world.[23]

Ghosts R Us: "Traditional" Ghosts and Their Worldview

The above survey provides us with the necessary context for locating Ashutosh Mukhopadhyay's collection of traditional ghost stories. The urban intellectual of this period very literally went into the depths of rural existence in search of ghosts, talking beasts, and beautiful princesses. The moment these unsuspecting creatures were located, they were promptly bagged and incorporated into collections, journals, and meticulously researched books. The ghosts, on their part, were not wholly unfamiliar with this behavior. The tales in Ashutosh's collection demonstrate that this tradition of the dead being duped by the living was particularly strong.

Of the recurrent themes, captivity narratives form the most pervasive of these tale-types. The basic format is as follows: a human encounters a ghost and is initially frightened by them. Then, by a sleight of hand, the human captures the ghost or threatens them into perpetual bondage. The ghost either ends up being sealed away in a place of confinement or is indentured into servitude to enhance the material prosperity of the mortal. In the tale "Kalshir Bhut" (The Ghost in the Urn), for instance, a poor fisherman (*jele*) nets a little copper urn.[24] Thinking it to be full of gold, he unscrews the lid only to reveal a terrifying ghost that emerges out of the urn and threatens to kill the poor *jele*. The *jele* quickly thinks on his feet and asks the ghost how he managed to fit his enormous body into such a tiny vessel. The unsuspecting ghost boasts of his demonic powers to shrink himself at will and—as the *jele* insists on a demonstration—puts himself back into the urn. The *jele* of course tightens the lid back on and throws the whole thing back into the sea. Similarly, in "Bhuter Bichar" (The Ghost's Judgment), the ghost ends up in a little tube and is confined there forever.[25]

In the more common form of captivity, however, the ghost is enslaved to serve the needs of the mortal. In "Bhutmedh Yajna" (The Ghost Sacrifice), for instance, an indigent barber or *napit* encounters a fearsome ghost in a forest. The ghost, delighted to have found dinner at last, starts to dance. The shrewd *napit*, not to be outdone, also begins dancing and tells the ghost that it is *he* who was delighted to have found the ghost. The king of the realm, the *napit* continues, was about to perform the *bhutmedh yajna*, which required a hundred ghosts to be sacrificed. The *napit* had already captured ninety-nine of them, and this ghost would complete his collection. Upon being asked to furnish proof of his captives, the *napit* brandishes his mirror. The ghost takes his own image to be evidence of other ghosts being held prisoner in this object. He begs the *napit* not to capture him and ends up as the *napit*'s slave for the rest of his life, keeping the *napit* and his family in luxury by supplying them with riches.

A similar fate awaits yet another indigent *napit* in the tale "Henre Bhut" (The Gruff-Voiced Ghost). The unfortunate ghost in this tale is a *mamdo,* or a Muslim ghost, whom the clever *napit* tricks in the end to wait on his every command and bring him a weekly supply of seven jars of gold sovereigns, no less. The tales "Tatai Patai" and "Khona O Batul" follow the same plotline, to the advantage of the humans and the misery of the dead.

Let us review in this light the frequent descriptions about the ghosts being harmless or inoffensive. When the dead come across the living in these tales, the modern reader is thus more alarmed for the fate of the former than the latter, given the nature of outcomes of such encounters. It is not always servitude that the ghosts experience at the hands of the mortals; often it is simply raw physical pain. In the tale "Petnir Alta Para" (The Petni Being Bedecked with Alta), a *petni*, or a female ghost, has just been married to a handsome male ghost or *bhut* and is on her way, for the first time, to visit her in-laws. Like her human counterparts, she desires her feet to be decorated with *alta* before this momentous journey. So, when she chances upon a *napitani*, the female barber, who customarily performs such services for the human bride, she of course asks the *napitani* to shave her legs and apply *alta* to her feet, for which impromptu pedicure she promises the *napitani* payment in cowrie shells. This particular *napitani*, however, was not fully equipped with her tools of trade and was not carrying any *alta*. Upon facing the fearsome *petni*, she devises a gruesome way out of her troubles. She scrapes chunks of the *petni*'s flesh in the guise of shaving her legs and uses the *petni*'s own blood as *alta* to decorate her feet. The *petni*, even though in intense pain, suffers bravely for the sake of beautification and in the end pays the *napitani* for her services as promised. In the tale "Bhute Paoa" (Ghostly Possession), again, a poor *bhut* is branded with red hot iron ladles for wanting fish from an old woman. Similarly, in the tale "Thalu-Malu," the two sisters, Thalu and Malu, along with their grandmother, sear a *petni*'s face with a heated iron plough.[26]

What lesson do these tales embody? For ghosts, clearly, that they should stay well away from humans. For historians, however, what emerges distinctly out of these stories is the close resemblance between the world of the ghosts and that of the rural poor. Coerced, unpaid labor, *begar* or *beth-begar*, existed in many forms throughout the Bengal presidency, its effects especially pernicious on lower castes and indigenous peoples. Similarly, extraction of "gifts" and taxes from the peasant as *nazranas* (gift), *abwabs* (extra tax), and other forms of arbitrarily imposed dues by the rural elites was a common occurrence.[27] While brutalized by these violent relations of land and labor in the real world, in the tales, the poor reverse roles and exact their vengeance on ghosts. Or perhaps the ghosts mirror their own condition and enrich the bonds of kinship and solidarity between the worlds. Storytelling, Walter Benjamin has pointed out, is intimately connected to labor. Boredom, which envelops the worker during the labor process, was for Benjamin the "dream bird" that hatched stories. As weavers and spinners worked their looms, the peasant worked the field, as the "rhythm of work" "seized" the worker, they

FIGURE 1.1 · Woman with fish and ghost: from Ashutosh Mukhopadhyay's *Bhut Petni*

listened "to the tales in such a way that the gift of retelling them . . . [came to them] all by itself. This . . . is the nature of the web in which the gift of storytelling is cradled."[28]

These relations of extended kinship between ghosts and humans, "cradled" in work rhythms and life, were part of the warp and weft of precolonial storytelling and stories. As far back as in the sixteenth century, we have an excellent description of a "unique bazaar for ghosts" ("*aparup preter bajar*") in the lyric ballad, *Chandimangal*. In the ballad, after a particularly bloody battle between the king of Ceylon and an army led by the goddess Chandi, the humans lose the war, and the battlefield is strewn with mortal corpses. The ghosts and demons then descend on the scene and start up a market to deal in the dead bodies:

> A unique market for ghosts
> Some dice and some slice   some weigh and some dispense
>   Some just deal and trade in meat
> The flesh is sold raw and cooking   some even buy it by hawking
>   Human heads, like so many coconuts.[29]

Besides being adroit businesspeople, premodern ghosts also had other social skills that mirrored the world of the living. They married other ghosts—as evidenced in the case of the *petni* and her episode with the *alta*— and even gave birth to baby ghosts, defying any Brahmanic notions of their genesis. For instance, a commonly told tale in the nineteenth century was of the two sister *petnis*, Kuni and Buni. The former lived in houses while the latter lived in the wild. One day a poor Brahman on his way home through a forest encounters the towering Buni. But instead of the usual threats of dinner and neck snapping, Buni asks him, rather shyly, to carry a message to her sister, Kuni, that she had just given birth to a beautiful baby boy. The Brahman, not overtly pleased to have met Buni in the dark, runs home as fast as he could. Once home he recounts this odd experience to his wife, and as he was narrating the alarming tale, a similarly huge and terrifying creature, Kuni, rushes out of the interior of the Brahman's home and asks him delightedly about news of her new nephew.[30]

If ghosts can be born, it follows, then, that they can also die. In the tale "Bente O Khenre," the ghost named Bente drops his rival Khenre into the river, whereby poor Khenre drowns and dies. Deaths are also duly ritualized in *sradhdhas* or funerals. When the king of ghosts wants to have a funeral for his late father in "Bhuter Baper Sradhdha" (The Funeral for the Ghost's Father), he is initially told by his ghostly subjects that there is no tradition among ghosts to have funerals. The king summarily dismisses such an idea and wins over the masses with the following argument:

> RAJAH: What do you mean there is no tradition? I say there is. Humans hold really bad funerals; I will easily outdo them. The true purpose of a funeral is to have a feast, to feed people, and that is what I shall do.
>
> REST OF THE GHOSTS: O king, does that mean we shall all eat too?
>
> RAJAH: Certainly. Now let us prepare for this ritual.[31]

The ghost-priest, the Brahmadaitya, is summoned, and a sumptuous feast of corpses, human flesh, and sweets then follows. Food and feasting are indeed important links that connect the human world to the ghostly one. The "traditional" ghost was not interested in fear for fear's sake alone. They descended on the human world usually in search of food or such material needs. A distinct pattern then emerges about this spectral world of the "traditional" ghosts: it is very much like our own. The claims of kinship that we sensed from both Rabindranath's account and that of Rajendralal Mitra now ring ominously true. They demonstrably suffered from hunger, physical pain, and social vanities as much as the next living person.

The hallmark of a modern ghost story is that we start off with an elaboration of the death that will become central to the rest of the narrative; it will "explain" the presence of the ghost, overlay even the preliminary proceedings (i.e., before the appearance of the ghost) with an sense of intense unease and, usually, as the deaths are frequently accidental or untimely, hauntingly bring home for us the needlessness of the end of life. Simply put, they are about death and the terrorizing concept of life ending.

This modern mode of narrativizing the dead is markedly different from that of our traditional ghosts. The most remarkable feature of these Beings, also their chief difference with their modern counterparts, is that we are narrative participants in their *lives*, not their deaths. The older ghosts, as we saw, lead regular "lives" and were collective social beings. Their deaths are incidental to the plot, most often unreferenced. It is their lives that we hear about, their social norms are described, their trials and tribulations documented. The stories were embedded in and arose from a society in which such Beings were inextricably woven into ritual life of the subaltern. The immensely popular festival of *charak*, so abhorred by British to merit its outlawing, for instance, consisted of the important ritual of *dāno bārāno*, or resuscitation of the dead. The chief devotee propitiated the village ghosts by taking food "to a tree standing in some lonely meadow, and the food [was] poured on a plantain leaf and left for the ghosts to devour," while others impersonated the ghosts themselves, donning masks, and reciting verses, "My name is Ram Sol, I shall be burnt and resuscitated again."[32]

These Beings were autochthonous citizens of a familiar landscape, equal to humans in all their formal activities; and, to paraphrase a classical mode of understanding the "other," when you tickled the "traditional" ghost, they too laughed; if you poisoned him, he too died; and if you wronged her, she too sought revenge.

"The Old Nurse's Tale": Servants, Stories, and the Supernatural

Who were the tellers of these tales and how were these tales received by the English-educated Bhadralok gentry of Calcutta? Unfortunately for us, the nineteenth-century ethnologist did not always signpost their findings such that we can easily locate the sources of these tales. But accounts of colonial childhood lead us to believe that most of the stories were either collected from the countryside or, if from the cities, from domestic workers and nurses.

Following the success of *Peasant Life in Bengal* (1874), Richard Temple,[33] the keen folklorist from the Bengal Staff Corps, commissioned Lal Behari Day to compile a collection of "those unwritten stories which old women in India recite to little children in the evenings."[34] Being "no stranger" to the "*Mährchen* of the Brothers Grimm" or to the works of other European folklorists, Day began to search, in his own words, for his own "Gammar Grethel" and found her finally in the person of a "Bengali Christian woman" who, when young and "living in her heathen home, had heard many stories from her old grandmother."[35] She, although a "good story-teller," failed to provide Day with the requisite variety of tales. Day gives us an outline of where and how he finally found his stories: "An old Brahman told me two stories; an old barber, three; and old servant of mine told me two; and the rest I heard from another old Brahman. None of my authorities knew English; they all told the stories in Bengali, and I translated them into English when I came home."[36]

But before he compiled these tales into the collection, Day had serially published them individually in his journal, the *Bengal Magazine*, between 1875 and 1878. There he had provided a more detailed account of the sources, which he, for reasons unknown, left out from his book manuscript. From their previous publication, for example, we learn that the "Story of the Brahmadaitya" was told to Day by one Manik Chandra Das, "a barber of Sonepore in the district of Burdwan," on December 21, 1877;[37] while the tales of "Hiraman" and "The Origin of Rubies" came to him from "Baburali, a Muhammadan of Santipore in the district of Nadiya," told to him on December 31, 1877, and January 31, 1878, respectively.[38] Similarly, "The Ghost Who Was Afraid to Be Bagged" was recounted by one Mrs. Kedarnath De of Chinsurah in August 1878, and the tale "The Field of Bones" by Kailas Chandra Banerjea of Sonatigri in the Hooghly district on September 17, 1878.[39]

The tales were thus collected from one or more of the following categories: from outside the urban center of Calcutta; from non-English-speaking people, hence people without access to higher education; and from multiethnic, multireligious and multicaste sources. This geography of social disadvantage is further highlighted in contemporary autobiographies.

The famous Brahmo reformer, Shibnath Shastri, recalls in his autobiography the tales that his childhood nurse Chinta-dasi told him about a particular coconut tree in their yard where a *dakini* (a variety of female ghost) had made her home. According to Chinta, this creature rode on the tree to travel to far-off places. Shibnath and his friends were thoroughly alarmed not only because there was fearsome *dakini* in their midst, but also at the possibility that she might lose their tree in her travels.⁴⁰ Rabindranath's nephew, the famous artist Abanindranath Tagore, in his trademark lyric style, recalls yet another nurse and her tales:

> The *dasi* [servant] sits at the far end of the room and weaves her fairy-tales — The tales are clearer in the memory than the *dasi*. . . . She says that her name was Manjari. . . . I see Manjari . . . leaning against a red leather bound trunk with her legs stretched in front of her. . . . Manjari nods sleepily and starts to speak: "once upon a time . . ."
>
> The terrace then appears like a dark primeval forest. . . . There the otter dances on treetops every evening and the Brahmadaitya plucks fresh jasmine flowers from the sky and ties it to his hair as he spreads his enormous legs between terraces and meditates. Through stories such as these I saw so many wonders.⁴¹

It is worth mentioning here that exploits of the Tagore Brahmadaitya came to the young Rabindranath himself through stories told by servants. It was not only the children of Bhadralok households who were privy to this world of ghosts. Many accounts exist of English children in India being frightened by such unenlightened ghost stories told by their equally backward native nurses and servants. J. D. Anderson (1852–1921), later distinguished professor of Bengali at Cambridge, spent his childhood in Calcutta in close company of a Hindu *ayah* (nurse) and a Bengali Hindu (male) servant, Hare. Later in life, the noted academic recalled how Hare would tell him frightful ghost stories at bedtime, causing him to squeeze his eyes shut with terror.⁴²

The underprivileged — servants, Muslims, lower castes, women — then, in ways however limited, provided a narrative bridge that allowed our old ghosts to creep into urban experience.⁴³

Multifaith Worlds, Heterodox Ghosts

The nineteenth-century Hindu Bhadralok scholar often despaired at the widespread religious miscegenation that marked everyday life for peasants and lower castes. Folklorist Dinesh Chandra Sen lamented how, in a form of ritual music in which singers went door-to-door recounting the glories of the Hindu goddess Lakshmi, the hymn singers were "not Hindus, as it should be, but Muslim mendicants."⁴⁴

This was the multifaith world in which nested the traditional ghosts. What was the significance of this world fluidly composing and recomposing itself to shape material and affective life?

It is now well established that, in Bengal, rather than being introduced by the sword from above, Islam had to engage existing, local traditions and accommodate itself into the molecular structure of the indigenous faithworld.[45] It was able to develop local roots in Bengal relatively easily because of the region's Buddhist past, which had weakened Brahmanic influence. It was not uncommon for popular texts of medieval Bengal, such as the Sufi poet Saiyad Sultan's (1615–46) *Nabi Vamsa* (The Prophet's Lineage) to portray Hindu gods like Vishnu, Bramha, and Shiva as Muslim prophets or Nabis.[46] Difference or even conflict between religious traditions was not glossed over but resolved in unexpected and delightful ways. In the Hindu poet Krishna Ram Das's *Raimangal* (1686), a struggle emerges between the tiger-demon Dakshin Roy and the Muslim fakir Barakhan Gazi over who should have control over the forests and waters of the Sundarbans. God himself has to come down from the heavens to resolve this dispute, but the form god takes as mediator is of interest. Half of him is the Hindu deity Krishna and the other half is the prophet Muhammad:

> One half of his head has dark hair   while the other has a top knot
>   Bedecked with flowers
> One half of his body is white   while the other is dark
>   He carries the Koran in one hand and the Puran in the other.[47]

Folk deities such as Satya Pir, Gaji, and Banabibi ruled over this multifaith universe, their origin stories as well as the communities of their faithful easily flowing over sectarian divides of faith and worship.

Asim Roy's formulation of Muslim "cultural mediators" is of use here. According to Roy, the exogenous Islamic tradition, embodied in Perso-Arabic literary cultures, failed to sink roots in a largely Bengali-speaking local audience. The cultural mediators—the numerous Muslim pirs, composers, and poets—consequently opted to present Islam through the local language, Bengali, and through a rich, complex mixture of Islamic and indigenous tales, legends, and religious doctrine. The syncretic mosaic contained, in equal measure, elements of Tantric Buddhism, non-Brahmanic local gods and goddesses, Islamic legends, and select but transmuted components of the Brahmanic tradition. Roy astutely unpacks the simple category of a Muslim pir—normally understood as a spiritual guide or mentor—and offers us instead a much more culturally dense pir-template, the figure of whom "extended far beyond the range of . . . mystic guides, saints and holy men . . . [as] this amorphous label [pir] came to cover a vast motley of popular objects of worship and supplication, not all of them being saints, or Sufis, or religious personages, or Muslims or even human beings." The template thus encompassed not just saints and religious figures but also "apotheosized soldiers, pioneering settlers on reclaimed waste lands in deltaic Bengal, metamorphosed Hindu and Buddhist divinities, and anthropomorphized animistic spirits and beliefs."[48]

Roy's processual account of cultural mediators and pir-ification can be employed to reveal two important aspects of religious procedures that determined the mapping of the precolonial ghost world. First, that the boundaries between gods, malevolent spirits, and ghosts were permeable, and figures moved frequently from one category to the other; second, that we need to modify the category of cultural mediators to include practitioners who *maintained* the multifaith mosaic through ritual practices that consciously refused to obey boundaries. In this category I include the *rojas* and *gunins*, community healers and ghost-doctors who were called on to exorcise ghosts, cure snakebites, and, overall, manage the relationship between the lived world and the world of spirits.

It made practical sense for ghosts and gods to have interchangeable status. After all, both were capable of affecting the lives of their followers when angered, pleased, or simply called on. This intimacy of functions left its trace in language. The word for gods, *debata*, and ghosts, *deo, deota*, was often the same in peasant society. Undoubtedly this linguistic intimacy was because of braided histories of the Indo-European family of languages, where Deva and Daiva were the word for god in Sanskrit and Avestan, respectively, while Deo was demon in Persian. Abanindranath Tagore recalls seeing a shadowy figure drifting by his moving palanquin on one of his night journeys through Orissa. When he called out to his palanquin bearers to ask if they too had seen the figure, their counsel was to ignore it as he was a "deota." "They call ghosts deota," Abanindranath concluded with some bafflement.[49]

Colonial ethnographers such as Herbert Risley pointed superciliously to this ambiguity between good (gods) and evil (ghosts) among peasants and indigenous tribes as a sign of cultural backwardness. Imagination of the tribal Oraon people, wrote Risley, "tremblingly wanders in a world of ghosts. Every rock, road, river and grove is haunted." The village bhuts who, Risley claimed, "have various names" were worshipped alongside more regular goddesses and gods.[50] Similarly, for the Bhumij there was not much difference either in worship or function between the powerful goddess Jahir-Buru "capable of blasting the crops if not duly propitiated" and Bagh-Bhut, who "protects his votaries from tigers."[51]

Risley could have saved his derision. Instances abound in the premodern world of the emotions fear, love, and veneration being consubstantial when it came to the worship of deities. The Rabbinical scholar Bernard J. Bamberger reminds us that "the contrast and antithesis between the expressions *fear* and *love of God* felt by later ages was not present in the minds of . . . Biblical authors. . . . The two terms are practically synonymous and interchangeable." Indeed, Bamberger further claims that both love and fear had "the general meaning of religion . . . [as] there is no abstract term in Old Testament Hebrew for religion."[52] Correspondingly, Jianto Ren and Andrew Lambert's discussion of the concept of "awe" in Confucian thought shows that for Confucius it is the governing principle that forms the bedrock of reverence for both territorial and divine authorities.[53] Heonik Kwon, noting the fluidity and regularity with which gods, demons, and ghosts changed places in Vietnam, called such evolving Beings "transformative spirits."[54]

Interchangeability between ghosts and gods, then, was not a sign of confusion but rather the expression of a philosophical regime profoundly different from that of the modern. Bamberger's insight that the biblical authors lacked an abstract term for religion is important. In the syncretic universe of the peasant and lower caste, *religion* was not *a set of beliefs derived from texts and rules*, but what was embodied in *practices of veneration and worship*. The severely practical nature of such religion (for lack of a better word), meant that it was also brutally consequentialist, meaning that its normativity was shaped by how the subject of veneration, god or ghost, could or could not advance the welfare of her or his votaries. Such subjects rose and fell with local needs. New goddesses, Sitala and Olaichandi, for instance, came into being when smallpox and cholera epidemics started to devastate villages. Further, since these goddesses and gods were so deeply imbricated in the rhythms of everyday *working lives* of their devotees—tiger ghosts/gods to fend off tiger attacks while chopping wood, snake goddesses to defeat snakes while working in forests, the ghost Pencho to ensure the welfare of newborns—it made little sense for the community of worshippers to be divided along more orthodox religious lines of Islam or some version of Hinduism.

Ghosts and demons as companions of established gods further unsettled the borders between gods and ghosts. Widely worshipped Hindu gods such as Shiva, Durga, and Kali in Bengal all traveled with ghosts of various kinds. The medieval narrative poems, the Mangal Kavyas, composed between the fifteenth and the eighteenth centuries, carry vivid descriptions of such Beings. Bharatchandra Roy's (1712–60) description of Kali summoning her forces in *Vidyasundar* is a representative example of this genre:

> When they were summoned to war   The joginis rushed in
>   Shrieking and howling in glee.
> Dakinis Hakinis bhuts   Shakhinis Petnis Duts
>   Brahmadaityas, Bhairabs Betals.
> The Pisaches, Bhairabs are on the move   The Yakshas and Rakshas are leading
>   Ghantakarna, Nandy and Mahakal.
> Shaking their matted manes   Roaring in laughter
>   Their eyes whirl like discuses
> Hungry tongues leap out   Fire burns on their faces
>   Fearsome teeth grind in fearsome mouths.
> Their jaws are open wide   Blood streams from them
>   Corpses of infants adorn their ears.
> They carry Falchions, human heads and divine assurance   In their hands
>   Severed human heads form their necklaces.[55]

Such evocative, synesthetic description of ghosts and demons is only partially due to the poets' genius. The sculpting material for these gorgeous portrayals existed in the popular consciousness of peasant society. The ferocity of life's adversities demanded ferocious Beings who could provide protection and comfort.

Consider the figure of the Jugini, who was revered in some regions as a ghost and in some as a handmaiden to the goddess of smallpox, Sitala. Anthropologist P. K. Bhowmick studying non-Brahmanic cults found the Jugini to be the dreaded executor of Sitala's wrath on a village. She devoured the flesh of her victims and retained their souls. Her appearance is equally fearsome and bears close resemblance to ghosts: "During summer . . . she strolls . . . in lonely fields. . . . She has no head, but her eyes are fixed on her breast. . . . [Others] think that she is a middle-aged woman with . . . breasts hanging down to her waist. . . . This spirit is sought to be averted by occult practices."[56]

Sitala herself was associated with the Sheora tree, universally acknowledged in Bengal as a tree favored by the female ghost, the *petni*. Kaibarta fishermen worshipped Sitala by setting up a "rough block or slab of stone . . . under a pipal, banyan, or seorha tree, smeared with red lead and bathed in clarified butter or milk . . . [representing] an ill-defined, but formidable power."[57]

The goddess at Kamakhya, with her temple in the Assam hills, was perhaps patriarchy's most dreaded female goddess. Nineteenth-century Bhadralok imagination teemed with visions of an untamed goddess luring men to their deaths or striking them with impotency. Such ideas were so ubiquitous that when the Assamese historian Haliram Dhekial Phukon wrote what is now considered the first empirical history of Assam in 1829, he felt he had to dispel a range of myths about the goddess. She was famous throughout all nations, but no one, he lamented, had any real information about her. Wild tales of "walking trees, men being turned to sheep and magic charms" were so prevalent about the Kamakhya goddess that most were reluctant to visit her temple.[58] Kamakhya, like many other religious figures, was undoubtedly a pre-Aryan mother goddess, feared by later Brahmanic and bourgeois cultures alike. For us what is important to note is her close connection with death and ghosts: "As the innumerable names of the goddess are mostly names of local goddesses both Aryan and non-Aryan, it may be suspected that the formation Kama in Kamakhya is of extra-Aryan origin. There is a strong suggestion of its correspondence to Austric formations like the following: Kamoi, Demon; Kamoit, Devil; Komin, Grace; Kamet, corpse."[59] Fear of female sexuality, monstrosity, and death were intertwined in the processes that shaped both ghost-making and god-making in this world.

Kunal Chakrabarti's work on mother goddess worship has stressed the egalitarian and distinctly non-Brahman nature of mother goddess cults in pre-Brahmanic Bengal. According to Chakrabarti, a conscious effort, in the form of a set of practices that he calls the "Puranic process," was made by the Brahmanic order to assimilate these wild pre-Aryan goddesses into their religious regime. The goddesses were often virgin deities, "sporting on the mountains . . . inaccessible forests and caves . . . followed by ghosts, associated with wild beasts such as tigers and lions." Brahmanism had to somehow acknowledge these figures or risk being unable to reach their already established votaries. The newcomers then, Chakrabarti elegantly demonstrates, "had to adjust with the prevailing tradition, . . . [adopting] these goddesses with suitable modifications, . . . [transforming] them into brahmanical divinities." The process was both uneven and often incomplete, whereby a new fair-skinned goddess who was more mother than warrior existed side by side with the older figure of the dark warrior goddess who was hard drinking, angry, and valiant. This, Chakrabarti rightly claims, was a "deliberate juxtaposition of opposites" that created a complex, composite figure who could encompass "a whole range of images, emotions and loyalties."⁶⁰ Risley records this process empirically in his study of the cult of Thakurani Mai: "Already Thakurani Mai, the 'blood-thirsty tutelary goddess' to whom, only twenty years ago, the Hill Bhuiyas of Keonjhar offered the head of the obnoxious Dewan of their chief, has been transformed, in Singbhum and Lohardaga, into the Hindu Durga, to whom a Bhuiya priest makes offerings of goats, sheep, etc., which are afterwards partaken of by the worshippers."⁶¹

We can begin to see now why there existed an easy fluidity between ghosts and goddesses. It also explains why precolonial ghosts were not often the lost souls of particular individuals, but were autochthonous creatures with no particular origin story. The word *fairy* in the British context, similarly, emerged as a catchall category for diverse Beings. Shifting through the scholarship, Jason A. Josephson-Storm has deduced that the term *fairy* was not "a particular class of magical beings, but first and foremost a general reference to the unusual, fated, bewitched, or enchanted," so much so that, in the early days of British folkloric studies, fairy tales and folktales were treated as synonymous, the category expansive enough to include all magical creatures.⁶² In the case of Bengal, by calling all such Beings "ghosts," I am, for the sake of modern intelligibility, rather shamefacedly, following the lead of the colonial ethnographer. This should not occlude the fact that the nineteenth-century classificatory grids, developed and employed by the British and the Bhadralok alike were, as Foucault reminds us, "linking together . . . things that are inappropriate."⁶³ Stanley J. Tambiah's discussion, pace Hilary Putnam, of *concepts* versus *conception* is also of use to us here. Putnam takes the word *temperature* as an example to explore how we can map the meaning of the concept from the world of early modern scientists to the present day. In doing such a mapping, Putnam asks us to attend to the fact that "the seventeenth-century scientists . . . may have had a different *conception* of temperature, that is a different set of beliefs about it and its nature than we do, different images of knowledge, and different ultimate beliefs about many other matters as well."⁶⁴ Thus, when the subaltern informant used the word *bhut*, the meanings and affect that radiated from the word would be very different from how the word was heard and interpreted by the nineteenth-century ethnographer.

Consider the *dakini*, a Being who started being catalogued under "ghost" but deserved her own place in the firmament. We have already seen her as an object of terror for the child Shibnath Shastri, who believed her to be living in his family's coconut tree. Bengali proverbs, in similar fashion, painted her as a figure of dread. A mother-in-law described her daughter-in-law as a *dakini* to express her extreme distaste for the newly wed:

bou na re bou na garal dakini
Diner bela manusher chcha rat hole dakini

She is no bride, no bride is she, but a poisonous dakini
By day she appears human, by night a dakini.[65]

But who or what was the *dakini* who sometimes accompanied goddesses such as Sitala or Kali and sometimes was understood simply as part of the pantheon of ghosts and demons that haunted everyday life?

Dak is a Tibetan word for knowledge, making a *dakini* a woman with knowledge, or a wise woman. This is clearly a legacy of Buddhist Tantrism of which tendency Bengal was a nodal point from the eight century onward. Many texts that were to become the Tantric canon were composed in Bengal between the fourteenth and seventeenth centuries.[66] Goddess worship was a vital part of this tradition. Many of the female ghosts and demons we find in folk narratives, like the *dakini* and *hakini* of Bharatchandra, have their origin in Tantrism. But how did the powerful goddesses of one tradition become dreaded monsters? Our answer can be only tentative and exploratory.

First, and most obviously, demonization of powerful female goddesses was Brahminism's answer to integrating figures that were harder to assimilate than others. While assimilation was the project of the "Puranic process," many tribal goddesses clearly resisted the process, thereby ensuring their "demotion" to demon-hood. But we must be careful about the meaning and scope of this "demotion." As we saw earlier, the worship of gods and ghosts was based on a *spectrum of reverence* rather than on their being polar opposites. Hence, many of these figures may have lost their goddess status, but they lingered on as subjects of both ritual worship and respect. Speaking about the agricultural caste, the Kurmis, Risley pointed out, "The animistic beliefs characteristic of the Dravidian races are overlaid by the thinnest veneer of conventional Hinduism, and the vague shapes of ghosts or demons who haunt the jungle and the rock are the real powers to whom the average Kurmi looks for the ordering of his moral and physical welfare."[67] What Risley prognosticated about the Kurmis held true for the vast majority of the agricultural and working classes of Bengal.

Second, the assimilation of tribal goddesses may not have been complete from the point of view of the Brahmanic order from above, but a different kind of assimilation did happen, a process we can call *assimilation from below*. Tantric norms, pre-Aryan goddesses, and Muslim pirs intermingled to form a unique composite mosaic of ghosts and gods. Ghosts followed the lead of the living in terms of religious amalgamation. Muslim ghosts lived in harmony with Hindu ones and plagued hapless villagers with equal determination. The *mamdo* and *mamdi*, respectively a male and female Muslim ghost, were beloved fixtures in Bengali folk tales and legends.[68] *Dakinis* and *hakinis*, originally of Tantric extract, coexisted with Brahman ghosts like the Brahmadaitya. As the reviewer for M. J. Walhouse's essay "On the Belief in Bhutas" observed disapprovingly, "Brahminical religion is spread like a thin veneer over all, but the old affections of the lower classes survive. . . . Notoriously . . . the lowest classes have their own deities, and indeed are incorrectly called Hindus in the Census."[69]

If we pick a single thread of this tapestry and try to trace it to its origin, we will miss the contribution of that particular thread to the overall beauty of the design. For instance, we can trace the history of the Sheora tree in order to find why it came to be associated with female ghosts and, from the evidence, deduce that this was because it was originally associated with fearsome pre-Brahmanic goddesses. But this linear approach can only feed the "demotion" thesis—once-mighty goddesses being reduced to ghosts who were ritually impure and socially to be avoided. Such an approach fails to grasp two structuring facts about premodern ghosts: one, that they are not clinically cleaved from the world of the living; and, consequently, two, that the fear of ghosts was on an equal plane with the fear of gods, both kinds of spirits being capable of bringing good or harm to the community.

Such a complex, ever-changing faith-tapestry, with multiple histories interacting on a granular level, produced its own practitioners, women and men who maintained its multireligious tessellation while at the same time initiating new rituals that integrated and deepened these arrangements. The *roja* or *gunin*, the exorcist found in all villages, was such a ritual practitioner, to whose presence and practice we now turn.

Tantra, Magic, and the Unbearable Burden of Enlightenment

In the world of the educated nineteenth-century Bengali, no two figures evoke more curiosity, concern, or wonder than the twin figures of the *tantrik* and the *ojha* (or *roja*). The first is usually a figure invoking awe and fear, while the latter conjures incredulity and/or wonder. The most celebrated literary representation of the former is Bankimchandra Chattopadhyay's *kapalik* in *Kapalkundala* (1866). In the novel, the eponymous heroine is raised on a desert island by her adoptive father, a fearsome *kapalik*, in Miranda-like isolation till she meets a handsome shipwrecked (and conveniently) educated Bengali man. *Kapalkundala* is referred to in contemporary literary reviews as "among the most popular of Bengali books." Sales were perhaps assured by the sensational descriptions of at least one of its characters in the contemporary book notices. The *Calcutta Review*, for instance, declared the *kapalik* to be a "member of one of those strange sects which practiced the wild and terrible Tantric forms of worship—whose temple is the burning ghat, and for whom no rite is too bloody and disgusting."[70] The famous missionary scholar John Farquhar called *kapaliks* the "skull-men," referring to the *kapalik*'s use of human skulls as instruments of worship.[71] To this colorful religious accoutrement one need only add the spice of transgressive sexual practices and we have a figure as steeped in thrill and mystery as someone out of an Indiana Jones film.

The *ojha* (*roja* or *gunin*), however, does not fare so well in contemporary literature either of the British or Bengali variety. Once commanding respect and fear in the village, where he was the sole interceder for the spirit world on behalf of humans, the *ojha* underwent a dramatic loss of face and fortune in the nineteenth century.[72] An important section in Kaliprasanna Singha's *Hutom Penchar Naksha* is devoted to *bujruki* or fraud. The irrepressible Hutom, ever vigilant against social wrongs, prefaces this section thus:

> When Hinduism reigned supreme and people were ignorant of [scientific disciplines such as] pharmacology, chemistry and geology, practices like these [claims to resurrect the dead, ability to read minds, communicate with ghosts] were believed in. Today, thanks to English education these things are rarely seen. Calcutta, however, is a city of wonders, there is nothing that cannot be found here, no gods here go unworshipped, so alchemists and exorcists alike often find their way into this city to make a living. They show their wares in several places and then finally learn a lesson when exposed.[73]

The chapter itself is a hilarious portrayal of various instances of magical fraud. The common framework for each story is the following: someone arrives at the city claiming magical powers. He then fascinates and awes the gullible for several days. Women and men without modern education constitute the vast majority of the gullible. Someone of superior intellect, usually a "college boy" or "Medical college student," then exposes the *ojha*, and he is forced to apologize and leave.

According to Kartikeya Chandra Roy, *ojhas* were also a threat to public health. If an infant fell ill while still in the birthing-room, instead of doctors it was the *ojha* who was summoned to administer to the baby: "A sick infant was diagnosed usually as being possessed by a little ghost called a Pencho. Men were not allowed into the birthing room, therefore whatever miraculous events the ojha and the duped females claimed to have transpired therein, were believed by all."[74]

According to Dinesh Chandra Sen, most *ojhas* were Muslims. With the help of incantations, mantras, and charms, they cured snakebites and spirit possessions. In his *Folk Literature of Bengal*, Sen analyzed in detail two representative collections of such mantras, both published and edited by Muslim authors from minor Calcutta presses. It will be worth our while to pause to reprise Sen's analysis.

The first collection was edited by one Mir Khoram Ali from Masjidbari Street in Calcutta. Ali claimed to come from a long line of such practitioners who had generationally passed down the mysteries of the tradition to their descendants. Fearing that he might be the last of the adepts, Ali decided to recruit the modern device of print to create a permanent record for his art.

Ali's mantras contained words in Prakrit indicating their pre-Islamic roots, as well as Arabic incantations invoking the Prophet Muhammad. They summoned the aid of powerful non-Brahmanic goddesses such as Manasa and Kamakhya in concert with appeals to older Brahmanic gods such as Shiva and Krishna. There were also references to Balluka Sagara, a Buddhist shrine. Non-Brahmanic ancestries were more clearly etched than others. For example, the Hindu goddess Chandi is referenced in Ali's text as the daughter of a Hadi (sweeper/scavenger caste). The reference, Sen rightly analyzed, reflected Chandi's lower-caste roots, which were suppressed when she was shoehorned into the Brahmanic pantheon as an incarnation of Durga. A similar text, by Munshi Enayetulla Sircar, recording the origins of the Fever Demon, Jarasura, and the ways to ward him off, is marked by this multifaith universe of meanings. The Fever Demon, or god, if you will, Sen records, was born of a Brahman mother and a Chandala father. The text, although by a Muslim author, is like Ali's text replete with Hindu invocations and symbols.[75]

If we go back to our proposal of *rojas* functioning as cultural mediators, the work of exorcism, then, was serious business. Men such as Mir Khoram Ali and Munshi Enayetulla Sircar probably had distant Hindu or

Buddhist pedigrees, their families having converted to Islam sometime in the fourteenth or fifteenth century. But what makes the texts and the actual practice of this kind of exorcism so significant is that these practitioners consciously transgressed faith barriers and *produced* a community of believers around these shared fears and the means to allay such fears. Ghosts and gods created and integrated close communities that were both sacral and social.

The *roja* was first and foremost a part of the working life of the village. William Hunter in his statistical account of Medinipur includes the *gunin* in his section on "village artisans" alongside more regular professions such as blacksmith, carpenter, and barber.[76] How did orality and concrete social relations produce such multifaith communities? Spoken words, as Walter Ong has reminded us, derive their meaning and explanation from the nonverbal elements embedded in the specific context of utterance, from "who is speaking to whom, on what occasion, with what sort of force, with what gestures, what facial expressions, and so on."[77] While applicable to all spoken word, this holds all the truer of ritual incantations. Incantations have what linguists call illocutionary force, meaning that utterance itself is the action. When a ritual specialist, under "felicitous conditions," utters certain words, the words embody the action. When a minister (specialist) who has the authority to marry people (felicitous conditions) speaks the words "I now pronounce you man and wife," the union is, as though magically, constituted—the couple is married to each other. The conditions are important. If I uttered those same words at a social gathering at my home for my favorite couple, I would not be able to marry them. For spells and incantations to be performative utterances, then, certain conditions must be fulfilled, the person uttering the words must be qualified to do so, the spells must use the correct words and right ritual materials, and the utterance itself must be correct in diction, cadence, and emphasis.[78] Being an *ojha* was thus not an easy operation.

The Jesuit priest Father Dehon observed that almost every Orao village had a school for training *ojhas*. The guru or teacher was from the Lohar, bhuniyar, or Turi community. The training, Dehon noted, was so rigorous that "only the cleverest and most persevering among them" could become *ojhas*:

> Every evening they spend three, four and sometimes five hours learning the mantras and the names of the deotas and the bhuts. The guru is generally a renowned ojha—a man with a strong imagination and the gift of the gab, who gives fearful descriptions of the bhuts and their doings, until the heads of his pupils are stuffed with all kinds of weird-looking imaginary beings. They are taught how to work themselves into a trance,

and some having more (*gun*) disposition to hypnosis than others, can pass their examination after one year, whilst others have to learn for two or three years. Of course, they do not know the mysteries of hypnotism and attribute everything to deotas and bhuts. When a pupil is ready to pass his examination, he has to recite all the mantras and incantations, give the names of all the deotas and bhuts and gurus, and perform all the duties of the ojha. When the candidate has done well he brings a fowl to sacrifice to the deota whom he has chosen for his special patron. . . . The fowl that the successful candidate has brought is then sacrificed in honour of his patron, and the guru, dipping his finger in the blood of the offering, marks with it a big line on the forehead of the future ojha. From that time, he can begin to practice.[79]

We have already seen how the language of the incantations enclosed their multifaith roots. The words, Sen noted, had remained largely unchanged through time, proving the need to retain their illocutionary force. Muslim *ojhas* thus routinely invoked Hindu gods, local deities, and Islamic prophets in the same breath to cure snakebites or rid a household of a troublesome ghost. "It is a curious thing," writes a somewhat perplexed Sen, "that the Muhammadan prodigy in the use of spells recites *Ohm Swaha Phat* like a Hindu Brahmin."[80] An incantation to cure a jackal bite might call on Krishna, "Oh Lord Krishna . . . let the poison be diluted," while another to cure a scorpion bite might call on Allah:

> Oh, the poison of the scorpion
> Listen to what I say.
> Allah may haunt you;
> If you withdraw the poison, Allah, the creator of all will protect you.[81]

Approaching Allah in this magical, rather than liturgical, manner was widespread. Sen reminds us that, in the medieval poet Ksemananda's *Manasa Mangal*, a copy of the Quran, along with other amulets and charms, is used by the protagonists to ward off evil.[82] In a similar vein, an 1898 report tells of an *ojha* from Sylhet using the Quran to deal with ghosts:

> A circle is described round the affected person with a stick, charms being recited at the same time; a verse from the Koran is read over a quantity of mustard oil, and a wick smeared with the oil thus charmed is burnt and the smoke out of it is thrust into the nostrils of the affected person. To the *bhut* this is unbearable and so it speaks through the possessed. The

sorcerer (Ojha) then asks the *bhut* his name and whereabouts and how he came to have possession of the person, and he gives replies. The sorcerer then makes the *bhut* promise in the name of Suleman Badshah, the sovereign of *bhut*, that it would never more enter the body and then, when he is satisfied, he cuts the magic circle and the *bhut* goes away.[83]

Like the incantations themselves, the "work" of the *ojha* scrambled religious borders in mirroring practices from multiple religious and folk traditions. The folklorist Sarat Chandra Mitra (1863–1938) noted the similarity between "Hindu exorcism" and "Muslim exorcism," in an ironic misrecognition of the syncretic world to which belonged the *ojha* and his art.

In direct contrast to Hutom's urban derision for the *roja/gunin*, in reality, then, as a figure producing and entrenching community life across sectarian divide, the *roja* continued to exert authority in the working life of Bengal's villages throughout the colonial period. Colonial officials and European missionaries alike were duly impressed by the power they exerted over both ghosts and communities.[84] There were, of course, material reasons for the *ojha*'s importance to the village. In an account of his childhood in a South Bengal village in the 1930s, anthropologist P. K. Bhowmick recalled how, with the nearest health center being twelve miles away, the villagers depended on the *gunin* for all medical and social emergencies. The villagers came to him with cases as varied as "theft, snakebite, ghost-possession, warding off the evil effects of planets, evil eye or witches," and although *gunins* came from lower castes, "by virtue of their profession and efficacious skill" they had "a high status in . . . society," so much so that they were "respected even by the Brahmins," who took "the water 'consecrated' with the puff and spittle of the gunins, in case of predicaments, without any hesitation, rather with reverence."[85]

As we circle back to the printed mantras of Mir Khoram Ali and Munshi Enayetulla Sircar, the irony of committing such a fluid oral tradition to the permanent and binding order of the printed word was perhaps not lost on these authors. The tradition of taming the natural and supernatural world with incantations was more than simply an oral tradition; but, precisely because it was so, it meant that the act of utterance had social force. Orality and oral traditions are by their nature participatory. They assume a face-to-face, non-distantiated universe wherein speaker and listener share not just a narrative but a social relationship. Print, in contrast, produced and sustained an unknown, anonymous audience.[86] These men seeking to preserve their art through such a medium signified something more profound than simple conservation. It indicated the fraying of the multifaith community that had been, in equal parts, produced and protected by such magic.

Past Imperfect: Old and New Ghosts

That there was a pronounced difference between the ghosts of old and their newer counterparts was first acknowledged in the autobiography of the prominent lyricist and writer, Kartikeya Chandra Roy (1820–85). Having lived through a crucial period of historical change, Roy was in an ideal position to notice this transition from the old to the new. By profession Roy had, for most of his life, served the royal family of Nadia variously as a private tutor, music instructor, and, finally, as the *dewan* or principal revenue officer. But, like several sophisticated men of his times, Roy combined in himself multiple talents as social historian, composer, and general man of letters.[87]

The section in his autobiography that deals with ghosts is titled, significantly, "Sekal O Ekaler Bhut" or "Ghosts of the Past and the Present." The terms *sekal* (past) and *ekal* (present) had a significant referential history. In 1874, the noted Brahmo reformer Rajnarayan Basu (1826–99) gave a lecture at Hindu College titled "Sekal ar Ekal." The lecture was a tremendous success, resulting in its appearance in print form in a pamphlet bearing the same title, which, again, sold rapidly, and even Rajnarayan himself was nicknamed "Sekal-Ekal" in certain young circles. The reason for this enormous popularity was because, in this lecture, Rajnarayan had managed to lucidly articulate the popular mood toward modernity. The past (*sekal*), in Rajnarayan's lecture, was celebrated as a predictable, happy time when society was governed by "mutual sympathy" among men. The present (*ekal*), by contrast, was suffused with such evil practices as loss of respect for the Bhadralok and unseemly cultural icons such as the Western-educated woman, demanding and shrewish in her interactions with her husband and in-laws. The most significant aspect of this argument was what Rajnarayan saw as the definitive dividing line between *sekal* and *ekal*: introduction of higher education in English.

Sumit Sarkar's pioneering work on the theme of Kaliyug, the last epoch before the apocalypse in Hindu mythology, persuasively demonstrates how millenarian dreams and social resentments found expression in nineteenth-century literature through a depiction of the present in apocalyptic language.[88] Rajnarayan's critique of *ekal*, ironically coming from a man who was one of the first to benefit from modern social changes, fed into an already existing discourse about the decadent present.[89] The use of the terms *sekal* and *ekal* thus had singular social resonance beyond a straightforward temporal debate.⁹⁰ Both these chronological templates came packed with social judgments, to the extent that use of them served as a shorthand reference to the original discourse about the dissolute present; we need to bear this in mind when we engage with these terms as used by Kartikeya Chandra Roy in his reference to ghosts.

Kartikeya Chandra devotes a small part of his autobiography to ghosts and their historical transformation. He begins in the traditional mode of human interactions with ghosts: by telling a ghost story.

Kartikeya Chandra was traveling with friends along the riverine networks of Bengal, and their boat eventually arrived at Murshidabad, the precolonial capital of Bengal. The city that had been the dwelling place of the "supremely powerful ruler of the three enormous provinces of Bengal, Bihar and Orissa," the city that had routinely forced the mighty English and French to "bow their heads in the presence of its throne," had awakened hope in the voyagers that it would show them many "wondrous sights" in keeping with its history.⁹¹ They were instead met with a necropolis. It seemed to Roy as though the "life of the city had been drained along with its power." Massive palaces, once the heart of a humming urban existence, now lay like "so many corpses." The living, numerically few, roamed the derelict city streets in their "emaciated bodies and ugly visages." The city had been reduced to "a home for ghosts and demons."⁹² The ghost story that he relates is set against this powerful portrayal of Murshidabad and its adjacent suburb of Kasimbazar, at once a description of urban decay and a coded indictment of the cause of decay: British rule. It is only fitting that this silent theater of a dead past, Kasimbazar, shall be haunted—as much by its pastness as by its deadness.

The ghost story that follows was related to Roy by a Bhadralok, thus in his mind erasing any doubts as to its veracity. The narrator, a devout Brahman by birth, had arrived at ghostly Kasimbazar just as evening had begun to darken the already dark landscape of the ruined town. Unsuccessful at finding shelter in a number of homes, he finally reached a house where someone answered his urgent call for refuge. The voice of the unseen proprietor came from within the darkened house, cordially inviting his guest to make himself at home and apologizing for his inability to be a more active host due to illness. As the guest settled in with a quiet smoke from the hookah and tobacco that were thoughtfully provided, the host called out to him once more, this time with instructions about dinner. The increasingly suspicious visitor was now told that since no guest should go hungry, he was to milk the cow in the attached shed and, with the rice and sugar stored in the alcove, make a rice pudding. That he should make "enough for two people" was the concluding part of the order. By now, of course, the visitor had become uncomfortable at both the persistent invisibility of his host and his nasal tone, an established characteristic of the speech of the dead. As soon as this thought had formed itself in the conscious part of his brain, his "host" dropped all pretense and said to the unfortunate guest, "You are correct in thinking what you are thinking; however, no harm will come to you as long as you follow my instructions. Place one bowl of the rice pudding on the porch and eat from the other one. You will be in grave danger if you do not do as I say."[93]

Left with little say in the matter, the Brahman wisely did as he was told and ate his dinner. From slurping noises in the dark, he realized that his host too was indulging in the delights of rice pudding. The placid regularity of this harmless domestic scene was, however, rudely shattered when the guest saw a gigantic arm, more than twenty-four or twenty-five times normal arm-lengths in size, emerge from the dark porch and dutifully do the washing up, drawing water from a waterhole. And yet the ghost was not quite done with the Brahman. His last instruction to him was to visit the ghost's living brother and ask him to offer the customary ritual rice cakes (*pinda*) for his soul in the holy city of Gaya, such that his ghostly existence could be ended, and he could find liberation. A failure to do this would result in the traditional ghostly revenge: the snapping of the Brahman's neck.[94]

As far as Kartikeya Chandra himself was concerned, there was no doubt in his mind that the above was a "fabulous tale." Later in his autobiography he leaves no doubt in our mind as to which side of this debate on faith he was on. "We were told so many tales by the *prachin* [old] about *Brahmadaityas*, *Bhuts* and *Sankchunnis*," he recalls. But "English education and Ramtanu Babu's influence" tore the veil from his eyes and revealed such tales as what they truly were: lies.[95] Armed with reason, Kartikeya Chandra and his fellow acolytes then proceeded to "debate vigorously" with the *prachins*, such that their minds too "could be rid of such erroneous beliefs."[96]

Kartikeya Chandra Roy's confident rhetoric about belief and reason initially follows a predictable nineteenth-century route, aligning belief with the past (as *sekal* or *prachin*) and reason with the present (as *ekal* or *nabin*). But all is not well with this neat division, as doubt creeps into Kartikeya Chandra's account when he delves deeper into the practices of *ekal* regarding ghosts. "Just as people of the past had 'seen' ghosts and claimed to have had communicated with them," adds Kartikeya Chandra with a certain amount of narrative disquiet, so too "some well-educated and wise men" of the present were claiming to have done the same.[97] And just as bhuts and Brahmadaityas were said to "visit" the *prachin* folks, so "spirits both good and evil" were paying visits to the distinguished and the educated of contemporary times. If this was alarming news for those cheering for the rational present, all was not lost. Unlike the bhuts and Brahmadaityas of earlier times, who had been deemed unconditionally unworthy by those who claimed knowledge of them, the new ghosts visiting the present-day Bhadralok were actually being praised for their civilized behavior by their advocates. The rationalist Kartikeya Chandra adds ruefully that this was perhaps because men of old were generally unworthy and uncivilized themselves, resulting in ghosts of similar nature, whereas, given the present age of enlightenment, it was not surprising that ghosts too would shed their traditional unruliness and copy the *bhadra* world of mortals. But the greatest epistemic discomfort that Kartikeya Chandra has for us is saved till the end. What if, he asks in the concluding part of his section on ghosts, the "traditional ghosts" were to come to us moderns and argue the following: "It is clear that you believe in the ghosts of *ekal*; but then by what offence have *we* been rendered non-existent?" Kartikeya Chandra's answer is a tortured one. "My simple mind," he writes, "does not have a good answer to that charge." As the section on ghosts ends, this response stays with us, an unhappy reminder of the irresolution and tragedy of the modern consciousness.

TWO
—

The New Spirits

MASTER: Man will turn God the day European science and technology unites with the spiritual self-control of India. Thereafter such science and technology will be put to more positive use.

PUPIL: Will man ever see such a day?

MASTER: Why certainly! You Indians are eminently suited for this purpose. It is all in your hands. If you so desire, you could be the Masters and Leaders of this world.

—BANKIMCHANDRA CHATTOPADHYAY

A second important seance we had was in 6/4 Anath Nath Dev's Lane, in a haunted room. The defunct hostess of the house which has now changed hands, has not yet left her favorite room. But ten minutes after the sitting, she began communicating and frankly gave us a bit of her mind. She was rather getting fond of the palmist friend of our automatic medium, Mr. S. Chaudhuri, the Secretariat clerk. The pious gentleman the palmist was rather non-plussed at the prospect of this Spiritual amour, which no human laws can declare illicit, in spite of the fact that he is already a family-man with a devoted-wife looking up to him for support. The amorous lady being a Hindu, did not see any objection to his taking a second wife, by way of digression, so to say. The object of her love, however, strongly objected to this sort of arrangement and very earnestly prayed for exorcism.—*Hindu Spiritual Magazine*, 1918

By "modern" ghosts and their advocates, Kartikeya Chandra Roy was referring to the notable rise in occult practices among the ardently "rational" Bhadralok world of the late nineteenth century. People from diverse religious traditions from orthodox Hindu to liberal Brahmo; from varying political affiliations from loyalist to nationalist; and with disparate personal histories all tried their hand at communicating with the dead in some form, with nothing in common between them except their Bhadralok social location. We are not referring here to marginal members of this group. Men as prominent as Raja Digambar Mitra (1817–79), leading businessman and the first sheriff of Calcutta; the noted Brahmo reformer Keshab Chandra Sen (1838–84); the novelist Peary Chand Mittra (1814–83); journalist Shishir Kumar Ghose (1840–1911); and several of the Tagores were all intensely engaged in various aspects and practices of the occult. Séances were held in private homes and scholarly articles on the subject published in leading journals. Engagement with the occult by the great and the good in Bengal had become so intense by the latter part of the nineteenth century that the satirical magazine *Basantak*, mocking the regnant practice of séances among the educated, remarked, "These days there is a great new fashion in town, previously the only famous object here was the *choti* [slippers] from Taltola [a neighborhood in North Calcutta], now we see that this Planchoti [Planchette] has completely robbed it of its fame."[1]

Shishir Kumar Ghose, firebrand anti-imperialist journalist and founder of the popular nationalist daily, the *Amrita Bazar Patrika*, could easily have been *Basantak*'s target. His nephew Mrinal Kanti Ghose's *Paroloker Katha* (Accounts of the Spirit World) (1933) is a detailed account of his family's experiments with the occult, with séances held regularly to communicate with loved ones who had passed away. But the most significant feature of this account is the trope of empirical science in which Mrinal Kanti framed his narrative. Communicating with spirits was seen as an illustration of modern technology:

> Just as we receive news from our loved ones travelling abroad through the postal service and Telegraph, so too it has become easy to receive news of our departed friends and relatives through séances; Just as Science has empowered us to converse with people at a distance over the telephone and hear their voice, in a similar manner, with the help of a Medium we can converse with a departed Soul and even hear their voice. . . . Hence there no longer remains any real reason to mourn the passing of a relative or friend.[2]

For the Bengali Hindu Bhadralok, self-appointed vanguards of reason, séances were appealing because they were a means to "scientifically" explore the world beyond death. They were communicating not with "ghosts" but with "spirits," the souls of their loved ones. The perceptual elevation of ghostly Beings into spirits is a significant one, and we will have more to say on this later. For now, let us note how the new occult practices of the English-educated Bhadralok cohered a new *science of spirituality*. While Spiritualism had its origins in Europe, in Bengal it acquired a specific valence: a means to advance the inherent superiority of India over Europe in matters of the spirit. A new science was birthed and nurtured in tandem with another new entity, an emerging nation.

The Scientific Supernatural

In his contemplative text *On the Soul: Its Nature and Development* (1881), Peary Chand Mittra made explicit the connection between the world of the dead and the new religio-philosophical discourse of Spiritualism. Peary Chand lost his wife in 1860. The loss, he admits, "convulsed me much" and made him take "to the study of spiritualism which, I confess, I would not have thought of otherwise nor cherished its charms." His grief made him seek out prominent Spiritualists of his time, including the famous American jurist and chief justice of the Supreme Court of New York, John W. Edmonds. But it was the coming to Calcutta of one Dr. Bérigny that cemented Peary Chand's relationship to Spiritualism:

> We had weekly séances at his house. At one of the séances, I was developed as a medium. . . .
> It is too late in the day to discuss whether we can communicate with the departed, or whether spirits can appear before us in materialized form. These are all accomplished facts. The spirits can do much more than we can think of in showing their supremacy over matter which falls within the domain of *occultism*, and this occult power we can show when we rise above the mediumistic state.[3]

Almost every leading intellectual of late nineteenth and early twentieth-century Bengal, especially the ones with reformist or Brahmo backgrounds, dabbled in the occult. The dead, they all claimed, frequently communicated with them in such settings; they imparted knowledge, insight, and often simply consolation. But unlike the older ghostly Beings and their rascality, these somber "spirits," summoned in polite circles through mediums, were part of a wider project of scientific inquiry that destabilized, yet again, the boundaries of the natural/supernatural. With modern Science as their interlocutor, these intellectuals tried to "scientifically" account for the world of the dead—thereby corralling the world of spirits/ghosts back into nature in a way that made this world the purview of both religion, in a modified sense, and natural science.

Since Tanika Sarkar's important work on gender illustrated the victory of Hindu "revivalists" over the Hindu "reformists" in the battle for the political soul of the new nation, several scholars have sketched out the connection between modern secular thought and this newly minted Hindu nationalism.[4] In the case of Bengal specifically, Partha Chatterjee and Sudipta Kaviraj have long drawn our attention to processes and practices in the region that, from the mid-nineteenth century onward, contributed to the production and consolidation of a new public sphere through which a new secularized Hinduism became the dominant political language of anticolonial nationalism.[5] For our purposes, it is important to note the social fusion between those who dabbled in Scientific Spiritualism and the architects of the new Hinduism.

A discourse of "Hindu science," in formation since the mid-nineteenth century, brought together a complex of social ideas and groups shaped in part by imperial racism and cultural self-assertion from Hindu Bhadralok society. Gyan Prakash's incisive study of this phenomenon locates its origins in eighteenth-century "Orientalism" but shows its subsequent mutation as a launchpad for the future nation: "Helped by its status as the product of academic research, the notion of Hindu science won influence beyond the circle of religious reformers. References to Hindu medicine, mathematics, astronomy, and chemistry became ubiquitous in the elite culture. Journals and pamphlets returned to the past to search for the scientific contributions of the Hindus, identifying India with Hinduism and seeking Hinduism's transcendent value in its science."[6]

As in other colonial societies at the intersection of "tradition" and "modernity,"[7] the discourse on science in Bengal did not easily map on to any discrete separation between various binaries—Europe-India, traditional-modern, or religion-science. Bankimchandra Chattopadhyay was influenced by Comte's positivism but tried to render it legible through the indigenous philosophical tradition of Samkhya. In 1866, Rajnarayan Basu, a leading Brahmo scholar-activist and close associate of Debendranath Tagore, published "Prospectus for a Society for the Promotion of National Feeling among the Educated Natives of Bengal," in which he advocated for a "school of Hindu Medicine, where Hindu Materia Medica and practice of physic will be taught freed from the error and absurdities that disfigure them."[8] Akshaykumar Dutta, editor of the Brahmo journal *Tattabodhini Patrika* for twelve years (1843–55), not only wrote the first science textbook in Bengali (1856) but, more significantly, in an uncanny mirroring of seventeenth-century

European scientists, declared that it was not the Vedas but nature herself we must regard as scripture (*shastra*): "The starlight, as fast as thought and yet taking a million years to reach our earth, is our shastra; the minute drops of blood that the heart pumps and circulates, is our shastra. The entire natural world is our shastra, pure knowledge our acharya (teacher)."[9]

There were two components to this epistemology: First, that any intuitive approximations of the divine ought to be regulated through reason; and, second, that it followed then that the relationship between religion (versions of Hinduism) and science was dialectical rather than oppositional. Bankimchandra Chattopadhyay, in his widely read *Dharmatattwa*, tried to articulate Hindu spirituality through a lexicon of the European sciences and reason. "Science and Reason," in capital letters, for Bankim and others, however, remained on a strictly European register—the point was to indigenize them. In this, two intellectual tools came to the aid of the neo-Hindu Bhadralok: first was to vernacularize scientific pedagogy and, second, to trace the roots of Science to a mythical Hindu past.

Bankim's journal, *Bangadarshan*—which, along with *Nabajiban*, *Aryadarshan*, and *Prochar*, Amiya Sen has termed the "neo-Hindu Press"—carried, as we will see below, a unique blend of popular science, Hindu metaphysics, and political philosophy. Bhudev Mukhopadhyay, another keen student of this new variant of Brahmanic Hinduism, fiercely advocated for a vernacular science education for Bengal. Besides writing science textbooks, in his popular essays for the *Education Gazette*, such as "Samajik Prabhandha" (1892), he leveraged his role as an inspector of schools to tie the fate of the nation to the acquirement of a scientific education.[10] While acknowledging the superiority of Western Science, he nonetheless suggested that science was neither inconsistent with nor oppositional to ancient Aryan knowledge. He saw "no inconsistency whatever between science and religious philosophy of the Aryans." Indeed, he proposed a historical relationship that many would follow: that "modern scientific postulates of Europe" were "anticipated in the Shastras . . . [and European] science . . . [would] have to advance itself considerably to reach anywhere near the truths . . . evident in the Shastras."[11] It was not coincidental that avowedly Hindu journals mushroomed in this same era in tandem with journals on popular science,[12] allowing later scholars to conclude that, from this period onward, "a conscious effort was made even by the more orthodox (Hindu) press to defend certain aspects of Hindu religion and philosophy by drawing upon analogies from modern science."[13]

The career of Kshirod Prasad Bidyabinod (1863–1927) is a testimony to the intersection of the newly articulated Hinduism, modern science, and

Spiritualism. Kshirod Prasad was a star student at the University of Calcutta and, after earning his master's, taught physical science and chemistry at the eminent General Assembly's Institution in Calcutta from 1892 to 1903. The fact that he taught science at this particular educational institution is of significance. Founded by the missionary Alexander Duff in 1830, General Assembly's Institution was seen from its very inception as steering a clear path toward European knowledge, particularly scientific knowledge.[14] Kshirod Prasad not only taught science but was also its hands-on practitioner. In 1913 he advertised his invention, Limodine, a water-purifying chemical, which he claimed he had produced through several years of "researching and collecting mineral water from various parts of the country" and by distilling its health-giving minerals through "advanced scientific instruments." A few drops of Limodine added to drinking water could "completely cure acidity, indigestion, diarrhea, cholera and other digestive illnesses." Indeed, Limodine added to wells during a cholera epidemic could arrest its deadly spread.[15]

Given this background in the hard empirical sciences, Kshirod Prasad was perhaps the least likely candidate to found and edit a journal on the occult, miracles, and Spiritualism. Yet that is precisely what he did. The journal *Aloukik Rahasya* (Mysteries of the Supernatural) sought to kindle in the emerging nation a sense of duty toward its own theological and spiritual past through the medium of modern science. Science, so far a handmaiden of empire, a preserve of European commentators and researchers, was suddenly reformatted as a discipline that ancient Hindus had had all along; and it was Scientific Spiritualism that partly facilitated this groundbreaking domestication of Science.[16] As Kshirod Prasad put it, the goal of journals such as *Aloukik Rahasya* was "to firmly establish the fundamental unity between the Natural Sciences and Spiritual Science," a methodology that allowed "[our contributors] to venture into areas of spiritual science established by Aryan *rishis* [sages, wise men]."[17]

In the introductory editorial to the journal, Kshirod Prasad clarified the mission of *Aloukik Rahasya*. The modern-day Hindu, he lamented, had lost his way in that he now considered the daily duties of a devout Hindu, such as "Sandhya [evening prayers], Bandana [song of praise], Sradhdha [funeral ritual], and Tarpan [the sacrament of offering drinking water to the gods]" to be useless, and was even repelled by them. But Kshirod Prasad had a unique solution:

> The only way the *sanatan* [ancient] Hindu *jati* can be saved, is by reestablishing firmly the fundamental unity of Natural Science and Spiritual

Science. Luckily for us, the very Western Science that we had used as an excuse to lose sight of our own indigenous jewels, that Western Science has now changed its tune. Western scholars are now attentive to the Supernatural and the Miraculous and are making an effort to reveal their mysteries. The resulting deep secrets that have been discovered and are being discovered through their extraordinary initiative and perseverance have ushered in a new era in the world of Science.

So that the Bengali reader may have some faint idea of such theories and mysteries and with the help of them reach our lost *Sastric* knowledge-rays and thereby be able to illuminate their hearts to whatever small extent—we have decided to publish [this journal] *Aloukik Rahasya*.[18]

While acknowledging a debt to the West for recognizing Spiritualism as a scientific discipline, Kshirod Prasad firmly situated his project in indigeneity. "Our curating efforts," he stated, "will not be limited to following Western scholarship alone"; instead, the journal was committed to collecting data on "many supernatural phenomena" that were yet to "become rare in this country." It was simply a lack of "initiative and indifference to scientific methodology" on the part of his countrymen that prevented the scientific analysis and public dissemination of such phenomena and knowledge, a lack the journal was eager to overcome. Kshirod Prasad's list of supernatural phenomena that the journal was going to cover included, among others, Spiritualism, clairvoyance, animal magnetism, mesmerism, mysteries of death, hypnotism, various tantric rituals such as spells of Maran-Uchatan to vanquish/kill an enemy, ghost sightings, miracles by saints, and witch lore.[19] It was published every month between 1909 and 1915 and, by all accounts, was very popular among its rather niche audience.

Aloukik Rahasya embodied the ideological shift from the old ghostly Beings to the new spirits. Its premise, like many journals of similar stripe, was the revival of a specific version of Brahmanic Hinduism as both a bulwark against European Enlightenment and the launchpad for a new nation. A new Scientific Supernatural was produced and recruited to serve this goal.

Authenticating and citing sources in the various supernatural accounts and reports was a key strategy *Aloukik Rahasya* used to stamp their articles with veracity. It was an obvious mirroring of empirical methods. To be published, authors had to provide names, places of employment, and details of the supernatural event they were reporting. Sometimes even that was not enough. An editorial note to one Girijaprasanna Sen Kaviraj's story about dueling ghosts stated the following: "We have published this story because names and place details were provided as authentication. Nevertheless, we need to be furnished with further proof. While we do not question the supernatural nature of these events, we do require signatures from all parties related to the events. We hope the author will provide us with these as soon as possible, for if not we will be forced to mark this account as untrue."[20]

Often the stories were accompanied by written testimonies from leading members of society. An account of spirit summoning was certified by a Rai Bahadur, government pleader at the Dhaka Bar,[21] while a piece on clairvoyance carried a medical doctor's eye-witness testimony: Dr. Ohdedar admitted that, during his "professional career, extending over nearly 27 years," he had never seen "another case which appeared more like that of 'possessed'" and that he was "unable to offer any explanation" for "certain things that happened in . . . [his] presence."[22] The latter testimony was printed in English, the master language perhaps offering further proof of reason.

Caste and class were important implicit validators of these accounts. Every essay and report in all five volumes of the journals, barring none, were by educated upper-caste authors. In one issue, the editor even expresses great surprise at having heard two lower-caste janitors discuss philosophy![23] During the complete run of the journal, two pieces were by women, all the rest by men. Authors came from various walks of life, often schoolteachers and court officials from small towns, but also prominent figures such as Manmathanath Ghosh, one of the few Indians to travel to Japan in the early twentieth century to learn industrial arts.

Validation through empirical proof being the dominant framework of the journal, grounding articles that set the tone for the journal, either by Kshirod Prasad himself or by one of his close associates, employed this method to explain the supernatural. A running series, *Dadamashiyer Jhuli*, probably by Kshirod Prasad writing under a nom de guerre, captured the methodology. It was written in the popular style of a dialogue between an old man, Taracharan Bhattacharya, versed in the Hindu *shastras*, and a young nonbelieving college student, Byomkesh, trained in the Western sciences. "Do tell me," asks Bhattacharya of Byomkesh, "what makes you think ghosts are not real/imaginary?" "Easy," comes the response. "What cannot be seen is surely imaginary." Bhattacharya's answer to the young man expressed succinctly the thrust of the Scientific Supernatural discourse.

When a glass is filled with ice water, Bhattacharya points out, droplets soon appear on its surface. Where do they come from? The standard scientific explanation of gas condensing into liquid, according to Bhattacharya, actually is an admission of defeat by science—an acknowledgment that "when matter is in its suksha [subtle] state it is invisible but when it sheds that state and acquires a sthula [solid] form it becomes visible again." Applying this basic scientific law to ghosts, one can see why "ghosts composed as they are of matter subtler than air, remain invisible to the human eyes," but once "ghostly matter condenses/solidifies" or "when human sight is deepened" ghosts become visible to us.[24]

Other essays similarly mounted a scientifically informed challenge to this so-called materialist view of invisibility being proof of absence. In "Suksha Sharirer Proman" (Proof of Subtle Body), the famous educator and Theosophist Hirendranath Datta asked his readers to consider the apparent monochromatic nature of sunlight, but that very light, when directed through a prism, reveals its spectrum of seven brilliant colors. This proves that we cannot "nullify the existence of things we cannot see." Hirendranath then discusses the case of Dr. Kilner, who had successfully invented a machine "with whose aid it was possible to condense the rays of the subtle body" or the human aura.[25]

One of the central planks for the Scientific Supernatural—namely, establishing the veracity of the afterlife and occult through scientific methods—was not unique to Bengal. Peter Harrison has outlined the conjoined history of religion, magic, and science as they emerged together in Europe but how "this initial cooperation collapsed as the science gained part of their respective notion of coherence in contradistinction to religion as an irrational belief system."[26] As early as 1678, the renowned chemist Robert Boyle wrote to Lord Tarbat, a Scottish nobleman, inquiring about fairies and supernatural Beings in Scotland. Boyle was also the intellectual patron for Robert Kirk, who under Boyle's encouragement wrote an influential treatise on witches, fairies, and elves.[27] Scholars such as Richard Noakes have detailed how many leading Victorians—scientists and Spiritualists alike—"used simple mechanical contraptions, precision electrical apparatus, vacuum tubes, photographic plates, and self-recording instruments to try to establish whether the striking physical phenomena produced through spiritualist mediums derived from known or unknown causes."[28] Dr. Kilner, approvingly cited by Hirendranath, was a case in point.

Walter J. Kilner (1847–1920), a medical doctor at London's St. Thomas hospital, was part of the nineteenth-century European project of using science to "prove" supernatural phenomena. At St. Thomas, he oversaw the newly introduced technique of electrotherapy, which created the basis for his investigations into electrical energy. In 1911 Kilner published his findings in his book, *The Human Atmosphere or the Aura Made Visible by the Aid of Chemical*

Screens, to great fanfare. He argued that the human body was "surrounded by a haze intimately connected with the body," which, until then, had been visible only "to certain individuals possessing a specially gifted sight, who have received the title of Clairvoyants." But now he had devised a machine that could study this haze or aura most scientifically—indeed by methods, he claimed, that involved "no more charlatanism in the detection of the human Aura . . . than in distinguishing microbes by the aid of the microscope." Given his official status as a medical doctor, Kilner was also eager to distance himself from any direct association with the occult. "It may as well be stated," he wrote, "that we make not the slightest claim to clairvoyancy; nor are we occultists; and we especially desire to impress on our readers that our researches have been entirely physical, and can be repeated by any one."[29]

European exploration of the supernatural with scientific means found its apogee in Theosophy, a new movement that combined these various elements, had an international appeal, and included several prominent public figures as adherents in both India and Europe. We discuss the movement in detail in chapter 5, but here it is important to state that, while the discourse of the Scientific Supernatural in Bengal and Europe shared many common features, the roots from which they drew sustenance were radically different and hence so were the fruits. It is to these roots that we turn next.

Hindu Spirits, Revivalist Souls

On a cold winter's night in December of 1875, nationalist journalist and campaigner Shishir Kumar Ghose paid an unannounced visit to Sir Richard Temple, the lieutenant governor of Bengal, at his home in Calcutta. It was a special night. Albert Edward, the Prince of Wales, was due to arrive in the city the next day. Whether Temple was surprised at the unorthodox nature of Shishir Kumar Ghose's house call remains unrecorded in Shishir Kumar's biography by his nephew. What the biographer does record is the momentous nature of his request to the lieutenant governor. "There are no industrial schools in Bengal," he put to the colonial official, "and now some of us have organized to remedy this." He then entrusted the lieutenant governor to announce this project at the much-advertised welcome ceremony for the Prince of Wales. In just two years, on April 28, 1877, Shishir Kumar's effective campaign strategies and extensive fundraising—he persuaded the lieutenant governor to provide a yearly grant of 8,000 rupees—resulted in the establishment of the Albert Temple of Science, an institution to provide technical education in Bengal. As science education goes, it is then hard to doubt Shishir Kumar Ghose's commitment to it. And yet, in a path analogous to many of his generation, this public advocate of science and scientific training also edited, from 1906 until his death in 1916, a popular journal of the occult, the *Hindu Spiritual Magazine*.

The mission of the *Hindu Spiritual Magazine* (HSM) is laid out in its editorial by Shishir Kumar Ghose. The first "object of HSM" was to "disseminate spiritual truths known in this ancient country but little known in the West, and those truths of the West which are similarly little known in the East." He credited the theosophists for having done "much to carry out this idea," but it was an area that needed more work. The other mission of the magazine was "to show that death . . . considered to be the greatest calamity that can befal [sic] man" was "in fact, the greatest of God's blessings to His creatures."[30]

Before we make further comments on the magazine, its editor deserves more of our attention. Shishir Kumar Ghose's fame as an advocate for science paled in comparison to his fame as a firebrand nationalist. His other more famous paper, the *Amrita Bazar Patrika,* was legendary for leading several social justice campaigns, including protesting oppressive labor conditions of peasants in indigo plantations and the racist Ilbert Bill. *Amrita Bazar Patrika* editorials by Ghose frequently referred to Englishmen as "jackasses" and "cowards."[31] When the British paper, the *Englishman*, known for its racist instigations during the Ilbert Bill controversy, campaigned to imprison Shishir Kumar for sedition, the *Dhaka Gazette* correctly predicted the nation's mood if such a thing were to come to pass:

> The great oracle of the Hare Street [the *Englishman*] seems to think that if the Editor of the Amrita Bazar Patrika is mulcted a sum of two or three thousands of rupees and made to rot for some weeks in some of the Indian jails, all the troubles would cease. We can only pity the man for his utter ignorance of the resources of the Amrita Bazar and the spring from which it draws its lifeblood.
>
> We would ask the *Englishman* and its followers to try the experiment once and for all. We would be no false prophet if we were to say here that as soon as the news spreads throughout the country that the Editor of the Amrita Bazar is in troubles, the whole country from Peshwar to Assam, from Himalaya to Comorin, will rise to one man to help him and send forth a growl that will shake the throne of the Queen-mother and make her look attentively into the affairs of India. Why, such a course of action, if followed up at all, will only lend to strengthen the cause which they propose to smother by all means.[32]

We need to be attentive to the breadth and depth of Shishir Kumar Ghose's popularity to appreciate the fact that it was the full force of his popularity, contacts, and public presence that he brought to bear on HSM. For instance, in its very first issue, the journal carried a fulsome endorsement from a scion of the Tagore family and a member of the legislative council of the governor-general, Maharaja Sir Jyotindramohan Tagore. "The importance of such a magazine," Jyotindramohan declared, "can never be overestimated." He invoked "that great statesman, Gladstone," according to whom psychical research was "the greatest and most important subject" that could "engage the attention of man." Jyotindramohan also referred to Shishir Kumar's already impressive list of books on religious thought to make his case about the journal:

> The Hindu Spiritual Magazine will certainly meet a want that has long been sadly felt . . . and will be hailed with joy by everyone who feels a craving for occult knowledge and spiritual research. . . . True . . . that you are widely known as a political character; that is by reason of your long connection with the Amrita Bazar Patrika, but the author of so many religious works breathing deeply of devotional feelings and high spirituality should be even more widely known in connection with spiritual culture.[33]

Both *Aloukik Rahasya* and HSM, to borrow Hirendranath Datta's sunlight analogy, were prisms that helped break down the different colors of the reigning discourse on Spiritualism. Discerning readers developed their own comparative models on how to assess both journals. One reader from Gaya found *Aloukik Rahasya* to be so popular and "necessary" that he was even willing to pay an increased subscription rate:

> Consider this: the annual subscription rate for Shishir Babu's *Hindu Spiritual Magazine* is 6 rupees, but the women in our families cannot enjoy it [it being an English-language journal]. Your magazine is only 1.5 rupees and yet the whole family can relish it. Indeed, it is so popular in my own family that when it arrives there is fierce competition around who gets to read it first. . . . [In] an age of vulgar materialism . . . [wherein] we have lost faith in the afterlife . . . your magazine is a like a lamp in the darkness.[34]

The preceding section analyzed the purported "scientific" claims of the discourse; here we unbraid its second constitutive skein: a revived Brahmanic Hinduism imprinting itself on to the present in creatively dangerous ways. Kshirod Prasad Bidyabinod's explanation for what happens after death is a good place to start to understand this strand.

In an editorial for *Aloukik Rahasya*, Kshirod Prasad, describing the passage of the soul from the moment of death into the afterlife, explained this crucial difference. According to Kshirod Prasad, those that have lived a life of excess, steeped in earthly desires and especially—of course—having indulged in copious sex, have difficulty detaching from those desires even after death; instead, they "act as if they were alive." These Beings "are commonly referred to as 'Bhuts.'" This state was extremely painful and polluting. But even the virtuous will pass though this stage (but will presumably emerge better behaved). Consequently, the raison d'être of "all religions" was to "avoid this state and reach salvation."[35]

"Let me tell you what a *Pret* is," says Taracharan Bhattacharya to the young Byomkesh, and thereby catalogues for us some of the key terms of this new discourse. Not everyone becomes a *pret* or a ghost. Only those whose *sthula sharir* (gross body) had fallen but "whose ordinary human instincts—such as sexual desire, anger and similar animalistic tendencies—remained" attained *pretabstha* or the ghostly state. While the living soul *Jibatma* is in this state, "its *Manomaya kosh* [mental sheath] starts to break down and its constituent elements then re-create a new body, or the Dhruba Sharir or the Jatana Sharir [Constant body, Body of pain]." The soul is "trapped" in this painful state for a while, prevented from moving on, which is precisely why, Bhattacharya emphasizes, the Hindu performs various funerary rituals, *sraddha* and *tarpan*, to "free their dear ones from this state."[36]

There were some important variations in the discourse to this puzzle of what happened after death, but most mirrored the widely accepted Brahmanic version of the afterlife: upon death, there is a period of dangerous death-pollution for twelve days when the soul takes the form of the *preta* (ghost/sprit); from this state they are rescued by appropriate funerary rites by the deceased's family and restored as a *pitr* (ancestor), after which, some argued, they begin their journey again on the cycle of rebirth.

Indologist Monier Williams, having interviewed several practicing priests and pundits, affirms in an 1876 essay the importance of *sraddhas* and restates the hegemonic belief in the trajectory of the departed soul:

> When a man dies his sthula-sarira or "gross body" is burned, but his soul quits it with the linga-sarira or "subtle body," sometimes described as angushtha-matra, "of the size of a thumb," and remains hovering near it. The deceased man, thus reduced to the condition of a simple individual soul invested with a subtle body, is called a preta, i.e., a departed spirit or ghost. He has no real body capable of enjoying or suffering anything, and

is consequently in a restless, unsatisfactory and uncomfortable plight. Moreover, while in this condition he is held to be an impure being. Furthermore, if he dies away from his kindred, who alone can perform the funeral ceremonies, and who are perhaps unaware of his death, and unable therefore to perform them, he becomes a pisacha, a foul wandering ghost, disposed to take revenge for its misery upon all living creatures by a variety of malignant acts.[37]

The terms and concepts mobilized here come mainly from post Vedic and Puranic texts. But Williams himself acknowledges that there was "much confusion of thought and obscurity, besides great inconsistency, in the accounts given by pandits of the exact object and effect of their [funeral] celebration." The reason for this "confusion" is that the dominant discourse on death, including that of the new Scientific Spiritualists, did not follow a linear development from one or other Hindu text but was a bricolage of notions composed from traditions that could even be at odds with one another.

Brahmanic texts themselves had little consensus on this issue. For instance, the Rig Veda alone had multiple views on the fate of the dead, from uniting with ancestors in an unspecified heaven to the body merging with the elements of nature. The notion of rebirth in the Rig Veda is, as one scholar put it, "at best murky," gaining its full scope only in the later Brahmanas (700 BCE) and even later Upanishads (600 BCE).[38] It is in these later texts, and through the intervention of contemporary religious traditions of Buddhism, Jainism, and the Ajavikas, that a jigsaw pattern emerge that can be loosely called a "Brahmanic" view of the afterlife. We should note the irony that while this new discourse of Scientific Spiritualism was fiercely committed to Vedic Brahmanism, a category that was itself hardly homogeneous or stable, scholars now assess that the entire architecture of rebirth may have originated not in Brahmanism or even Buddhism and Jainism but in the non-Vedic, tribal religions of the Gangetic delta.[39]

Scientific Spiritualists reflected this heterogeneity of traditions. Shishir Kumar Ghose, who, after his initial enthusiasm, had left the Brahmo Samaj in 1869, was perhaps reacting against its Vedantic and Upanishadic training when, unlike Kshirod Prasad, he strongly rejected the theory of rebirth in his magazine:

> A Hindu correspondent cannot understand how the Editor of the *Hindu Spiritual Magazine*, who is also a Hindu, should oppose the theory of re-birth, when Hindu Shastras . . . proclaim it. We have said it more than once that the theory of re-birth is of Buddhistic origin and had only been

incorporated in their creed by latter day Hindus. Our Shastras enjoin upon us that the Veda is the supreme authority, . . . not only there is not a trace of the theory of rebirth in the Vedas, . . . that supreme authority advocates immortality of the soul, pure and simple and reunion of the beloved in the other world.[40]

But if there was no rebirth, what did the afterlife look like? For Shishir Kumar and his many followers departed souls went to three *lokas* (abodes): "earth bound souls" went to Hell, "souls of ordinary men" went to Hades, and those of "superior men" went to Heaven. The neat classificatory model allowed this discourse to similarly explain and classify the conduct of such departed souls as they came into contact with the living. Spirits in Heaven "rarely came to communicate with mortals" except occasionally to provide us with "inspirations, intellectual and religious." Spirits from "the second sphere" came to us only when summoned and could thus "give warning of . . . danger" or help in practical matters like "the discovery of a lost article" or "the detection of a criminal." Spirits from the "lowest sphere" either came to the human world "of their own accord" or were "summoned by . . . black magic." It is this lower class of spirits, if you will, that were responsible for things like "demoniacal possession" and other such harmful phenomena. But even such cases, "though . . . dreadful to the victim" were of "great use to mankind," as they "completely establish the survival of men after death—a knowledge most precious to mankind."[41]

This is a remarkable set of observations, for it establishes two distinct projects for Scientific Spiritualism: first, the Hinduization of existing folk rituals; and, second, it hews its path away from such local or folk traditions. The precolonial ghostly Beings, their playfulness and petty vengeances, could now be explained as lower class "souls," thus firmly tying them to an Hinduized afterlife. Similarly, existing folk traditions, such as *rojas* magically finding lost household objects with the aid of ghosts they commanded, could be folded into this highly ethicized framework of a Hindu afterlife.

Unsurprisingly, *bhut*, a word that carried echoes of the past playful, vengeful creatures, was rejected by the new Scientific Spiritualists. *Atma* or "soul" was their preferred term, a term that severed connections with the precolonial tree-dwelling Beings and established a new one with Hindu *shastric* texts. Akshay Chandra Sarkar (1846–1917), a close associate of Bankimchandra Chattopadhyay and an important member of the intelligentsia, wrote a remarkable essay in his journal *Nabajiban* in 1884, making this case.

Akshay Chandra titled his piece, after a poem by the famous Sakta poet Ramprasad Sen, "Bol dekhi bhai ki hoi mole," or "Tell me what happens after death," and he used the opening lines of the poem as his epigraph:

"Tell me what happens after death / Some insist we become bhut-pret / some assume we will go to heaven / and yet others claim we will attain Sāyujya [a state of conscious unity with the divine in Sakta philosophy]."

Akshay Chandra used the interrogative trope of the poem to great polemical effect. He is horrified at the prospect of the first, that is of transforming into a bhut after death:

Become a bhut? What! What a terrible plight! Shall I become a creature that evokes only terror and disgust in human beings? That which travels in cremation grounds, in ritually unclean spaces? That lives in the dark, in trees, and speaks in nasal, unclear and yet horrifying tones? A creature, simply thinking about which stirs up disgust, is that what I will become?[42]

Let us note here the repeated use of the word "disgust," *ghrina*, and mark it for the caste marker that it is. Further analysis of Ramprasad's poem, as well as a "careful review" of "ancient philosophies," however, assured Akshay Chandra that he would not be subjected to such a destiny. His body after death would go back to the elements but his soul—his "immortal, ageless, infinite, unalterable" soul—would continue on and eventually merge into the Para Brahman (the Supreme Brahman of the Vedantas).[43] Similarly, when Shishir Kumar cited his contemporary and colleague Kaliprasanna Ghosh's views on the issue, he was, in effect, speaking for this generation of Bhadraloks. "Kaliprasanna Ghosh Vidyasagar (Companions of the Order of Empire, CIE) of Dhaka," wrote Shishir Kumar, "did not like to use the word 'pret.' He preferred 'atma' to show respect to the departed. To be honest, it is painful to designate our respected ancestors as 'bhut pret.'"[44]

Kshirod Prasad similarly carried forward the campaign against lowly bhuts in the very first issue of his journal. Accounts of bhut sightings in India, he noted, came most frequently from the lower orders, the "uneducated masses," and were therefore unreliable and impossible to verify. In his journal he therefore only published accounts from England and America, where several "educated, discerning, subtle, and scientific minded" men had "investigated and observed such phenomena" before recording them.[45] When he did publish Bengali authors on the subject, there remained no doubt in those accounts that the sightings were of somber, Hindu "spirits"—Shishir Kumar Ghose's *atmas*—rather than playful bhuts. An employee of the reputable scholarly society Bangiya Sahita Parishat, Binodbihari Gupta, published one such account of how, as a child, he was frequently visited by a "40–45-year-old, very handsome" man, who had the sacred thread around his neck and was a figure of "great beauty and comeliness."[46] Most Bhadralok accounts of ghostly visitation described similar figures who, rather than evoking terror or disgust, appeared to learned men as sources of solace and validation. When Debendranath Tagore was criticized by some important family members for converting to Brahmoism, his dead mother came to him in a dream, telling him how proud she was, thus assuring him of the righteousness of his chosen path.[47] From descriptions of séances organized by Shishir Kumar Ghose's family, it is impossible to tell whether they were invoking spirits of the dead or participating in a traditional Vaishnavite devotional moment. Highly devout *atmas* joined in the family's singing of Vishnu's name and glories, while the medium in the family, Motilal Ghose, when possessed by spirits, was overcome by trances that were very much like Vaishnavite devotional trances.[48] While in London, Bhupendranath Bose (1859–1924), president of the Indian National Congress and later the vice chancellor of the University of Calcutta, was a regular participant in séances held at Holland Park by the Psychic Society, where he managed to communicate with his deceased parents, brother, and his much-beloved son. His son, in a trope common to all similar encounters with the Bhadralok dead, assured Bose that death was not a state to be feared, presumably for those from his class and caste background.[49]

It is unsurprising then that the new spirits followed strict codes of class and caste. According to Mrinal Kanti Ghose, when "low class" spirits appeared at their family séances, the medium, the spiritual-minded Motilal Ghose, "suffered greatly," as the plebian spirit would force him to "flay about, yell, and curse in dreadful unrefined language." By contrast, "high class," *pabitra* (holy) souls brought spiritual joy and abandon to these gatherings. One such soul, Haridas, upon coming, would transport those gathered into throes of spiritual ecstasy, they would spontaneously burst into devotional songs (kirtans) and gain a sense of blissful peace.[50] Lesser-known authors repeated this trope of strictly classed spirits. One even suggested that there was a correlation between the class of the medium and that of the spirit they summoned; respectable men from the upper classes attracted "godly spirits," while lower class spirits had their way with lower class people.[51] Unlike their premodern counterparts, these spirits were so godly that they even came to earth to participate in scripture reading.[52]

But, while saintly, the new spirits were not impervious to either commerce or nationalist politics, arenas both constitutive of the new Bhadralok modernity. The journal *Pandit*, which proudly declared itself to be a propagandist (*pracharak*) for the "Aryan religion," carried an advert for a "wondrous ghostly device" called the "Planchette Machine." The advertiser, the Indian Trading Company of Garpar Road, was offering the machine at the very affordable rate of three rupees only; this was particularly reasonable because, as the advertisement noted, when such machines first arrived in Calcutta, they were sold by European traders for very steep prices, sometimes five to ten rupees a piece. With the machine, one could call on the dead—and they would dutifully arrive—to ask them about "the past, present and future, actually anything, and they would answer all queries most satisfactorily."[53]

Akshay Chandra Sarkar, editor of the popular *Sadharani* and an ardent nationalist, wrote humorously about asking one such planchette machine pointed questions about the future: how long was the "kindly British Raj" going to rule over India, were Bengalis forever to be slaves to the British, and, finally, was Lord Northbrook for or against Bengalis?[54] What Akshay Chandra wrote sarcastically about was in reality colored by truth. Séance circles and the new Scientific Spiritualism were closely connected to developments in anticolonial politics and modern subject formation.

Two literary giants of anticolonial internationalism, Rabindranath Tagore and W. B. Yeats, for example, shared a passion for, and correspondence about, not just literature, but also the occult.[55] In a private letter to Kalimohan Ghosh (1884–1940), the manager of Santiniketan, whom Rabinandranath sent to study educational methods in England, W. B. Yeats expressed his great disappointment when a particular séance session had to be cancelled (figure 2.1). The imbricated relationship between anticolonial nationalism and the Theosophy movement is of course the clearest instantiation of this social blending between Scientific Spiritualism and the new nation (we study this in detail in chapter 5). The Rabinandranath and Yeats encounter mediated through Kalimohan Ghosh, however, gives us the opportunity to discuss a separate if related anchoring point for the new discourse of Scientific Spiritualism, namely the social networks that constituted and helped disseminate this discourse. Here I want to begin to trace the contours of this specific form of sociability.

In her autobiography, Sarala Devi Chaudhurani (1872–1945), Rabindranath's niece and a proto-feminist activist in her own right, noted that when the theosophical/séance circles waned in popularity, her mother, Swarnakumari Devi (1855–1932), threaded together a new women's rights group from the ashes of those circles with the women she had met through Theosophy and Spiritualism.[56] Séance and theosophy sessions provided what can be called *political sociability* in urban centers like Calcutta and Dhaka,

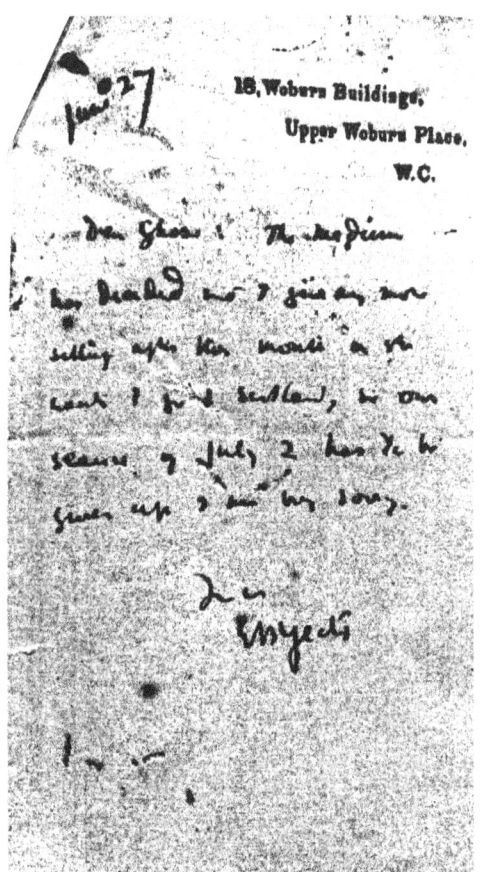

FIGURE 2.1 · Letter from W. B. Yeats to Kalimohan Ghosh: "June 27. Dear Ghose, The medium has decided not to give any more sittings after this month as she wants to go to Scotland. So our séance of July 2 has to be given up I am very sorry. Yours, W. B. Yeats."

as the authoritarianism of formal politics under the colonial regime forced the Bhadralok to carve out alternative spaces for sociopolitical expression. A burgeoning print culture, in Anderson's sense, then linked the developments and discourses forged in these capital cities to smaller local towns and regional centers, where scholars have noted the importance of newspapers published in villages and district towns as powerfully shaping consciousness, whether about the nation or the modern moment.[57]

Margaret Jacob's study of Masonic Lodges of eighteenth-century Europe, an authoritarian milieu in a different context, makes a wider claim about voluntary organizations and their role in shaping the politics of modernity that is of relevance here. Focusing on "nonparliamentary, ostensibly civic forms of behavior," Jacob finds "a discernably modern civic consciousness in voluntary associations in midcentury Britain, in the clubs to promote the 'useful' in the Dutch Republic . . . and similarly in secret societies (of both left and right) in the absolutist German states."⁵⁸ Closer to home, Dipesh Chakrabarty's study of the Bengali social practice of *adda* (social gathering of a particular kind) asks us to think about how informal spaces of sociability helped produce both a modern cosmopolitan space as well as the modern subject who was seeking a home in that space.⁵⁹ Here we raise a different question: What kind of work does *informality* as a social form do in this particular historical context? To go back to Sarala Devi's reminiscences, we note particularly her fond memories of her mother starting a women's Theosophy group to cohere and *socialize* with the wives and daughter of male Theosophists.⁶⁰ Consider a leading Scientific Spiritualist like Shishir Kumar Ghose, who was inserted into social networks with all the prominent intellectuals of his time, having easy access to the Tagore household, Brahmo networks, and of course the social networks he personally established through his political journalism. Adjectives can sometimes function as metrics of assessment. When we say a social space is *informal*, it conjures a map of related insinuations: we understand such a space to be produced through *diffused* social relations, *soft*, voluntary networks, gatherings bearing the *gentle* palimpsests of generations. Thought of this way, it is indeed a surprise how such soft forms of informality—social gatherings, voluntary associations, or secret societies—where participation was entirely guided by spontaneous choice, could produce such concrete (hard) modernities and modern subjects. But what if we, like processual archeologists, slightly blur the borders between the production of the artifact and the artifact sui generis, focusing attention on how the processes of production of these spaces shaped the kind of historical subject produced within them? If we do that, then we might find that the easy informality of these social spaces was achieved precisely because a difficult social preselection preceded such practices. Institutional exclusion of certain groups of people through the formal education system was as important as informal exclusion through a culture of performing book learning and high Bhadralok education. While institutions can be considered explicators for this exclusive informal sociability, caste, class, and gender remained the explanation; it was shared histories in shared social spaces *prior* to the formation of these associations that determined their easy sociability. In other words, the new ghosts emanated social power unknown to their precolonial counterparts.

In an earlier work on class formation in nineteenth-century Bengal, I showed how the term Bhadralok, far from being a homogeneous sociological category, was an "ethic or sentiment" that united in ideological coherence two very different sections of the petty bourgeoisie. The top layers of this class, the intelligentsia, held middle to upper positions in the colonial bureaucracy while the lower layer, the much-maligned *kerani*, held lowly clerical jobs in the same administration: "In 1833, the office of deputy collector was created for Indians, in 1837 that of principal sudder, and in 1843, the deputy magistrate. A large section of the intelligentsia, Bankimchandra Chattopadhyay, Shibchandra Deb, Vidyasagar, Bhudev Mukhopadhyay, Rangalal Bandyopadhyay formed a part of this layer. . . . While part of the same *class*, deputy magistrates, like Bankim, with their annual incomes ranging between £480–600 were . . . quite different from the junior clerks in government or private offices who barely earned Rs 30, a month."[61]

The upper layers of this class were members of literary, political, and in this case séance, circles that remained exclusive and alien to not just the peasantry and working classes but to the lower rungs of the very Bhadralok group. Inherited wealth and marital alliances maintained these hallowed circles:

> Pearychand Mittra's grandfather, for instance, married into the millionaire family of the Duttas of Hatkhola. Ramkamal Mukhopadhyay, principal clerk at Fort William's Engineering Department commanded substantial wealth and bought a huge property at Khidirpur and called it "Bara Bari" (big house). His nephew, Yogweshwar Mukhopadhyay, who later became a deputy magistrate, was Bankim's classmate and married Bankim's niece. Their daughter was to marry the famous poet Hemchandra Bandyopadhyay's son. Hemchandra, Bankim, and Sanjibchandra Chattopadhyay all met at Bara Bari to discuss the arts. Rajnarayan Basu . . . also married into the Dutta family of Hatkhola. He was also related by marriage to the Young Bengal icon Ramgopal Ghosh. Haragopal Sarkar, another diligent reformer, was married to Ramtanu Lahiri's niece. The Tagores were related by marriage to the leading men of the age like Asutosh Chaudhuri, Pramatha Chaudhuri, Janakinath Ghoshal, and so on. The various educational institutions like the Sanskrit College and Hindu College, and later Presidency College served as key areas of class mobilization.[62]

We need to be attentive to the caste-class location of the Scientific Spiritualist discourse to understand the careful social strategies adopted by the upper Bhadralok to distinguish this saintly discourse from its two main counterpoints: the lower classes and the lower Bhadralok. A campaign against "superstition" or, rather, what they claimed was superstition, took care of the first.

That India was a morass of superstitions and false gods was a well-established British trope employed by a wide range of colonial figures, from officials to scientists and missionaries alike. The only variation to the theme was in deciding where the rot began. For some the condition was endemic to being Indian, while for others, influenced by "Orientalism," the decline was attributed to Muslim rule. The civilizing mission was thus either to lift those who had always been enveloped in darkness, or to do the same for those for whom the condition was more recent; for the latter the benevolent English Raj existed only to restore the natives to their previous Hindu golden age of enlightenment. When the English-educated Bhadralok took up the same campaign, some of these frameworks of Islamophobia and British munificence were maintained. They allowed someone like Gosto Behary Mullick, the secretary of the Burra Bazar Literary Club, to want to revive "the days of Elphinstones and Malcolms, Thompsons and Metcalfs, of Joneses and Wilsons and Bethunes . . . who came to India not for its rice or cotton, indigo or jute, shell-lac or lac-dye, sugar or salt-petre, but to raise from the depths of ignorance and superstition—fruits of years of foreign [Muslim] domination—a race whose venerable relics of literature and science play fantastically like the dazzling coruscations of a polar winter athwart the mysterious gloom that shrouds the dark night of ages."[63]

This is not to claim that the crusade against superstition was an uncomplicated one. In the hands of women, albeit from the same class, the targets of criticism were often patriarchal practices such as polygamy or social norms that barred women's access to the written word.[64] What is worth thinking about, however, is in what ways the war against superstition aggregated the upper Bhadralok across religion and gender and how peasants, lower-caste groups, and women were uniformly relegated to superstition, while the upper Bhadralok emerged bathed in the light of modern science; how clear borders were drawn between the different forms of believing, between what emerged as faith and what remained as superstition; and how Hindu Science, and the allied Scientific Spiritualism, helped craft and patrol such borders.

In 1869, in his lecture to the scholarly Canning Institute, Mahendralal Sircar, medical doctor and social reformer, argued passionately for a Darwinian worldview while mocking ruthlessly the Hindu idea of rebirth, which, according to Mahendralal, was about "spirits floating and flying about everywhere," in search of a suitable body "either from choice, or doomed . . . by an unalterable fate, or by an irrevocable curse of some greater being."[65] Mahendralal was a vigorous advocate of science education for Indians and founded the Indian Association for the Cultivation of Science (IACS) in 1876 to promote scientific research. Among the early investors in IACS were Brahmo figures such as Keshab Chandra Sen and leading intellectuals like Bankim,

Ramendrasundar Trivedi, and Rabindranath. But while scientific reason, for Mahendralal Sircar, cleaved a clear path away from superstition, reason's relationship to Hinduism was equally clear and entrenched. In his prospectus for IACS, he reproduced the same fall-from-glory framework of the old "Orientalists" but enlarged the canvas for what could be considered as a scientific discipline. Most branches of modern science, he argued, owed their origin to ancient Hindu rishis, but Indians had woefully fallen behind in their pursuit, ceding such ground to Europe. His catalogue of sciences included astrology, algebra, geometry, Ayurveda, chemistry, botany, palmistry, psychology, chemistry, and musicology. The inclusion of astrology or palmistry as fields of scientific study reflected the already existing compact between the natural sciences and Scientific Spiritualism that flourished in nineteenth-century Calcutta.[66] For Mahendralal, as for many of his contemporaries, science dispelled superstitions while drawing one close to comprehending god's divine plan, thus making science a "moral force" for national regeneration.[67] The *Indian Mirror* referred to the proposed IACS as the "temple of science" that would lead the inquirer from "nature to nature's God."[68] And this science was definitely Hindu.

Once science could be established on a secure footing with Hindu ideals, it became clear which social groups needed its ameliorative effects. British Science had already declared that "few, if any, of the inhabitants of the globe . . . [were] more completely under the control of superstition in its widest sense and in its most absurd forms, than the natives of Bengal,"[69] but Hindu Science was keen to disaggregate the generalized colonial condemnation of "natives" into a specific condemnation of particular social groups. A letter to the editor of the reform-minded *Somprakash* captured the Bhadralok zeitgeist. Superstition, defined the author, "was firmly believing in something without judgment or reasoned discernment." While every country had its share, superstition was particularly dominant in India, causing people to die of "smallpox while refusing vaccines" or "snake bite for depending on rojas and their mantras." Belief in "ghosts and witches" compounded the problem and provided a barrier to true *shastric* knowledge and national uplift.[70] To put an authorial stamp on such discussions in his paper, the editor Dwarkanath Vidyabhushan (1820–86) himself came in on how "letters to the editor," had greatly improved as a genre and now had as much of an edifying influence as actual articles; one no longer had to wade through letters claiming "O Mr. Editor, so and so's wife has been possessed by a bhut" or "such and such roja has exorcised three bhuts."[71] The subaltern, as Prakash correctly established, was either "silenced or made to speak only through superstition."[72]

Survival of the Repressed

Sanitization processes, as we know, are notoriously messy affairs and that which is sought to be exorcised often ends up haunting spaces and leaving traces. So it was with the old ghostly Beings and practices that honored their existence. In a satirical piece in *Basantak*, the editor's wife warned that if the editor "abolished" bhuts, "all mothers would turn against him."[73] Hunter and Risley both testify to the presence of *gunins*, *rojas*, and *kapaliks* at the village level, while hand-wringing from the upper Bhadraloks about superstition continue unabated well into the twentieth century. Even with the editorial guidance of Vidyasagar and Vidyabhushan, *Somprakash* may have been too hasty in declaring victory over such dark myths. In 1863, for example, it carried an anxious letter from an unmarried "Vaidik Brahmin" man deeply worried that his bachelor status in life would make him a Brahmadaitya upon dying.[74]

Certain strains of religious practice were more hospitable to the older Beings than others. Many *shakta* families among the Bhadralok maintained tantric practices that brought them in close contact with such Beings. Dinesh Chandra Sen's grandfather, Ramanath Sen, was, for example, killed by a ghost. The set of events leading to his death must have left a deep impression on his scholar-grandson, for Dinesh Chandra takes some pains in trying to accurately reconstruct the incident as he heard it from his grandmother and Ramanath's wife, Gourmoni Debi:

> It was winter. My husband and his friend went out in the evening. It was a Saturday and an *amabasya* night [new moon]. They had acquired two *chandal* [low caste] corpses and planned to sit on them and meditate. . . .
>
> I woke to the sound of great commotion and instinctively knew that the greatest misfortune had befallen me. My husband was carried back to the house on a stretcher. He was groaning and on his left cheek was a mark of a great blow, the imprint of five fingers stood out clearly, his neck had probably been snapped as his entire face was tilted to the right. . . . Everybody said, he was meditating atop a corpse, a ghost's slap had brought this to pass.[75]

Although Dinesh Chandra expressed some skepticism about the true cause of his grandfather's death (speculating it might have been related to his line of work as a police inspector) his uncertainty on this matter of ghostly murder is at best remarkably mild. The Sen family's involvement in Tantric practices was by no means an anomaly, and the sensational events leading to Dinesh Chandra Sen's grandfather's death in the hands of ghosts offers us a way to conceive of the multiple forms of Scientific Spiritualism's troubled relationship to the older ghostly Beings.

Unlike the upper layers of the Bhadralok, who communed scientifically over séances, there existed a strain of Scientific Spiritualism that uneasily straddled the increasingly divergent worlds of the older Beings and the new spirits. This version of the discourse, coalesced heterogeneously through books, journals, and pamphlets, shared some key features. Ideologically the texts reproduced Scientific Spiritualism in its broad strokes in that they all attempted to align Hindu *shastric* knowledge to questions of the afterlife, rather than elaborate on or give accounts of older bhuts. The authors, almost uniformly, were upper-caste men, but they belonged to a different social class—and hence to different social circles—from the upper Bhadralok. The first clue to a different social milieu was the authors' location, both geographical and social. Many of these texts were published from outside of the metropolitan center of Calcutta, from towns such as Baranagar, Uttarpara, Bali, Chittagong, and Dhaka. The authors were often schoolteachers, minor pandits, or, in the case of one Ramankrishna Chattopadhyay, a practicing astrologer. They differed from the main strain of Scientific Spiritualism in a crucial way: along with all the discussion on Hindu *shastras* and their relationship with modern science, they provided practical guidelines on how to ward off the older bhuts. If this confluence between the new spirits and the old Beings seems to be an uneasy one, we have to attend to the social context that made this co-constitution possible. Outside the hallowed circles of the upper Bhadralok and their metropolitan center in Calcutta, the older Beings were often alive and well, and one needed practical advice on how to deal with them. Who best to authorize this advice but upper-caste Hindu men who came from these very milieus?

Take the case of one Rasikmohan Chattopadhyay, prolific writer and resident of Butni in the Dhaka district. He edited the journal *Arunodaya* (1890–nd), which promised articles on "Yoga, Astrology, horoscope making, tantra, incantations, puranas, vedas, nyaya, smriti, shaddarsana, . . . Dayabhaga law, . . . worship procedures for multiple gods, magic, mesmerism, spiritualism, [and] palmistry," among others. The journal was structured in a way that placed articles denouncing kulinism right next to ones sharing ingredients and spells to charm women (Stree Vashikaran) "potent enough to tame even Tilottama." The same spell apparently also took care of "mosquitos, rats, lice and bedbugs."[76] The journal detailed the usual Spiritualist methods for summoning *spirits* through mediums, but unlike our high society Spiritualist journals, such as HSM, it also published advice and mantras on *bhutchcharan*, or exorcism of bhuts. Exhortations to follow Manu sat alongside practical advice on how to protect against witches.

A slew of such books that dis-ordered the neat division between the old Beings and the new spirits poured out from the Battala presses. They were curio-cabinets of discourses, pulling from multiple traditions with little regard for uniformity. If the overall framework was Brahmanic, in that they were usually studded with comments about India's glorious Hindu past, they carried distinctly heterogeneous ideas about the afterlife and accommodated local beliefs alongside of *shastric* diktats. One such book, *Bibhuti Vidya*, even classified ghosts into "shastric" ghosts and local varieties, while providing practical remedies and advice on how to deal with the latter. "Bhut-Prets," according to the author, "could be divided into two main jatis. First, those who are companions to Shiva and Parvati and second, those that are the ghosts of dead humans. The first kind only perform good deeds for humanity while the latter try to torture us."[77] Tantric incantations formed a key part of these texts, recommended by the authors as essential for exorcism rituals.

Tantra, as Imma Ramos has recently shown, was neither a homogeneous nor unilinear tradition till the British and the Bhadralok recast it as such in the nineteenth century and claimed it as part of Hinduism. While the colonial authorities uniformly condemned Tantra as composed of obscene sexual rituals and therefore indicative of the lascivious nature of Indians in general and Hinduism in particular, it was not so easy for the Bhadralok to do the same. Through its Buddhist roots in Bengal and Assam, Tantric traditions had been part of the palimpsest of faith and worship in the region for centuries. As with Dinesh Chandra Sen's grandfather, many members of Bhadralok families were practitioners.[78] According to Sumit Sarkar "Disreputable, yet often deeply attractive, Tantric . . . traditions . . . had a powerful appeal for lowcastes and women—while providing at the same time a kind of secret second life to many high-caste men."[79] Tantric traditions, with their emphasis on religious fluidity, women's sexuality, and *bamachar*, had a highly transgressive charge. Panchkori Bandyopadhyay, in an article for *Prabahini* in 1915, noted the existence of "several, highly skilled Muslim tantriks" and made a special mention of Dayab Khan, a practicing Muslim tantric whose "*Gangastotra* was read by Bengali Brahmins on a daily basis."[80]

The Battala texts that hovered between the old and new ghosts then performed a double role. On one hand they popularized Scientific Spiritualism as a discourse, diffusing its Hindu-inflected Science and Spiritualism from hallowed Calcutta circles to less salubrious spaces. On the other hand, they nourished older traditions of ghostly beliefs, offering advice, incantations, and spells on how to deal with ghosts who were more unruly than those found in séance sessions. It was common for these authors, sometimes as prolific as their upper Bhadralok counterparts, to publish both a book on Hindu philosophy and an edited collection of spells.[81] The result was an uneasy heterogeneity. But we must attend to that uneasiness, make analytical room for it. I make this plea because, by the early twentieth century, Scientific Spiritualism is not only the dominant discourse about the afterlife, but also one that births new social practices, modifies or rejects older ones, and of course produces and sculpts spaces for its own enactment. In this theater of apparent victory, it is important for us to mark and honor the little cracks and fissures that allowed our unruly older Beings to "live."

THREE

Deadly Spaces

Haunted Homes and Haunting Histories

In his autobiography *Apan Katha* (My Own Words/Stories) (1946), the renowned artist and writer Abanindranath Tagore (1871–1951) imputes an amazing historicity to space. An ancestral home, writes Abanindranath, "lives" only through the "company of people." In his characteristic lyrical style, Abanindranath further elaborates this connection between history and location:

> As long as there are people in the house, who make the stream of the past, present and future flow, the house continues to change its appearance, its history. It fills itself up with memories and the house-memories constitute the being of the house. All objects in the house get tied to *ekal* (the present, or the modern) through the sinews of memory. In this way ages pass, and then one day when people leave the house, the cobwebs of memory fly away in the wind; it is then that the house truly dies.[1]

What can we make of this beautiful connection between location and history or space and time? In particular, what do we make of his transposing the organicity of living and dying onto space in this evocative manner? In this chapter I advance Abanindranath's claim about this relationship between history and spatiality in the context of Calcutta as a colonial city. I argue that spaces acquired a certain kind of past-ness or the patina of antiquity through a very specific rhetoric related to death and dying—that of haunting. We look at haunted spaces as locations of history from two perspectives: British and Indian; this dual perspective is necessary, because each side was invested in sets of very different arguments about Calcutta's status as a city with a past, or its respectability as an old city. Ghosts, both Bengali and British, I argue, determined and/or disputed the antiquity of the city and in turn questioned or consolidated the future of British rule.

Early British accounts of the city never fail to relate the story of the city's most prominent ghost: that of the first governor-general, Warren Hastings. In terms of social standing, one could not hope for a more exalted spirit. Evan Cotton's history of Calcutta (1909) recounts the legend in vivid terms. "It is said," writes Cotton, "that the great Governor-General drives up the avenue every evening in a coach and four and upon alighting walks through the house in evident search of something by which he lays considerable store."[2] "Hastings House," as it was popularly known, was indeed more famous for its dead governor-general than for its living ones. Located in fashionable Alipore, a very white part of Calcutta in the eighteenth and early nineteenth centuries, the house was a palatial building with sprawling grounds. High vaulted ceilings, clustered columns, and pointed arches gave the building the required gothic air. A contemporary Indian account further embroiders on the existent legend by adding yet another essential gothic element to it: the love of a woman. In his volume *Indian Ghosts Stories* (1917), S. C. Mukerji describes the haunting thus:

> While living in this house Warren Hastings married Baroness Imhoff sometime during the first fortnight of August about 140 years ago. "The event was celebrated by great festivities"; and, as expected, the bride came home in a splendid equipage. It is said that this scene is re-enacted on the anniversary of the wedding by a supernatural agency and a ghostly carriage duly enters the gate in the evening once every year. The clatter of hoofs and the rattle of iron-tyred wheels are distinctly heard advancing up to the portico; then there is the sound of the opening and closing of the carriage door, and lastly the carriage proceeds onwards, but it does not come out from under the porch. It vanishes mysteriously.

The only other haunted house in the city mentioned by Mukerji was famous for "its windows in the first floor bedrooms [which] open[ed] at night spontaneously."[3] Unfortunately, besides hair-raising accounts of what transpired within when mortals chose to defy the powers of the dead, Mukerji fails to provide for us any further details about the house itself, such as its exact location.

Worth noting is that most of the British accounts of haunting place the ghosts, naturally, in British or colonial towns. British ghosts also tended to reside in, visit, and prefer the indoors. Rattling windows, rustling curtains, spectral carriages—all underscored the dead's great liking for the home, the greatest haven of safety for the modern bourgeois self. If one recalls Freud's reflections on the uncanny, it is precisely the spectralization of the *heimlich* that creates profound unease in the modern.[4] Neither of these two features, given the generalization of the attributes of what constitutes a modern ghost story, would seem so odd if not for the radically different spatiality of the Bengali ghosts.

The chief feature of a traditional Bengali ghost was most certainly his or her out-of-the-home location. Trees were a great favorite site, as were marshes, ponds, and forests. Locations and domiciles, however, were not arbitrary. Like the rigid hierarchies of premodern societies, a clear classificatory universe existed for the dwelling of the premodern ghost. Particular trees, for instance, were associated with particular species. The saintly Brahman ghost, the Brahmadaitya, preferred as his abode the Bel tree, a plant of ritual significance as its leaves are traditional offerings to Siva. We have already noted the *petni*'s preference for the Sheora tree.

Autobiographies of the great and the good of nineteenth-century Calcutta were filled with accounts of childhood experiences of the ghostly. Rabindranath Tagore's account of his childhood, *Chelebela*, as we noted, began with the tale of the Brahmadaitya. Similar denizens of the ghostly world inhabited marshes, heaths, cremation-grounds, forests, caves, or even wells.[5] The place of the dead in premodern tales and perception was, clearly, the wild, not the home.

The first change to this pattern in the world of the Bengali ghosts comes with the creation of the modern gothic as a literary genre. The previous chapters have dealt with the characteristic differences between the new gothic apparition and the more traditional ghosts of folklore and oral culture. Here I simply point to the difference in location.

Rabindranath Tagore was the first to create a string of extremely successful and atmospheric gothic short stories. The most famous of them, *Manihara* (1898) and *Kshudita Pashan* (1895), were translated immediately and anthologized several times. Both embody the classical features of a Victorian Gothic tale: large, brooding, almost sentient mansions, simmering and displaced eroticism, a deliberate psychologization of fear, and, of course, the requisite unquiet, restless souls. The remarkable point of unity of all these stories, however, which set them scrupulously apart from the premodern ghost stories, was that the location of fear had shifted from the trees, heaths, and marshes and was now the home.

Manihara is the story of an unrequited, lonely wife, Manimalika, whose childless life is filled with a pathological attachment to her jewelry: "Like a thick-leaved and fast-growing vine, Manimalika, by divine decree, remained without fruit, unable to have a child. In other words, God did not give her that which she could understand and feel for more than the jewels in her iron safe."[6] It should be clear, given where the narrator's sympathies lay regarding ornaments and breeding, that Manimalika's life was not going to end well. It does not. She dies a lonely violent death at the hands of a distant cousin who murders her on a stormy night for her jewels. We will not go into the details of the haunting that begins after this murder; it is an exquisite delineation of unfulfillment, as both a material condition and an ontological state. What is important for us here is the role domestic space plays in this haunting.

The climatic point of the story is reached as Manimalika's dejected widower husband enters their "deserted bedroom" and proceeds to wait for his dead beloved. The passage of waiting describes the bedroom in its minutest detail, carefully outlining and emphasizing the quotidian materiality of clothes racks, tea tables, empty soapboxes, and lamps. It is a purposive description, because space plays a central part in the subsequent paragraph:

> Even she who departs, leaving everything bare behind her, leaves so many signs, so much history, so much of her lively self, her careful touch! Come Manimalika, come and light your lamp, light up your room, stand in front of the mirror and put on your *saree* with careful pleats. All your possessions are waiting for you. . . . Spread your glory on all these scattered things and with your life yoke them together and infuse them with life in turn. These inanimate things cry out mutely, making this very house a cremation ground![7]

It is not merely the house, but the *home*, the bastion of modern safety, the heart of bourgeois selfhood, that is rendered unstable here. The narrative moves even further to shatter the peace of domesticity as the bereaved husband, Phanibhushan, hears an eerie sound of "jangling . . . jewel[ry]." The domestic space is not offered any possible respite from this deep unsettling fear:

> The sound crossed the guardless gates and entering the inner chambers of the house began to climb, round and round the circular staircase, across the wide veranda, stopping for a while as it came to the door of the bedroom.

> . . . The sound crossed the threshold and entered the room. Where the *saree* lay pleated on the rack, where the lamp stood in its niche, where the box with dry *paan* lay upon the tea table, and near the cupboard with its strange collection of things—the sound paused at every step, finally stopping by Phanibhushan.[8]

Why does fear need to caress every familiar object in the room, tightening the circle of dread around the hapless husband? Why does the specter need to underscore its intrusiveness, as evidenced in the meticulous description of its passage from the outer world to the inner? The answer lies in Rabindranath's prescient metaphor of the house as a cremation ground. Manimalika's restless spirit is definitely not the *petni* of folklore, nor does she behave like any of the premodern ghosts that inhabited the trees and marshes. What makes the dead Manimalika fearsome in the above passages is that she brings into a space of comfort the dark wildness of the outdoors. She turns the home, associative of life, into the dead space of the cremation ground. There is no longer any assurance that closed doors will keep the outside out—the dead will cross the threshold and contaminate the safety of the living.

The modern domestic space, then, is extremely particularized. This is not unexpected, as under modernity the domestic sphere, for the first time, is evacuated entirely of production and becomes solely a site of residence, leisure, or consumption. The scrupulous separation of home and work, private and public, transforms the home into a nonproductive zone and turns it into a space of "phantom objectivity," where the real relationship between people is obscured by a relationship between things.[9] This object-filled home is primarily self-referential, wherein each "thing" merely accentuates the relationship of each object or each part (tea table) to the whole (well-appointed home). The reason the modern ghost creates such fear is not simply because she or he is crossing into a sacred space where only the bourgeois family is allowed, but also because the new presence lays bare all that is wrong with the home. When safety is revealed simply to be an ideology, the objects that were previously markers of security themselves turn threatening. Manimalika's presence not only invades the home, pulling down revered partitions between private and public, but also actually negates the home as an adequate habitat for the bourgeois self, which knows no other.

The relationship of modern ghosts to modern homes was, however, not entirely antagonistic. A comparison between British and Bengali ghost stories of the nineteenth century reveals a very consistent pattern in the location of haunting. As mentioned earlier, all the British stories were set either in Calcutta or in similar company towns, while all the Bengali stories were set outside these new settlements, in houses, mansions, and old buildings that were almost always in precolonial towns or villages. Of the British part, Kipling assures us, "Nearly every other Station owns a ghost. There are said to be two at Simla, not counting the woman who blows the bellows at Syree dâk-bungalow on the Old Road; Mussoorie has a house haunted of a very lively Thing; a White Lady is supposed to do night-watchman round a house in Lahore; Dalhousie says that one of her houses 'repeats' on autumn evenings all the incidents of a horrible horse-and-precipice accident."[10]

Both *Manihara* and *Kshudita Pashan* are set outside of an urban locale. *Manihara* is explicitly set in an unnamed "village," while *Kshudita Pashan* is set in imaginary Barich. The mansion where the story of *Kshudita Pashan* unfolds is described as "a marble palace in solitary grandeur amidst the foothills. There is no habitation nearby. Barich village and its cotton market are quite some distant from there." It is not enough to say that these locations are nonurban; what clearly sets them apart from urbanity is their age. Manimalika's house is set by a "crumbling decayed embankment by the river." The house itself is described as an "enormous mansion with broken windows, and a veranda that hung precariously from its supports"; as though this description was not enough, it is twice referred to in the same page as "decrepit" and "dilapidated." In *Kshudita Pashan*, we are told more explicitly that the mansion is specifically pre-British, it was built "nearly two hundred and fifty years ago" by the Mughal emperor Shah Mahmood the second. Time and, more specifically, age give the narratives an authenticity that can be called by only one name: history. It is a past that bears a deep resonant connection to the present, a past that can be narrativized, that transposes itself onto the space of haunting, giving it a validation and a rootedness.

One can now see why none of the Bengali stories are set in Calcutta. The city does not count to the Bengali mind as a valid city, let alone an old one, till the mid-twentieth century. Most of the middle class retained their ancestral homes in their villages of origin as the venues for major family ceremonies for most of the nineteenth century, using their Calcutta homes as temporary abodes.[11] Most early accounts of the city by the Bengali middle class were extremely unflattering. Calcutta was seen to be godless, unhealthy, and relentlessly modern and anxious.[12] History did not get made there and hence neither did ghosts.

British accounts of the city, on the other hand, are very different. The eighteenth century is referred to in a late nineteenth-century account as "a period when we had opulent merchants . . . days when gold was plenty . . . and not an indigent European in all Calcutta."[13] The determination with which Calcutta was deemed a "city of palaces" by the English, in the face of malaria, cholera, smallpox epidemics, open sewers, and alarmingly high mortality, is astonishing. The remarks of an early governor-general, the Marquis of Wellesley, are relevant in this context. He considered that "India should be governed from a palace, not from a counting house" and "with the ideas of a prince, not with those of a retail dealer in muslin and indigo."[14] In other words, the city had to be turned from an upstart town with no history to a city endowed with a past and a tradition. British ghosts hence almost never strayed out of British towns. Englishmen encountered indigenous ghosts in the wild, but the true Englishman never haunted anything less than an English town/city. Haunted houses lent to new insignificant towns the validation of a past and the glory of history.

Legislating Death: Law, State, and Mortuary Practices

The British lawmakers in the town of Puri, sacred as a pilgrimage destination to Hindus, faced an unusual dilemma in 1863. The execution of prisoners condemned to death by capital punishment usually took place in front of the city jail. When a Brahman prisoner was sentenced to death in 1863, however, a storm of controversy arose regarding the place of execution. The native population claimed that spilling Brahman blood within the limits of the "Kshetro," or the sacred Circle of Puri, would render the entire town unholy, and any god-fearing citizen would be forced to desert such unhallowed territory. So strong was public opinion on this matter that, according to an English sessions judge, if the "whole population of the District" were to be "polled on the subject," he doubted there could be found "a single dissenting voice" on the matter. According to this upright English judge of course such "aversion" was founded on "religious feeling," and he strongly felt that the course of the law should not be impeded by such "fictitious objections."[15]

Regulation 16 of 1795 exempted Brahmans of the province of Banaras from the death penalty—a gesture by the new colonial state to uphold the "traditional" status of the Brahman. This exemption was limited to Banaras alone and was actually revoked by Regulation 17 in 1817. What remained of this privilege was that Brahmans were not allowed to be executed within the city limits, as a concession to "Hindu" law, in order to comply with the religious and spatial convictions of the townsfolk. Until 1861 this custom was maintained by the local Faujdari Adalats (criminal courts) and was undoubtedly approved by the Sadr Nizamat Adalat, staffed by several Indians who had a say in the dispensing of justice.[16] The Indian High Court Act of 1861 created new high courts at Calcutta, Madras, and Bombay, staffed mostly by the British, and initiated a new regime of jurisprudence. The year of our case, 1864, was clearly still a period of transition to the new system, one in which the rules were not particularly obvious. The lieutenant-governor of Bengal hence sought to clarify "whether under the existing Law it . . . [was] for the Court or for the Government to decide as to the place in which capital executions . . . [were] to be carried out."[17] He did not receive a satisfactory answer to his query. As it turned out, no allusion was made in the new form of warrant to the *place* of execution. Nevertheless, the superintendent and remembrancer of legal affairs, E. G. Birch, thought that it was up to the High Court—that is, the exclusively British judiciary—to determine the place of execution.[18] One would have thought that, given a free hand to decide on such "superstitious" matters, the higher administration and the judiciary would rule in favor of upholding the sacred "rule of law." In reality, however, the government submitted to the depth of popular feeling, and the lieutenant-governor, in agreement with the judges of the High Court, decided that all convicts, Brahman and non-Brahman alike, were to be henceforth taken beyond the sacred "Kshetro" of Puri to be executed.[19] It allowed the government to save face in a certain way by claiming that, in the eyes of the British law, there were no distinctions between criminals on the basis of caste. But it was also clear that the colonial administration, still shaky after 1857, was not willing to test the strength of the so-called native prejudices regarding the specificity of their chosen place of dying.[20]

The place of death—the actual physical and geographical location where the body gave up its vital breath (*prana*), or life, was of paramount importance in several versions of Brahmanic Hinduism and, by extension, in popular or folk belief. This was because at the specific place of death, the dead produced, as we noted, both intense ritual pollution and a potentially malevolent ghost unless their funeral rites were appropriately conducted. Since the place of death was thus marked as a potentially volatile zone, it followed then that it could be used as a weapon to serve the living. Funeral rites might be suspended to facilitate the haunting of an adversary, or the body physically placed at an enemy's property in order for the ghost to pursue justice for the living. Bishop Heber, the lord bishop of Calcutta, noted in his famous travelogue the account of a peasant who had killed his wife on a piece of disputed land "in order that her death might bring a curse on the soil and her spirit haunt it after death, so that his successful antagonist should never derive any advantage from it."[21]

Although a considerable volume of literature exists on the ritual significance of "place" in the South Asian worldview, it is important to outline here certain specificities in our particular argument about location and place.

Spatial organization and the production of a suitable geographical landscape have always been indispensable aspects of capitalist development. Scholars such as David Harvey have demonstrated how, since its inception, capitalism has relied on "spatial fixes," or "geographical reorganization [as] both expansion and intensification" as forms of solutions to its inherent crises. Capitalism, according to Harvey, "builds and rebuilds a geography in its own image," creating a "produced space of transport and communications, of infrastructures and territorial organization," the ultimate goal of all of which is the accumulation of capital.[22] The historical activities of the bourgeoisie, even at a commonsensical level, are demonstrably geographical. One cannot envision the history of capitalism without the voyages of discovery, the "rounding of the cape," and, later on, its expansion into colonial markets in distant lands. But space is also "produced" at a more immediate experiential level, and on a much more continuous basis. Henri Lefebvre's concept of "social space" is of use here.

According to Lefebvre, social space is "not a thing among other things, nor a product among other products: rather, it subsumes things produced and encompasses their interrelationship in their co-existence."[23] In trying to understand the mechanics of social space, Lefebvre makes a primary distinction between "works" and "products." The former he rudimentarily defines as "unique, original and primordial," and the latter as repetitious, artificial, and "associated with instruments which are both duplicatable and designed to duplicate."[24] In terms of urban spaces, Venice as a city is one that he argues can be considered a *work*, while modern suburbia is an exemplifier of the *product*. These distinctions, however, are strictly at a primary level. In reality, Lefebvre rightly and elegantly points out, there exists a dialectical relationship between works and products as the two modalities of "occupied space." All works occupy and create space, whereas all products, while occupying space, also circulate within it. Under this analytic, if we go back to the case of Venice, we see the city for what it really is: a city of great beauty, architectural unity, and spatial expressivity, but one that is buttressed by "sinking pilings, building docks and harbourside installations." Behind "Venice the work," thus shows Lefebvre, "there assuredly" lies "production." At an even deeper structural level, the space of Venice as human habitat (city) cannot be separated "from a vaster space, that of a system of commercial exchange which . . . took in the Mediterranean and the Orient" and would eventually encompass the globe (capitalism).

The social space of a city, any city, then is produced and reproduced in connection to the forces and systems of production. But these productive forces, it is important to realize, do not give rise to space in any causal way. Mediators in the form of historical actors, levels of knowledge, and ideology play crucial roles in producing this space. Let us now come to a fuller definition of social space as outlined by Lefebvre. He maintains that "social space contains a great diversity of objects, both natural and social, including the networks and pathways which facilitate the exchange of material things and information. Such 'objects' are thus not only things but also relations. As objects, they possess discernible peculiarities. . . . Social labour transforms them, rearranging their positions within spatio-temporal configurations."[25]

The spatiality of a city thus must be conceived through what we might call an archeological lens. The arrangement of buildings and the distribution of the population are held together in a continuous but changing unity by deeper historical processes and concepts. As Lefebvre puts it, the representation of space (natural boundaries, buildings) and representational space (social relations, distributions of wealth) are "mutually reinforcing."[26]

The "place" of death in the indigenous perception, as we saw above, had a potentially dangerous cartography limited to the vicinity of the deceased's physical remains. But the social space of colonial capitalism that contained Calcutta as a city within a vaster world of the British empire was a spatial determinant that was fast becoming the sole rubric through which people and things negotiated their place in time.[27] In determining the historicity of haunting, it would then be remiss to ignore the material contours of governmental policy that attempted to mark the spatiality of death in the city of Calcutta.

From the mid-nineteenth century onward, a concerted effort was made on the part of the British government to "cleanse" the urban limits of Calcutta from any unsavory associations with the actual physicality of death. In the words of the contemporary municipal authorities, appropriate means had to be devised "for making the burning of human bodies . . . as unobjectionable as possible."[28] Consequent to this new ideological imperative a bylaw was passed by the Calcutta Justices of Peace in June 1864 stating that, "no person" was allowed to "throw, or cause to be thrown, any corpse or carcass, into any River or Nullah, or Canal . . . within the limits of the Town of Calcutta." As part of the new strictures, even deaths of animals had to be reported to the conservancy overseer of that particular municipal division. Any lapse on the part of the citizens would result in fines up to 20 rupees and, for continuing offences, "rupees 10 for every day after such notice during which such offence is continued."[29]

Sanitation reform, particularly after the revolt of 1857, was one of the major concerns of the new British Raj. Veena Oldenburg, in her study of urban Lucknow, has argued that post-1857 urban reconstruction had three main prerogatives: safety, sanitation, and loyalty.[30] These processes of urban transformation in India from the mid-nineteenth century have been amply catalogued by scholars as acutely politicized processes through which the British colonial regime restructured the physical and social environments of cities and established their domination there.[31]

The policies to "clean up" the city were thus not without their deeper political implications, a point well understood by the native population of the city. In March 1864 the *Somprakash* ran a series of articles on the controversy regarding the proposed government reform to try to ban the cremation of dead bodies within the city limits of Calcutta. The paper claimed that F. R. Cockrell, the officiating secretary to the Government of Bengal, had sent an unequivocal letter to the Justices of Peace for Calcutta prohibiting the cremation of corpses within the city. Consequently, at a meeting of the justices, the firebrand orator Ramgopal Ghosh proclaimed that, in banning cremations at places like Nimtala Ghat, the government was directly interfering with the religion of the Hindus. A heated debate then followed at the meeting, with some members arguing the government's case on grounds of health and sanitation while other members stridently opposed such a move. The *Somprakash* summed up the issue in this lengthy editorialized comment:

> The question to be asked is this: do the last rites of the Hindu consist solely of the cremation of the body by any means? This is clearly not so. Hindus have a set of specific mortuary rituals, the *Anteshti Kritya*, in accordance to their religion. First, the dying person is taken to the Ganga. There are certain rituals, such as the *Baitarani*, that need to be performed *before* death. During the time of death the dying person's body has to be half on land and half immersed in water and the ritual of *Antarjali* performed. After death the corpse has to be ritually bathed to the chanting of certain mantras. Those who have faith believe that it is only these rituals, performed by the river Ganga, will allow the soul of the deceased to be free.[32]

Clearly, according to the *Somprakash*, these intricate ceremonies could not be performed if cremation were to be banned within the city, as only within the city did the people of Calcutta have full and easy access to the Ganga. If the government was suggesting that one ought to perform the Antarjali and so on by the river, and then carry the corpse out of the city to be cremated, that too was patently impossible. The corpse, in accordance with Hindu rites, had to be carried by blood relatives only, and they had to perform this very important function barefooted. The paper rightly claimed that it was a hideous demand to impose on people to walk barefoot, carrying a corpse, for more than 3 to 4 kroshes, for that would roughly be the distance that one would have to travel from the Ganga to the outer limits of the city.[33] The most important part of this article was, however, its conclusion, in which the *Somprakash* clearly linked the procedures of dying to the birth and life of the future nation.

The lieutenant governor, Cecil Beadon, the paper stated, had done Indians a "serious and grievous injury" by attempting to pass this law. Echoing Ramgopal Ghosh, the paper predicted that, if the government were to pass similar laws in places such as Kashi, then "the displeasure of its subjects would become universal; even a revolt was not out of question." In conclusion, it was important, said the *Somprakash*, that Indians be part of the decision-making process at every level of policy enactment, for only the presence of Indians in the committee of the Justices of Peace had prevented this catastrophic act from being instituted.[34]

It is important to realize that the sole node of contradiction here is not simply Hindu tradition versus British sanitation drive. Or even an effort on the part of the state to reconfigure urban space in order to enact better control. Besides trying to organize the city to prevent any future mutinies, the British were also trying to "modernize" the very process of dying.

Philippe Aries, in his famous monograph on death and dying, was the first to alert us to a history of the transformation in perceptions of death from the premodern to modern times. According to Aries, changes in notions and structures of the family as a unit prompted a change in the way an individual was "prepared" for death. In premodern times, a dying person was made to confront the knowledge of his impending death, publicly, in the comforting presence of his family and friends. "As soon as someone fell ill," Aries tells us, "the room filled with people-parents, children, friends, neighbours, fellow workers." Even strangers came to be at the bedside of the dying. From this publicness of death, the process of dying increasingly became a more private affair, wherein the immediate family gradually became the sole arbitrator in matters of death, to the extent of even excluding the dying person from the knowledge of his coming end.[35]

Aries's description of the very public death scenes of premodernity gives us a similar historical perspective for what the *Somprakash* report seems to be drawing our attention to. Procedures of death encoded in the various rituals that the paper outlined were still extremely public and probably not sufficiently "modern" for the colonial government. Shibnath Shastri recalled that, sometime in the 1850s, his great-grandfather Ramjay Nayalankar intuited his death a few days prior to the actual event. He immediately made arrangements to summon all of his family, even those who were away from home, like his grandson, Shastri's father. He then gave detailed instructions on how to place him out into the courtyard of the house, such that death pollution would not contaminate living quarters. Relatives tried to tell him that he would be taken out when "the time came," but he would not listen. At his insistence he was placed out in the yard, and there he lay "chanting the name of god till death bore him away to heaven at the age of 103."[36] Similarly, Abanindranath Tagore recounts the case of a family friend, Purna Mukherjee, who decided to undertake a Gangayatra or journey to the Ganga in order to die. He was placed on a platform made of bamboo just as though he already were a corpse. As he was carried out, he merrily waved farewell to friends and family and said his goodbyes.[37]

It was not just that efforts were made to keep the dying in a public context; the procedures of dying were so structured as to need public participation. The rituals themselves were often visceral, and no attempt was made to secrete away processes that brought the living into physical contact with the corpse. Another Brahmo reformer, Bangachandra Roy (1839–1922), describes how as a grieving eleven-year-old he had to oil his mother's corpse to prepare the body for cremation.[38] The apogee of such physically involved rituals was of course the *kapal-kriya* or the rite of the skull, in which the chief mourner had to literally crack open the skull of the deceased, using a bamboo pole from the bier that bore the body.

Back at home, Victorian Britain witnessed a flurry of community activism and research around mortuary practices during this time. Voluntary organizations such as the London Association for the Prevention of Premature Burials (LAPPB) sprang up, focusing public scrutiny on the time and manner of death. Coffin patents aimed to deodorize the corpse, while laws such as Birth and Death Registration Act of 1873 endeavored to streamline and keep track of death informationally. It is thus no surprise that the essayist Joseph Jacobs remarked in 1899 that the "most distinctive note of the modern spirit" was that death had "lost its terror" for the British people.[39]

In keeping with the new spirit of disassociating the materiality of death from the civic life of the living, new equipment was proposed to dispose of corpses in such a manner that their corporeality could be both minimized and sanitized. In 1865, for instance, the Burning Ghat Committee of the Justices of Peace for Calcutta experimented with a new apparatus that was "found to consume completely, the body placed, therein . . . [and] burnt without any offensive odour," and the smoke was conveyed by an underground flue and up through a chimney.[40]

In our specific argument about the sanitization of death, it is important to note two parallel, if apparently contradictory, developments. First, that legislating against the corporeal excesses of dying created an ahistorical register for death. While the effort was to barricade civil society from any visual reminders of dying as a physical reality, the effect was that discourses of physicality grew delinked from issues of mortality. Death thus became invisible to the public gaze, turning exclusively into either a matter of civic concern or an issue limited to the sphere of sentiments and emotions. So insistent was the demand to hide the "remains" of the dead that, according to certain medical opinions, it was better to cremate than bury the dead, as in cremation "man 'ceases to do evil' and learns to do well. The gases evolved go to build up vegetable life; while his ashes may manure mother earth."[41] Secondly, this process of concealment and sanitization led to the confinement of the dead to the spectral sphere alone, unconnected from everyday life and its realities. The dead, lacking in historicity, could look only to their ghosts to give deadly spaces a sense of history.

Mortality and Morality

A historical fact that is often overlooked about the nineteenth century in Bengal is that it was a century of numerous famines and epidemics and, hence, a very high rate of mortality. It is thus not surprising that the first modern ghost stories by Bengali authors came into being in this period. But while "spirits" like Manimalika were still relatively new to the geography of haunting, older ghosts still clung to their traditional hunting grounds. The location of ghosts was very important to indigenous thinking because ghosts, like certain animals, had their extremely specific habitats and would not be found outside of it. Kipling, being aware of this, commented in 1888:

> There are, in this land, ghosts who take the form of fat, cold, pobby corpses, and hide in trees near the roadside till a traveler passes. Then they drop upon his neck and remain. There are also terrible ghosts of women who have died in childbed. These wander along the pathways

at dusk, or hide in the crops near a village, and call seductively. But to answer their call is death in this world and next. Their feet are turned backwards that all sober men may recognize them. There are ghosts of little children who have been thrown into wells. These haunt well-kerbs and the fringes of jungles, and wail under the stars, and catch women by the wrist and beg to be taken up and carried.[42]

Modern spatiality, Lefebvre has famously argued, is devoid of time. Briefly put, he argues that, in nature, "time is apprehended within space . . . and natural space was merely the lyrical and tragic script of natural time."[43] With the advent of modernity, however, time disappears from social space. This "manifest expulsion of time," according to Lefebvre, is "one of the hallmarks of modernity."[44] At first glance, the tales of haunting of the new colonial cities seem to be doing exactly the opposite ideological work: that of ascribing time onto space. In reality, however, this is not so. The historicity that colonial spaces acquired from ghosts was necessarily spectral. It was not a history of the real social order but the manufactured time of colonial continuity. Indeed, as Francis Hutchins has suggested, the "illusion of permanence" as regards British rule in India became far more pronounced after 1857, with the transfer of power from the company to the crown.[45] One of the most spectacular architectural projects, the Victoria Memorial in Calcutta, which stamped the landscape with this sense of colonial/British historicity, was began under Lord Curzon in 1906 and completed in 1921. Unsurprisingly, Curzon was interested in establishing a marker for the "history of India itself . . . [of] the past two centuries."[46] This massive colonial building thus significantly combined aspects of European and older Mughal architecture, thus laying claim to both the antiquity and continuity of colonialism.

As we come back to our ghosts in the British stories, we find them thus laden with a brittle temporality that is as anxious as colonial rule itself and as eager to appear eternal. It is perhaps the unresolved murder of *real* history that would not let the spirits rest in the colonial mansions of nineteenth-century Calcutta.

FOUR
———

Enacting Ghosts

New Spirits, New Rituals

The death notices in Al-Ahram, the city's newspaper of record, run to thirty solid columns a day and often more: the saying is that a person cannot have died if their death goes unmentioned in Al-Ahram.—MAX RODENBECK, *Cairo: The City Victorious*

The various societies and associations with which he was connected passed resolutions in the memory of the deceased. The ... Vice-Chancellor of the University, paid a fitting tribute to the memory of the deceased remarking that "something more than a passing notice is due to the memory of Peary Chand Mitra." The Calcutta Public Library voted for an oil painting which is still now an ornament of the Metcalfe Hall.—"PEARY CHAND MITTRA," *Calcutta Review*, 1905

In this chapter, I continue to center Doreen Massey's beautifully phrased insight that space is "stretched out social relations" and use it as an important analytical infrastructure. It merits revisiting for two reasons. First, Massey's insistence on the "interpenetration of space and time" demonstrates both the inherent dynamism of spatiality and its historical imbrication with social power. It helps us understand fully her allied claim that the spatial organization of society is "integral to the production of the social, and not merely its result."[1] If the nineteenth century was, for Bengal, to use Sarah Nuttall's phrase, a "time of entanglement," then we need to apply this spatiotemporal analysis to institutions and spaces that helped cohere the self-consciously "modern" discourse of the period, or this newly minted sense of time and chronology.² In other words, while the invention of a new "history/time" has been the subject of much scholarly discussion, this literature has attended only marginally to the production of space and the institutions that created, scaffolded, and in turn reflected the new spatiotemporal regime. Second, we need to be attentive to Massey's argument about space and place not being discrete phenomena. "Place," Massey cautions, ought not to be conceived as the obverse of space, one being abstract/stable while the other is concrete/historical. Instead, place is a "particular articulation" of social relations. What constitutes place always extends out beyond it, thus challenging any "claims to internal histories or timeless identities."³

If a new orthodoxy of death and spirits was being constructed from the ashes of the old heterodox ghosts, then what were the new institutions/spaces that allowed for the enactment of these new spirits? I look here at what feminist scholar Leslie Salzinger calls a "process of repetitive citation," through which particular social forms, once produced, are socialized and generalized through the social body.⁴ What new social rituals, literary forms, instituted the new ghosts? How did the new ghosts become dominant over the old? The central question that melancholically animates this chapter is, what historical processes forged the path from ghosts as a part of everyday life to death as a concern for governability?

Governing Death, Producing Ghosts

The ghost of Gadkhali was the star of the Bhadralok ethnologist's notebook. She was so famous that she was catalogued in a contemporary *Dictionary of Superstitions* as "unquestionably recognized by the Bengal peasantry."⁵ The story went that an unfortunate worker in Calcutta was on his way to the countryside in south Bengal, possibly Gadkhali, to visit his wife, who was living with her parents in her natal home. The man knew of the cholera epidemic that had devastated the land around his wife's village, which was partly why he was anxious to check on his wife's welfare. Night had fallen by the time he arrived at the village, and all was eerily quiet. No one welcomed him at the small railway station or greeted him on his way to his in-laws' home. Once he reached the house, however, he was relieved to be met by his mother-in-law (or wife, in some versions), who laid out an elaborate dinner for the weary traveler. Many unnerving things begin to happen during this meal: the mother-in-law anticipates the man's needs before he speaks, brings him food that he merely wishes for but has not articulated, and so on. Finally, he asks for a piece of lime to spice up his daal. When the woman leaves to fetch the lime, the man follows her curiously into the kitchen and then, to his utter horror, watches as she extends an arm straight out of the kitchen window and plucks a lime from a tree several yards away. As he begins to lose consciousness, he realizes that all life in the village had been wiped out by the epidemic and only unhappy ghosts roamed the ruins of the necropolis.

That ghosts would germinate in the wake of epidemics was to be expected and followed global patterns of such narratives elsewhere.[6] In the context of Bengal, however, the policies of the colonial state, the roiling of life and death that followed such policies, made epidemics and its ghosts both biopolitical and administrative as never before. Recent scholarship has contributed greatly to our understanding of statistics as imperial statecraft. Ian Hacking's seminal work on the epistemology of statistics shows how early statistical surveys included "much information about lifestyles." As an academic discipline, statistics' reliance on discourses of typologies and classifications thus closely allied it with another emerging discipline, that of ethnography. Born of European explorations, the knowledge produced by statistical surveys, through typification, made legible for the colonial state unknown lands and peoples, and their bewildering practices. Edward Said was one of the first scholars to identify colonialism as an enumerative project that divided a people into "manageable parts."[7] It is unsurprising then that the disciplinary politics of statistics were first developed in Ireland, with William Petty's census operations of 1679.[8] By the nineteenth century, statistical studies were widely in use in both Europe and the colonies to pull together projects as disparate as health and sanitation, wage relations, crime, and land revenue, thus making it indispensable as both discipline and tool of civic control. Death in colonial Bengal was "processed" through these same administrative strategies of observation and classification.

From the mid-nineteenth century onward, as the colonial state was buffeted by successive waves of epidemics, enumerative operations took a new turn. Three distinct but related mechanisms of governability emerged, stripping death down to its numerical value.

First, the various epidemics were classified into an ordered set of reports and surveys. Faced with a series of cholera and malaria epidemics, the colonial medical bureaucracy, activating its vast networks of officials and amateurs, produced an endless stream of reports, statistics, and analyses. Death, disobeying the colonial bureaucrat's dry analysis, however, created architectures of gruesome horror in vast swathes of the Bengal countryside, constructing necropolises and inciting ghosts. Writing in 1875 about the Burdwan Fever, the Bengali doctor Gopaul Chunder Roy observed how villages that "once rang with the cheerful, merry tone of healthful infants" now resounded with "loud wailings and lamentations." Fields were littered with "the skulls of human beings . . . at every few yards' distance."[9] Even British reports could not help but mention the effect of epidemics on villages like Gadkhali. The Epidemic Fevers Commission noted how the fever "depopulated a large and populous village named Gadkhali . . . in 1840."[10] Gadkhali reappears in the writings of the nationalist journalist Motilal Ghosh, for whom the destruction of villages "like Gour, Gadkhali, Ula, Kanchrapara, Halishahar and Naihati within ten years from 1860 to 1870" was proof of a deeper history of colonial predation. In the 1860s, Ghosh was a student at Krishnanagar College, about a hundred miles north of Gadkhali. No one remained, Ghosh later wrote in his memoir, in the town of Krishnanagar "to burn or bury the dead bodies." So "cart-loads of them were thrown in the Kharia river or in the bed of the dead river Anjana. Heartbreaking lamentations were heard almost in every house of the town and to add horror to the situation jackals in packs howled during the day . . . having feasted upon the dead bodies."[11]

Second, a new bureaucratic language was created to account for and control the narrative about these epidemics. The colonial state created an elaborate map of bureaucratic correspondence on what it variously designated as Assam Fever, Nagpur Fever, Peshawar Fever, Amritsar Fever, and the infamous Burdwan Fever. This new vocabulary of configuration of disease produced the effect of classifying disparate bodily symptoms into recognizable, broad categories of "disease" in ways that scholars have correctly argued made epidemic a "flexible medical metaphor."[12] Such reports also allowed the state, faced with nationalist condemnation, to ascribe its own set of reasoning on the rise and spread of epidemics. Such reasons were usually a long litany of how the people of Bengal were the real cause of the disease — from "deficient ventilation" in their homes to their "excessive use of farinaceous food." It was the life of the people that was the responsible for their deaths.[13]

But the concrete presence of mass death, its corpses and its ghosts, also had a third effect. It incited in the state the necessity to track death in a way that abstracted it from the unfolding gruesome spectacles and record it in tidy numerical order, making death legible for the purpose of rule. It is unsurprising then that, precisely in this period, the colonial state insisted on instituting a system of birth and death registration, a move that, as Foucault has taught us, created out of a heterogeneous people, endowed with idiosyncrasies and particularities, a trackable *population*, with its "specific phenomena and its peculiar variables: birth and death rates, life expectancy, fertility, state of health, frequency of illnesses, patterns of diet and habitation."[14] Birth registration was first introduced in the Central Provinces in 1866, followed by Punjab and the United Provinces. In Bengal, while the state made several attempts to track births and deaths throughout the nineteenth century, the efforts became particularly vigorous from the mid-century onward, with the epidemics ravaging the land. Scattered and local attempts to tie biological processes to a grid of observations finally culminated in the Birth and Death Registration Act of 1873.

The act coalesced many of the colonial states' enumerative fantasies. District magistrates were mandated to appoint registrars for their districts, names of whom were to be published alongside their office hours in "a conspicuous place." The registrars were to be armed with notebooks in which to enter births and deaths of their area. Even the form of such entry was laid out in the law with terrifying obsessiveness: the "pages of such books shall be numbered progressively from the beginning to the end; and every place of entry shall be divided from the following entry by a line."[15] The law placed significant responsibility on the village *chaukidar*, the last stop in the colonial chain of command; he was, in the last instance, the person who gathered death-as-data and reported to the registrar. A chilling array of punitive measures undergirded the law, criminalizing areas of life and death never touched before. The *chaukidar* was tasked with obtaining in writing all the details of births and deaths from the families; if the families were not literate, they had to supply the information in great verbal detail. Failure to produce this record came with heavy fines, two rupees for the *chaukidar* and up to five rupees for families. As death was run as numbers through the system, strict time limits were imposed on the reporting process:

> The nearest male relative of deceased present at the death, or in attendance during the last illness of any person dying, within such area, or in the absence of any such relative, the occupier of the house, or, if the occupier be the person who shall have died some male inmate of the house in which such death shall have happened, shall within eight days next after the day of such death, give information either personally or in writing to the registrar of the district, or by means of the *chaukidar* or other village-watchman . . . according to the best of his knowledge and belief of the several particulars hereby required to be known and registered touching the death of such a person . . . [16]

Unnatural deaths, the purview of ghosts, were subjected to particular surveillance. Hunter documents villages paying the cost of carrying a corpse to the police station in case of "an unnatural death."[17] Heavy fines were charged for any infraction related to a draft of newly enacted laws pertaining to the disposal of the dead. For instance, one had to pay a fine of ten rupees for conveying a corpse along any road "unless it be decently covered and totally concealed from view." An even heavier fine of fifty rupees was levied if the dead body was not cremated within six hours of being brought to the burning ghat.[18] As death gradually became part of state business, those attending to or surviving the dead suddenly found themselves trapped in these skeins of state power.

Despite these measures, the project of enumerating death continued to run into problems. First, there was the problem of veracity as expected by the state. From as early as 1879 one "invariable complaint" of many British officials was that it was "impossible to improve registration."[19] The charge of incompetence of course fell on Indian officials such as *chaukidars*, so much so that, in several districts higher officials, "magisterial and police," during their tours of inspection, double checked their reports.[20] The state distrust of *chaukidars* grew to such an extent that in 1888 we find the district magistrate of Hooghly advocating for changing their recruitment base, for he believed that *chaukidars* "should no longer be recruited from Bagdis, Haris, Domes, Chamar and other of the lowest and most criminal classes, which have . . . a quasi-hereditary claim to the post."[21] All the caste groupings vilified by this magistrate were also, we should remember, those who ritually handled death and cremation and, prior to these official moves to ensnare death, were responsible for maintaining registers at cremation ghats and graveyards.[22]

Reaction against this governmentality of death was so widespread that it can be counted as its second constitutive feature. Due to the punitive nature of various laws regulating death, the living tried their best to avoid them or in some instances to make them work in their favor. "A very prevalent crime" among the "natives of Bengal" wrote Norman Chevers, the secretary to the Medical Board at Fort William, was to cause "a person to disappear" and charge an enemy with their murder. A "putrid corpse" recovered from the river was often brought forward as the body of the disappeared individual.[23] Finally, and significantly for our purposes, rumors often started flying about "walking corpses" in parts of the Bengal countryside. An unidentifiable dead body would suddenly appear on the boundary line of a certain village, causing panic among the inhabitants for both otherworldly and worldly reasons. Was the dead walking? Or was it some enemies from a rival village using their dead to trap the living into the colonial web of laws and fines? Often the answer was unclear; what was clear was that ghosts continued to lurk on the margins of colonial biopolitics. Sacrosanct as death registers were to colonial governmentality, even they were not free of ghosts. Since denoting cause of death was the task of the *chaukidar*, certain kinds of death, clear to him as having been caused by a ghost, were catalogued faithfully as just that. One can almost see the colonial official shaking his head in despair while writing the following: "death caused by . . . *tetanus resnatorum* [are often reported as] *pachoa paoa*, literally attacked by a ghost," such comments ironically ratifying the popular Bengali proverb of "a ghost within the mustard" traditional antidote for ghosts, or a virus within the antidote.[24] The ghost of Gadkhali was not fully vanquished; she continued to haunt colonial records.

Nevertheless, we need to register a profound change in ghostly epistemology as it developed from the mid-nineteenth century because of these colonial incitements. What was key to "producing" a different kind of haunting was the abstraction of death through the enumerative and legal procedure of the state regime, hence an explanation is necessary here about the role of abstraction.

In one sense, we all process the concreteness of reality through a series of abstractions. To be *thought of*, reality must necessarily be parceled out by our senses. As the philosopher Bertell Ollman put it, our "minds can no more swallow the world whole at one sitting than can our stomachs."[25] But abstraction plays a specific role in capitalist/colonial modernity. According to Marx, capitalism presents us with political economic categories that are the "abstract expressions of the real, transitory, historic, social relations."[26] This is because the system operates through a process wherein different kinds of concrete labor—cleaning streets, making iPhones, teaching—are assigned a value, and, ultimately, payment, by making them commensurate with each other. Different kinds of labor are recognized only through this homogenization, thus making all concrete forms of work subordinate to its value form: "As money is not exchanged for any one specific quality, for any one specific thing, or for any particular human essential power, but for the entire objective world of man and nature, from the standpoint of its possessor it therefore serves to exchange every quality for every other, even contradictory, quality and object: it is the fraternisation of impossibilities. It makes contradictions embrace."[27]

Capitalism's indifference to the concrete form of labor—its presentation of all labor as abstract general labor alone—forms the basis of all social relations and organization under capitalism. The form that the state takes, the laws that are generated, the institutions and ideologies that dominate the relations between humans, not as people but as wage workers, all embody this fundamental procedure of the value form—transmogrifying concrete, discrete categories to their abstract and alienated form.

We can now make better sense of our earlier discussion on statistics and understand *why* it emerged in modernity in its reified form, suppressing through its enumerative operations the richness of lived experience and processing all experience in its specific, serialized modality. This is not to say that premodern states did not count, but to point out that numbers were qualitative rather than quantitative in premodernity. Take the case of death records in premodern Europe. In Britain, before the first national census of 1801, the birth and death records of a county were to be found in the Parish Registers, kept from the sixteenth century. But such records were of only limited use to the census officials of the nineteenth century because the Parish Registers were not records of births and deaths in the abstract, but specifically how such life events related to the life of the parish. They did not register births, only baptisms, and deaths were recorded only as interments in churchyards.[28] Numbers, in other words, reflected rather than suppressed life. The various registration laws in colonial Bengal reified death in this very specific modern way. They counted not individual people with names and life stories, but inert "bodies," each commensurate with the other. Serialized death in Bengal could thus be cast on a comparative scale with deaths in Madras through such homogenized, vital statistics.

What happens to ghosts through these procedures of law and state? They emerge, like bodies, like labor, without form or substance. They are smoky apparitions constantly escaping description and features. The colorful ghostly lives of the *ekanore*, the *mamdo*, the *petni*, are subjugated under the singular, solitary gothic form of the specter. There are no longer the various typologies of ghosts, just the one kind, recognizable through limited behavior recognizable across literary forms and lived experience, and it is to this spectral presence we turn next.

Literary Worlds of the New Ghosts

Rabindranath Tagore was undoubtedly one of the most daring of the twentieth-century figures to query and map the borderlands between the living and the dead—both in his life and in his art. While séances were part of his every day, ghosts abound in his writing. In this section we use his writing, particularly his short stories, as our key to understanding the new modern zeitgeist, especially as it related to the modern ghosts.

Although Rabindranath wrote the occasional short story in the 1870s, the bulk of his writing in this form was done in the last decade of the nineteenth century. Between 1891 and 1895 he published forty-two short stories in the Bengali-language journals *Hitabadi* and *Sadhana*, and a few others in the Tagore family journal, *Bharati*, thus earning his nomination from William Radice as "the first Bengali writer to think of the short story as a serious art-form."[29] Of these, about six stories can be considered to deal with the supernatural: "Kankal" (The Skeleton), "Manihara" (Lost Jewel), "Nishithe" (In the Night), "Kshudita Pashan" (The Hungering Stones), "Mastermashai" (The Teacher), and "Jibito O Mrito" (The Living and the Dead). These were some of the most popular stories of a particularly prolific author. For instance, the title of one of the first translated collection of his stories in English, published in 1916 by his close associate and friend C. F. Andrews, derives its name from one of the more famous supernatural stories, namely "*Kshudita Pashan*," or The Hungering Stones.

Popular though some of the stories may have been, they were not without their critics. It is noteworthy that all these stories, later to be deemed classics, were published in the various house journals of the Tagore family. The weekly *Hitabadi* was edited by Kaliprasanna Kavyavisharad, but according to Krishnakamal Bhattacharya,[30] the journal owed its inception to Rabinandranath Tagore's older brother, Dwijendranath Tagore (1840–1926); Rabindranath himself was appointed its literary editor in 1891; he also assumed editorship of the journal *Sadhana* in 1894 and later of *Bharati* between 1898 and 1899.[31] In other words, the stories appeared within the relatively safe confines of journals that were stewarded either by Rabindranath himself or by his close associates. This is because the newness of Rabinandranath's art form came with a price. Consider the example of the short story "Nishithe." After its publication in 1894, a leading contemporary literary critic, Suresh Kumar Samajpati, pronounced "Nishithe" to be "utterly lacking in narrative skill." The story, according to Suresh Kumar, did not work "because of the writer's lack of storytelling skill and inability to perceive what might be possible."[32]

Here Suresh Kumar inadvertently gives us the analytic lever to pry open a whole complex of questions about the "new" supernatural; we are suddenly presented with a new ontology of ghost stories—that which has to consciously navigate and ultimately transgress the "possible." This new ghostly ontology is different from our previous premodern ghosts in two important respects.

First, the previous ghosts did not raise questions about the condition or possibilities of their existence. They just were. *Their relationship to the world of humans was one of correspondence*: ghosts existed, just as wild animals existed, ipso facto humans needed to devise ways to protect against them. Indeed, the vast majority of the premodern ghosts, as we saw in chapter 3, were to be found in the "wild," as opposed to the new spirits, who haunt the most sacred of bourgeois spaces: the home.[33]

Second, and following from the above, the new ghosts proposed a new epistemology for humans to relate to the natural world. While the old ghosts were a part of nature, in a relationship of correspondence with humans, the new spirits existed despite, or in contradiction to, the laws of the natural world: they were *super*natural.

There emerge, then, two distinct ghostly typologies: one belonging to the class and tradition of Rabindranath Tagore's Brahmadaitya, and the "host" with the gigantic arm from Kartikeya Chandra Roy's tale; and the other the spirits, or *atmas*, that were called forth in the civilized settings of séances, in the presence of polite company, and within the elegant homes of the nineteenth century. Indeed, what was extremely clear from Kartikeya Chandra's account was that a remarkable difference existed between ghosts of *sekal* and those of *ekal*. But unlike the usual temporal condemnation of *ekal*, it was the ghosts of *sekal* that were disreputable in comparison to their modern counterparts. Of all the social creatures that had survived the temporal shift from *sekal* to *ekal*, including (but not limited to) women, youth, lower castes, peasants, or servants, only the ghosts, it seems, had improved their morals under modernity.

The Literary Worlds of the New Supernatural: A New Aesthetic

"Kankal," published in 1892, is Rabindranath Tagore's first supernatural story. It begins by fusing the fictional narrative with the actual life-memories of Rabindranath as a young boy:

> A complete human skeleton hung from the wall of a room adjacent to the one in which my three childhood companions and I slept. Its bones rattled in the night air. During the day we were the ones who rattled them. . . . A student at Campbell Medical School was tutoring us in osteopathic medicine.
>
> Much time has elapsed since then. The skeleton has disappeared from that room along with the knowledge of osteopathy from our brains.

Recently, due to lack of space elsewhere, I had to go back to that room to sleep. Sleep refused to come given the unfamiliarity of my surroundings. As I tossed and turned the big church clock loudly struck the many hours of night. Right then the little oil lamp in the corner flickered a few times and then died completely. There had been one or two accidents in our home in recent times. So, the dying of the lamp easily reminded me of death; I thought, just as the light disappeared into the darkness of this night, human life-flames being extinguished—sometimes during the day and sometimes at night—must appear similarly to Nature.

Eventually I thought of that skeleton. As I began to imagine what its life must have been like, it suddenly felt as if a sentient being was groping its way through the darkness and circling my bed and its mosquito net, I could hear its rapid breathing. It is as though they were looking for something, not finding it, and then circling the room in increasingly quickened steps. I knew for certain that all this was the product of my sleepless, overheated imagination, . . . but still I began to feel the first shivers of fear. To forcibly break through this unreasonable fear I loudly voiced: "who is there?" The footsteps came nearer to my bed, stopped there and I heard an answer: "It's me. I have come back to look for my skeleton."[34]

"Kankal" sets the terrain for how the new spirits were to be conceived, or socially enacted. Several factors mark their distinction from the older ghosts, and it is worth spending some time on this dissimilarity.

First, we note the uncomfortable braiding of fiction and life-memory in the opening paragraph, where Rabindranath invokes his actual experience—there was a skeleton in his family home that was used to educate him and his cousins—to carefully confuse the borders between the real and the unreal.[35] This porosity of the natural/supernatural divide is characteristic of all supernatural tales by Rabindranath. We are never certain whether the authorial voice is asking us to believe or disbelieve the supernatural events—but it is noteworthy that it is "belief," not reason, that becomes the arbiter of the narrative. Contrast this with the older ghost story, which could, and frequently did, begin with the unproblematized opening line: "Once upon a time there was a ghost."

The question of belief is further accentuated and complicated by the narrative style that Rabindranath adopts in "Kankal," one that he uses for all his other "ghost stories." The stories are told in the form of a dialogue between a believer—one who is committed to the world of magic and haunting—and a nonbeliever, who brings in the harsh light of science to dispel the hazy mists of belief. Science is thus literally brought into a dialogue with the supernatural, thereby destabilizing the veracity of both. We will have occasion to explore further the implications of this dialogue.

Second, the intense aestheticization of fear should be of note here. We are being asked to feel every frisson in the escalation of narrative tension as the church clock sounds its knell, the lamp goes out, and, finally, as the sounds of breathing and footfalls of an unknown Being approach the protagonist. This new inflection of fear is not merely a form of terror but an admixture of terror and pleasure, which can only be obtained through *reading*. I submit that these stories mark the tremulous beginnings of a literary genre being crystalized.

E. J. Clery has convincingly shown a similar, if contested, process of genre-making at work for supernatural tales in Victorian England. She argues that by the beginning of the nineteenth century "literary tales of terror were being affirmed as manifestations of an autonomous realm of the aesthetic, detached from the didactic function which had guaranteed the social utility of the realist novel."[36]

For Clery, this process was connected to *the material reality* of an expanding market for books in general, whereby certain books or genres could become "luxury items"; and *the ideological dimension* of capitalism as a system of mystification and spectrality that generated a chiastic relationship to the fictional supernatural. While the most famous example, what Clery calls "the spirituality of the capitalist marketplace," is Adam Smith's "Invisible hand," Clery uncovers an entire fabric of eighteenth- and nineteenth-century sources that imputed the rhetoric of "providential belief" to the emerging discipline of economics. For instance, in a textbook meant for the English royal household, one Josiah Tucker argued that the "system of Commercial Industry is equally the Plan of Providence with the System of Morals." Similarly, Edmund Burke proposed that the "laws of commerce" were in fact "the laws of nature, and consequently the laws of God." This leads Clery to propose that it is no coincidence that "the expanding taste for commercial fictions of the supernatural" in this period "and the project of a supernaturalized theory of capitalism" converged perfectly.[37] There is no doubt that, as in Britain, in Bengal, too, the process of genre formation for supernatural tales intersects with processes of a capitalist modernity in formation, but with important differences. We will have occasion to return to this question in the next section; for now I continue to catalogue their differences with our ghosts of old.

Unlike their premodern counterparts, the modern ghosts never make an appearance in the stories. The most important source of terror for the old ghosts was the way they looked and the inhuman feats they could achieve. The *ekanore* was known to all for his *kulor mato kaan, mulor mato dnaat* (ears as big as a kulo and teeth as long as radishes). Creatures were often referred to as having *bhantar mato chokh* (eyes as fiery as burning kilns). But the new ghosts are terrifying only in their absence, not in their presence.

We have already noted the ominous but muted signs that signal the shadowy coming of the spirit in "Kankal." Throughout the story the author never once sees the ghost. He hears her, speaks to her, and senses her through the opaque yet porous screen of the mosquito net that divides the living from the dead.

In "Nishithe," this allusive absence is what drives the narrative plot. The protagonist of "Nishithe" is the *zamindar*, Dakshinacharan, who is married to an ailing wife. As his enfeebled wife, in true Victorian fashion, lies dying with no apparent medical reason, Dakshinacharan falls in love with her doctor's young daughter, Manorama. The wife, whose name we never learn, sensing this budding romance and realizing that she is a barrier to her husband's true happiness, decides to make matters easy and commits suicide. Dakshinacharan manages to overcome his shock and marries Manorama. It is then that his haunting begins.

One evening in early autumn, Dakshinacharan is walking with his new wife Manorama in their garden. It is an "eerily dark" evening. Here in the shadowy garden, with only the sound of rustling *jhau* leaves, Dakshinacharan clasps Manorama's hand and declares his love for her. But this is the very same spot where he had once uttered similar sentiments to his unnamed, now deceased, wife: "I winced in alarm at my own words, remembering I had once spoken in the very same way to someone else. And that very moment, above the *bakul* tree, over the top of the *jhau* bushes, under the yellow slice of the moon, right from the eastern to the far western bank of the Ganges, the sound of laughter sped swiftly, a rolling laugh. I cannot describe that heart-rending laugh, the way it seemed to split the sky. I lost consciousness and fell from my seat."[38]

When he comes to his senses, he learns that what he thought of as supernatural laughter was only the sound of a flock of birds flying overhead. But these incidents of supernatural misrecognition keep repeating. Another time, when Dakshinacharan kisses Manorama,

> At once a voice resounded through the empty waste, asking three times, "Who's she? Who's she? Who's she?" I started in alarm, and my wife shuddered too. But the next moment we realized it was not a human voice, not

ENACTING GHOSTS 109

> a supernatural one either—just the call of the water-birds scouring the sandbanks. . . .
>
> Shaken by our fear, we hurried back. . . . We lay on our beds: Manorama was exhausted and quickly fell asleep. But someone came and stood by my mosquito-net in the dark, and pointing at Manorama with a long, thin, bony finger whispered ever so softly and indistinctly into my ear, "Who's she? Who's she? Who's she?"
>
> I sat up and struck a match for the lamp. Instantly a gale of laughter swept the shadowy figure away, shaking my mosquito-net, . . . turning the blood of my sweat-soaked body to ice.[39]

The new ghost, then, forever resides in allusions rather than emerge in the concreteness of a substantive form. She or he is hidden behind a thicket of literary description—so much so that it is the atmospheric narrative that can be said to raise the ghosts more effectively than any séance. The new ghosts, in turn, depend heavily on the literary genre that created them. It is unmistakable, from the patterned way the stories are structured, that very clear rules exist for the genre, rules that repeat themselves in all the tales of this genre.

We have already noted the absence of an actual creature in both "Kankal" and "Nishithe"; the same pattern can be found in all the other supernatural tales by Rabindranath Tagore, where the approach of the ghost is marked by nonvisual sensory triggers.

Sounds and smells, rather than sight, are powerful reminders that signal the approach of the specter. To return to "Manihara," when a scheming relative murders Manimalika for her jewels, she does not let mere death stop her from being reunited with her ornaments. With her murder, the husband, Phanibhushan, enters the sensory universe of allusions and signals that structure the new supernatural:

> At some point late into the night the rains had ceased along with the sounds of music from the village theatre. Phanibhushan still sat by the window as before. The world-enwrapping, complete darkness outside his window seemed like the towering gateway to hell itself, it seemed as though at this moment if one cried for things that had seemed forever lost, they might re-appear for once. . . .
>
> All of a sudden there was knocking sound mingled with the jangling sound of ornaments. It seemed just as though the sound was travelling from the river up to the shore. [Manimalika was killed while on a boat.] The waters of the river and the night had become one. . . .

Slowly the sound began to move from the riverbank towards the house. It paused in front of the house. The doorman had shut the main gates. . . . The knocking sound and the sound of jewelry began to pound at the gates, it seemed as though along with ornaments something hard was striking at the gates. Phanibhushan could no longer remain still. He went past the lightless rooms, went down the dark stairways and stood before the closed doors . . . and shook them with all his might, the contact with the door and its sounds startled him awake. He discovered that he had sleepwalked downstairs. His body was drenched in sweat and his limbs were as cold as ice. . . . Awakened from his dream he found that there no longer were any sounds outside, merely the quiet sound of the *Sraban* rains.[40]

The source of horror of the modern ghost, then, is simply their existence. Therefore they do not require any description in the narratives. The premodern ghosts had to evoke terror explicitly through their form and their fearsome deeds. When modernity has decreed death to be the end, a creature that insists on existing despite this coda needs no description; its very existence is the source of horror. The new ghost and the literary artifice that shapes it can be horrifying only under modernity—that which forbids its existence.

If thus far we have traced the procedures and histories of how the old ghosts were vanquished, the next section should offer some relief, for here we meet them again in their carnivalesque glory, drawn by some of the leading literary figures of the nineteenth and early twentieth centuries but, as we will see, changed irrevocably in their meaning and affective regime.

The Literary Worlds of the New Supernatural: Children's Stories

By all accounts, Damarudhar was a prosperous, respectable gentleman. His home, in a village south of Calcutta, was the center of sociability, a meeting place for all, especially during festivals and pujas. When such an upright member of society walks home with a nice fish and is attacked by ghosts, does he have any choice but to defend his property? Is he to blame if he happened to bite said ghosts? Ghosts, however, are toxic, and Damarudhar fell into a coma, from which he awoke after weeks to find that, in his illness, he had been cared for by none other than a "smallish, good-natured ghost." It is a great tragedy, then, that such a caring Being met his violent end by a carnivorous tree in Damarudhar's own garden. The tree attacked the gentle ghost, sucked him dry, and threw his ghost-husk on the ground.

"Ghost-husk? What is that?" asked Lambodar.

Damarudhar replied: "That terrifying tree had sucked the ghost dry of his bones, flesh and blood. Have you seen the husk of a bed bug? Or lentil husks? Ghost-husks are just like that, only bigger. Anyway, I got rid of that tree, otherwise I could certainly show them to you."[41]

The above story, by Troilakyanath Mukhopadhyay (1847–1919), a prominent literary figure of the time, at first gives comfort that the world of our old ghosts was not entirely lost. In the pages of Troilakyanath's numerous books we find them dancing, marrying, working—on notable occasions, forming private limited companies—and, of course, as the above tale chronicles, dying. Folk themes are reprised and forms common to oral narrative techniques implanted in these highly original stories. And yet, in this section I argue that, for all the homage he pays to older ghosts and the technologies of their retelling, Troilakyanath remains embedded in the Scientific Spiritualist framework. The old ghosts that he draws so deftly and sympathetically are there to serve an ideological function that only strengthens the bulwark of Scientific Spiritualism.

Troilakyanath was among a small but significant coterie of authors who rehabilitated the older ghosts and allowed them a life outside the gothic. We can count the polymath Upendrakishore Roy Chowdhury (1863–1915), the humorist Rajshekhar Basu (1880–1960), and the children's author Lila Majumdar (1908–2007) as members of this group. Not unlike his creation Damarudhar, Troilakyanath had a colorful life. He left formal education at eighteen and began work as a teacher in a village school in Birbhum (south Bengal). From Birbhum he moved around Bengal, working in several schools, at least one of which appointments was arranged by Debendranath Tagore. Then, in what appears to be a leap in many ways, he changed professions and got a job as a subinspector of police in Orissa. Working for the colonial carceral administration was becoming increasingly acceptable as a respectable job; by the 1880s, for example, Indian-run newspapers were lamenting the eagerness with which the Bhadralok served in colonial courts and prisons.[42] For Troilakyanath, this first encounter with the colonial state proved to be the beginning of a lifelong career. He served as a clerk at William Hunter's *Bengal Gazetteer* office, followed by positions in the Agriculture Department, the Revenue Department, and, finally, finishing out his career in 1896 as the assistant curator of the Indian Museum in Calcutta. He advised the government, traveled all over Europe, spoke multiple languages, and published several government reports and catalogues on Indian crafts and the artisans who produced them. In all this, he occupied, like many of his Bhadralok peers, a deep political contradiction—his livelihood depended on the very regime that dictated, or openly suppressed, all other expressions of life. His first, and arguably his best-known, novel, *Kankabati* (1892), embodied both these countervailing political currents, as well as reconfirmed his place in the Bhadralok literary milieu. *Kankabati*, upon release, was reviewed by none other than Rabindranath in *Sadhana*.[43] Although *Kankabati* is Troilakyanath's most discussed work, for our purposes of ghost-tracking, we must begin with "Lullu," a novella published in 1896, for it is a combined map, archive, and genealogy of such Beings.

Lullu was a "civilized, genteel, modern" bhut, who happened, one evening, to be casually resting on a terrace, when he spotted a beautiful woman appear on the terrace, taking her evening walk.[44] It was Lullu's lucky day, for soon after, he heard the woman's husband's voice from within the home urging him to "take the lady." As Lullu jumps to obey, carrying the beauty away from her husband into his lair, therein begins the adventure of the husband, an opium-addicted *aamir*, following Lullu's trail in search of his beloved, through many trials, tribulations, and final triumph. In his rescue efforts the *aamir* leads us through the lifeworld of ghosts, each more unique than the other. Take the lovelorn bhut Ghayngho who is pining for his one true love, Nakeshwari (the nose goddess), and who, with the *aamir's* aid, takes revenge on a fellow bhut, Gongo, for ruining his chances with her. Take Lullu himself, who, along with his friend, Gyente dada, are, in his words, truly "civilized, genteel, modern, bhuts never returning home before dawn," and always "showering with soap." The soap, a gift of the English, had made him so fair, that in a few days "none would recognize [him] . . . and all would exclaim 'this cannot be Lullu, this is a Saheb-bhut, must be the son of a Lord'" (figure 4.011). And of course we would be remiss if we did not mention the sumptuous feast at Ghayngho and Nakeshwari's wedding, attended by bhuts from all over India, that ends both the narrative and the adventure.[45]

Troilakyanath's brilliant evocation of older forms of storytelling is unmistakable and widely acknowledged. Sisir Kumar Das noted how Troilakyanath had "fully exploited" the potential of the old forms and had "the ingenuity to combine the techniques of the oral form with the modern art of narrative."[46] His most famous heroine, Kankabati, for example, enters a magical palace underwater, as in the tales of Buddhu-Bhutum and Manimala; she meets the fabled *khokkash* (figure 4.2); as in the Lal Kamal-Neel Kamal story, in "Lullu,"

FIGURE 4.1 · Lullu dressed as a white man: from Troilakyanath's "Lullu"

the *aamir* performs the popular folk ruse of capturing a ghost by tricking it into a bottle, and of course the novels are studded with creatures and Beings familiar to folk genres who behave in predictable ways.[47] But these tales are not folktales, and the creatures they enclose are not folk creatures. Troilakyanath, I submit, is not presenting new wine in an old bottle, he is presenting us with what Foucault calls "a new regime of discourses." It is not a case of quantitative difference — of more fearful older ghosts competing with less fearful, funnier ones, but to further evoke Foucault, "things were [being] said in a different way; it was different people who said them, from different points of view, and in order to obtain different results."[48] In the discussion that follows, I look at the corpus of Troilakyanath's work and tease out the ways in which the form of the old actually encloses new historical developments.

Let's begin with the role of humor in Troilakyanath, and how laughter organizes the lifeworld of his ghosts. Most scholars commenting on his work have drawn attention to Troilakyanath's mastery of the absurd. While Partha Chatterjee calls him an "outstanding humorist," Tapodhir Bhattacharjee actually points to the specific relation between humor and his ghosts: "There is nothing ghostly about them; rather they invoke our laughter."[49] The ghosts in

FIGURE 4.2 · Ghostly Being: Khokkosh, from Dakshinaranjan's *Thakurmar Jhuli*

Troilakyanath, while retaining certain formal allusions to precolonial ghosts, had undergone two important modifications. First, rather than creatures of the wild who invoked fear and incited protective measures, they were now constituent elements in a fast-congealing literary genre: fantasy.[50] They were no longer "real"; rather, they functioned as aestheticized, literary means to shape and reflect modern affective life. In a way they mirrored a death that had already come to pass; the old ghosts were gone, what remained were their ghost-husks. Second, because the ghosts were annexed to literature, the stories could easily embody multiple emotive scapes besides laughter — in the case of Troilakyanath, irony and satire.

Troilakyanath's ambivalent relationship to colonialism is best captured in his expert wielding of satire. In "Lullu," the *aamir* realizes how English education had robbed ghosts of their livelihood. The minds of people of "this wretched country" had been shaped so completely by English education that "when someone is possessed by a ghost or witch, they now claim that it is nothing but 'hysteria.'" In disgust, bhuts have unanimously refused to possess humans, and witches to devour them: "Bhuts and witches of India today are therefore silent and dispirited. The cremation grounds lie silent."[51]

In *Kankabati*, a paired skull and skeleton raise a similar concern about the English-educated and their loss of belief in gods and ghosts. To restore faith, the ghosts have established a private limited company, "Skull, Skeleton and Co," through which bhuts will "organize public lecture, publish books and newspapers." They were especially mindful that the company bear an English name, for only then would their business be taken seriously and result in an increase in both profits and respect.[52] The pathetic *saheb bhut* who keeps falling apart in "Birbala"[53]; Mr. Gamish the frog's insistence in *Kankabati* that he be addressed only in English[54]; Damarudhar, in a fix, pretending to be a *saheb* with a pith helmet because being a white man was the best protection against danger[55] — these are only some of the brilliant examples of Troilakyanath critically navigating colonial oppression through irony. It is, however, precisely irony and humor as literary forms that separate Troilakyanath's ghosts from their older counterparts.

The old bhuts in their world did not impart any moral lessons. In this they were part of global, pre-bourgeois, folkloric traditions in which, Robert Darnton reminds us, "without preaching or drawing morals . . . folktales demonstrate[d] that the world . . . [was] harsh and dangerous . . . they inhabit[ed] a world that . . . [was] arbitrary and amoral."[56] In contrast, Troilakyanath's ghosts never miss a chance to impart moral lessons. In "Lullu" we learn that bhuts are created when liquid darkness freezes into its solid form. The narrator wonders whether the powerful English, who had already invented a machine to freeze water into ice, might not invent a machine to make ghosts by freezing darkness. The human mind "is shrouded in unlimited darkness. If all this darkness can be shoveled out, gathered in baskets, and put into the machine, one could have a mass production of ghosts. Ghosts would be so cheap! . . . even the poor could afford a ghost."[57] The moralism is not arbitrary; it speaks to a specific framework wherein superstitions (darkness) are proscribed and modern beliefs stimulated. Throughout Troilakyanath's body of work, we can trace an identifiable schema that, while communing with the older ghosts, outlaws them from polite society.

Consider how the novels approach the new Hinduism. Characters who cling to certain "superstitious" versions of Hinduism — child marriage, denying education to women, bans against overseas travel — are shown to be villainous and corrupt; so much so that such characters are shown to violate basic ritual commensality and accept food from Muslims and even eat beef. The hero in *Kankabati*, Khetu, on the other hand, is the model of Bhadralok civility and religion. If we recall Scientific Spirituality's aversion to atheism,

Khetu denies being an atheist and is a devout Hindu of the right kind. He tops his classes, speaks perfect English without aping the colonial masters, refuses all ritually forbidden food, is a staunch supporter of women's education, makes his living though education (as opposed to land or moneylending), and saves every penny earned. Khetu also embodies a new masculinity. He is gentle and kind to the meek and infirm, mostly women, but fierce toward the unjust. There are instances of disturbing displays of rage by Khetu, where he wrecks whole buildings, which are portrayed as examples of his righteous manhood. Crucially, for present purposes, Khetu neither believes in nor declares his disbelief of bhuts—instead he laughs at them.[58]

Laughter, then, has a very specific ideological function. It does not trivialize bhuts; rather, it inserts them in a particular literary genre, humor. Contemporaneous literary critic Pramathanath Bishi (1901–1985) was prescient in his assessment of Troilakyanath:

> Ghosts and monsters are some key ingredients in his stories, . . . but he cannot be trivially dismissed as a writer of ghost tales. Ghosts are material for his work but his purpose is not to tell a ghost story. . . . [Like Jonathan Swift] Troilakyanath seeks to bring out the discrepancies of human nature. [Just as Swift] created gigantic and minuscule beings to show the absurdity in humans, bhuts are used by Troilakyanath for exactly a similar purpose. . . . His project is to mock humans, not tell a ghost story.[59]

His laughter mocked the world, but it was the humor of modern satire rather than the carnivalesque, earthy laughter of either the *rup kathas* or even the *mangal kavyas*, a distinction that Bakhtin first identified between the modern satirist and the folk comic:

> The people [in premodern festivals] do not exclude themselves from the wholeness of the world. They, too, are incomplete, they also die and are revived and renewed. This is one of the essential differences of the people's festive laughter from the pure satire of modern times. The satirist whose laughter is negative places himself above the object of his mockery, he is opposed to it. The wholeness of the world's comic aspect is destroyed, and that which appears comic becames [sic] a private reaction. The people's ambivalent laughter, on the other hand, expresses the point of view of the whole world; he who is laughing also belongs to it.[60]

Troilakyanath's genius was in creating characters and narratives with strong echoes of folk traditions but inserting them in a powerfully modern framework.

What did that modern framework look like? Unsurprisingly, very much like Scientific Spiritualism. In the nonfiction account of his travels in Europe, Troilakyanath takes up arms against the superstitious/irrational beliefs in ghosts that prevailed in India and how detrimental they were to the development of Indian children:

> The fear of ghosts, witches, and the whole brood of them is instilled into the tender heart of our boys and girls from their very infancy, which, acting on their mind like the iron shoe on the feet of a Chinese girl, warps the natural courage inherent in human beings. In after life these curdle-blooded men and women quiver with terror at the fall of a leaf or the rise of an owl when the evening shade has fallen upon the haunted garden. Whatever might have been in former times, the English children of the present day are free from such fears.[61]

Troilakyanath makes clear which ghosts he is at war with—the bhuts found in abundance in Indian "village life." With his trademark fierce irony, he even offers to classify them in true Linnaean fashion, arranging them under "classes, sub-classes, order, genera and species, in a separate chapter, entitled the 'Ghostial kingdom,' like the 'Mineral Kingdom,' 'Vegetable kingdom,' and 'Animal Kingdom,' of topographists." Lest we misunderstand, Troilakyanath follows up this vituperation with a further invective against bhuts, "I am against ghosts," he declared, "live or dead . . . male ghost or female ghost, child ghost or adult ghost, Brahman ghost or Islamite ghost, land ghost or water ghost, cow ghost or horse ghost, against all manner of ghosts."[62]

Except he was not. There was a certain variety of the dead, the new spirits informed by the revived Hinduism, that found a hospitable home in Troilakyanath Mukhopadhyay's life and writing.

Troilakyanath underwent a formal initiation ceremony, or *diksha*, with his family guru at Deoghar, which involved the usual ritual, receiving a specific mantra and mode of worship from his preceptor. As scholars have pointed out, he was also a regular contributor to *Bangabasi* and *Janmabhoomi*, journals that were strongly identified with Hindu revivalism.[63] These multiple but related discursive strands of anti-superstition, condemnation of old ghosts, and a newly minted modern that united Brahmanic Hinduism with English education come together in both his writing and his life to form a pattern that we can now easily recognize. Thus, it is unsurprising to learn that this vigorous denouncer of "all manner of ghosts" was also a firm believer in séances. Sudhirkumar Mukhopadhyay, in his biography of his father, recalls sessions where he served as a medium as Troilakyanath strove to communicate with the spirits of "great men" such as Rammohan Roy and Vidyasagar.[64]

On a similar note, while old ghosts were exiled into humor and satire, the gothic found powerful expression in Troilakyanath's writing. Gothic elements that we identified in the previous section were compellingly mobilized in stories such as "Pujar Bhut," "Bhuter Bari," and "Keno Eto Niday Hoile." While the "humorous" old bhuts were diverse in their gender, religion, and familial arrangements, the spirits or *atmas* in these tales, following established gothic rules, were strictly female. They sighed, whispered, and hinted rather than scaring or tormenting directly, like Lullu or Nakeshwari. Gender was a site and cause of terror rather than incidental to it. Troilakyanath's work with both kinds of ghosts tragically demonstrated how the "grotesque tradition peculiar to the marketplace [folk] and the academic literary tradition . . . [had] parted ways and . . . [could] no longer be brought back together."[65] If we return to his most popular protagonist, the young Kankabati, let us recall how Kankabati tries to escape old-world rogues who wanted to enforce a marriage on her in the name of obsolete rituals, who were against women's education and who, in their villainy, had fallen far enough to even consort with Muslims. Who should provide solace and support to our heroine against such formidable foes but the creatures and ghosts of old? Talking mosquitoes and frogs, ghosts and their relatives, chart Kankabati's path to her own true love, Khetu. But the ghosts can now exist only in delirium; they vanish upon her waking, leaving only an elegiac trace—as shadows, which, if the new world found offending, were "no more yielding but a dream."[66]

Mourning the Dead: Sraddha, Memories, and Sorrow

In 1914 the editor, author, and prominent advocate of Hindu revivalism, Panchkori Bandyopadhyay, wrote a piece about what he called the new "fashion" of memorial meetings, a scathing commentary that deserves to be quoted at length:

> Smriti Sabha or Smarak Sabha are now a fashion. When Bengali society was Hindu, the dead were remembered through conforming to proper rituals at sraddhas and through feeding Brahmins and the poor at these ceremonies. Now, thanks to English civilization, all of this can be done on the cheap. Five siccas will get you a tea party or an evening commemoration

event, spend ten or fifteen rupees and you have a Smriti Sabha. The usual suspects of Calcutta society are recruited to speechify meaninglessly to enthusiastic audiences. Men laugh, clap, speak—and boom! the sabha is done. . . .

Is this a memorial meeting? There is no meaningful discussion about the life of the man whose memory you want to preserve, what were the circumstances of his birth, . . . what were his views and are those views still relevant in society, if not then why not? . . . At the most speakers shower some praise on the deceased, praise thoroughly without any relationship to contemporary society. . . . The organizers install a famous man as chair, and familiar tropes and words are circulated and regurgitated. . . . The sabha adopts important resolutions, perhaps a marble bust for the deceased? Or a scholarship in his name? . . . but once the meeting is over you remain in the same dark as you were before. From the time of the death of Bankim Chandra and Vidyasagar, there are the same cheap dramas that pass as memorialization.[67]

There is much to unpack in Panchkori Bandyopadhyay's conservative critique of what he saw as modern modes of memorialization. The memory of past men, he argued, were preserved by two kinds of people: sons and disciples. Sons maintained the lineage through ritual *sraddha* ceremonies, while disciples preached their master's word, ensuring his place in history. Men lacking either disappeared like a "bubble in water." The English-educated missed this essential truth about memorialization: that memory could only be preserved through the social activity of people who were in an organic relationship to the deceased; by focusing on modern rituals by random strangers, such projects were doomed to failure. What stands out most prominently in Panchkori Bandyopadhyay's critique is an acknowledgment of the new, that there had emerged in society new ways of remembering the dead. By the early twentieth century, new social networks had revised and, in places, created new rituals of memory. While *sraddhas* of old had a festive quality, a new sobriety attached itself to the ceremony, manufacturing both a new civic sphere, as well as rules to govern grief for the modern self. In this section, we examine this shift from public, ceremonious *sraddhas* to civic memorialization, and the consequences of the emergence of an abstract "civic" from the ruins of a concrete and specific "public."

Nabakrishna Deb was the raja of Shobha Bazar and a close ally of the East India Company. A famous public spectacle of the eighteenth century, chronicled in multiple urban tales, was the funeral ceremony he held for his mother. The barrister Nagendranath Ghosh, writing the raja's biography in 1901, noted the event/funeral to be on an "imperial scale," a ceremony at which entire villages were "depopulated" as everyone traveled to Calcutta to have their share of the raja's munificence:

> There were full thirty days between the death and the Sradh day, and Navakrishna's countrymen made good this advantage. At first the professional beggars, Bhats and Pariahs, undertook the journey. Next those whose condition oscillated between decency and beggary, who hitherto wavered between going and not going, decided in the affirmative. Lastly men even in competent circumstances, tempted by large expectations, and urged by greedy wives, coupled with the small chance of being distinguished in the crowd, followed. Those who had to come from great distances, necessarily carried their homes about with them like the Bedouins.
> All the Pundits of Bengal and many even of Benares were invited, and came. . . . [The] confectioneering skill of the whole country were invoked to feed the motley mass of humanity. The entire pottery of the country was exhausted. All the plantain trees of the land were laid under contribution for plates for the eatables. . . . Piles of spices, the produce of all the betel-topes of Bengal disposed of in heaps, pottery that rivalled Babel, Himalayas of brass vessels and Alps of gold and silver things, all the shawls and broadcloth and other cloth of Burra Bazar, vast pyramids of sweetmeats and lakes of liquid sweets, kheer, dohee and milk, wore an imposing aspect. Everything bespoke barbaric profusion. The arrangements were as perfect as human foresight and wisdom could make, but the contest was unequal.[68]

In contrast to this spectacularization of death, the late nineteenth century saw a gradual move toward what historians of early modern Europe, in their own context, have identified as a privatization of grief.[69] Compare the full sensory spectrum of sights, sounds, and smells of Nabakrishna Deb's ceremony with the more modern funeral of Dwarkanath Tagore, marked with controversy precisely about ritual and sorrow.

Dwarkanath Tagore, among the last of the fabulous merchant princes of Calcutta, died in his London hotel room during a powerful thunderstorm in 1846. The gothic strains of this dramatic departure are continued in his son Debendranath's autobiography regarding the circumstances of how he received the news of his father's death. Debendranath was taking the air on his family pleasure-boat on the river when an immense storm hit the boat and nearly drowned everyone on board. When he somehow managed to get ashore, he received the news of his father's death and felt as though "struck by lightning."⁷⁰ Performing the *sraddha*, however, proved to be even more dramatic. Debendranath and a few of his brothers had already converted to Brahmoism and were thus committed to avoiding all idolatrous elements of a Hindu *sraddha*. This brought Debendranath into direct conflict not only with members of his own family, but also with all significant Hindu households of the city, who refused to sanction the ceremony with their presence and even threatened a social boycott of Debendranath. The resolution to this divide between social mores and moral conviction came to him on a grief-filled, sleepless night in the form of an apparition. As he lay in bed in the "twilight of sleep and awakening," a figure came to lead him out into the open air. The phantom took him across the world where all was "clean and bright . . . calm and peaceful" and finally paused in a quiet, silent room.

> Shortly afterwards the curtain of one of the doors in front of the room was drawn aside, and my mother appeared. Her hair was loose, just as I had seen it on the day of her death. . . . I felt sure that she was still alive. . . . She said, "I wanted to see thee, so I sent for thee. Hast thou really become a brahmagnani? Kulam pavitram janani kritirtha." On seeing her, and hearing these sweet words of hers, my trance gave way before a flood of joy.⁷¹

Debendranath's account does not simply strike a different note from Nabakrishna Deb's mother's funeral; it marks a significantly different way of organizing emotions following a death, a departure from public splendors to a deeply interiorized sense of grief, from a community celebration of life *and* death to death as finality and hence a moment of moral reckoning for the individual mourner. It is thus not a coincidence that, in this journey of redefining grief, Debendranath was assisted by the "spirit" of his dead mother—an apparition, who, unlike the old ghosts, brought peace and reconciliation rather than fear and horror.

The Brahmo movement has been rightly identified as an expression of "bourgeois Hinduism" that built some of the first bridges between belief and reason, using Vedanta as an exemplar of rational faith.⁷² The privatization of mourning sat well with this new worldview, in which death of a family member became an opportunity for self-reflection rather than community celebrations. Rajnarayan Basu, a close friend and comrade of Debendranath, noted how the death of his father turned Debendranath closer to ascetic ways. Instead of sitting at "tables groaning with the weight of best foods from the world over," from this period onward he chose to sit on the floor and eat just "plain daal and bread."[73] Even on the day of the much-contested funeral, he chose to spend most of the day away from the melee, praying silently in his room.[74]

It would be wrong to assume that this approach to death rituals was limited to the Brahmo milieu. Leading litterateur and critic Akshay Chandra Sarkar was a staunch Hindu and performed all the *shastric* rituals for his father's funeral. But in his autobiography, he described the days following the funeral as being "shrouded in fog." It was a "mist, but an empty mist—everything was empty, present but always absent." Akshay Chandra felt the same renunciatory pull of mourning as his Brahmo counterpart. "I felt empty of thought," he wrote, "of the ability to think. As though there was no "I." His wife slept in the bedroom with their children, but he spent his nights "on the open balcony, covered in a thin blanket."[75]

This is, I propose, a new interplay between social responsibility and selfhood unknown before the nineteenth century. The debate on whether the emerging sense of a national "public" in colonial Bengal was similar to or different from a Habermasian public sphere is a sterile one. That the colonial state was different from early European states and therefore bound to generate a different relationship between state and society in the colony seems so obvious as to be banal. The more interesting question to pose to theorists of "multiple" or "alternate" modernities is not *how* the colonial modern was different from a European one—that difference is expected—but rather what allows such theorists to diagnose the colonial modern *as modern*? This is not a question that can be answered by an empirical listing of such features alone but must involve a prior ontological dimension that allows us to map such features on a legible register. This a priori I understand to be a renegotiated relationship between the individual and their place in the world. How the monadic individual as "self" emerged under capitalism as the normative organizer of both state and society has been the subject of theorists as varied as Weber, Marx, and Foucault, each theorist denoting different implications for this development. For our purposes, it is enough to note the development and trace the procedures by which mourning from this period was both interiorized in the self, and freighted on to the other conceptual apparatus of modernity—history.

From Festival to Bereavement

The premodern *sraddha* ceremony, a necessarily caste-coded affair, was a soteriological enterprise involving both the religious actor performing the ceremony and his "community." The solemnity of the occasion, however, had a *ritual expression* rather than an individual or social one. Sorrow and bereavement were encoded in the *shastric* mantras and ceremonies, but rather than appear as an interiorized, private grief, the same ceremonies enforced a degree of sociality, preventing the bereaved to withdraw from the melee of activities. Indeed, it is doubtful whether sorrow, as we understand it in the modern sense, was ever supposed to be the tone and hue of *sraddha* ceremonies, the word being connected semantically to words such as "jivita (life), sukha (happiness), bhoga (enjoyment), yasas (fame), and dhana (wealth)."[76]

Sociability and hospitality were integral, if not the only, nonnegotiable parts of premodern *sraddhas*. Both high Brahmanic/Vedic and more renunciatory Sramanic traditions combined "ancestral offerings, milk-boiled rice offerings (thālipāka), divine offerings, and food given *in hospitality*" as central components of *sraddhas*.[77] The quantity and quality of the invited Brahmans who had to be fed as guests often determined the extent of protection and beneficence to the family from gods and ancestors. Some scholars have even argued that the purpose of the *sraddha* ceremony was, in the main, organizing and establishing the sacrality of the guest-host relationship.[78] In a society where the private had not yet been hollowed out of the public, the relationship between the householder and his *samaj* was both sacred and consequential.

But which *samaj*? A recent work persuasively makes the case for the premodern individual belonging to "multiple samajs at the same time" as "samaj did not mean society" in its modern, singular sense. Social groupings differentially predicated on class, caste, or religious affiliations all qualified as *samaj*.[79] As with *samaj*, so with the state. Sugata Bose and Ayesha Jalal have drawn attention to the stunning contrast between the premodern state, whose legitimacy lay in negotiating a "balance between different hierarchically arranged layers of sovereignty" and the modern state, with its insistence on absolute, centralized sovereignty.[80] Marx establishes an explanatory relationship between these twin observations about state and society. He sees in the modern state the fullest development of the state form, and an expression of the most complete form of alienation, whereby the state appears as "a separate entity, beside and outside civil society,"[81] or, as the Soviet legal theorist Pashukanis put it, as an "impersonal mechanism of public authority isolated from society."[82] Lacking this looming presence of the state over society in precolonial times, multiple forms of "society," or *samajs*, could coexist, not needing to collectively define, or defend, themselves against a singular, centralized state.

The colonial state is perhaps the closest kin to the early modern absolutist European state form, so it should not come as a surprise that the bilingual elite of nineteenth-century Calcutta tried to craft a new personhood for themselves, in which the private and intimate emerged in opposition to both the colonial state and a new civic-public. I am distinguishing between the "public" nature of precolonial ceremonies and the new civic-public of nineteenth-century Calcutta, because the previous sense of public did not carry with it a transactive relationship to the precolonial state and therefore did not define itself through and against it. While in precolonial times one could belong to multiple "publics," there was only one such public under modernity, which I am calling a civic-public. It is this new civic-public that provided the conditions for and orchestrated all forms of sociality, ceaselessly orienting the newly minted self toward it.[83]

When the doyen of modern Bengali literature, Bankimchandra Chattopadhyay, died on April 8, 1894, in his obituary for the Royal Asiatic Society, R. C. Dutt observed that not only was Bankim "mourned by his countrymen" but also that he had left "none behind him worthy to fill up his place in the literary world of Bengal."[84] Given Bankim's general acceptance as an institution in both English and Bengali circles, it is perhaps odd that a great controversy should have erupted over his memorialization. Participants in the controversy were Rabindranath Tagore and Nabin Chandra Sen, leading lights of the literary world themselves, making it safe to assume that this "debate" between them enclosed something of the current zeitgeist.

It all started when Nabin Chandra Sen, a close friend and associate of Bankim, refused to speak or preside at the public condolence meeting organized for the deceased litterateur. "A public meeting to express grief!" he wrote disparagingly, a phenomenon that was about "aping the English" like no other, and something a "Hindu" like Nabin Chandra found incomprehensible. He jokingly asked whether arrangements were being made to "reserve tubs to catch the public's tears." The real scandal about these public condolence meetings was that the so-called public came to these events to be entertained, "humming the latest show tunes, while chewing paan and listening to Rabi babu's effeminate singing." Expression of sorrow—for "us," Nabin Chandra clarified, presumably meaning Hindus—was not about displaying "black ribbons"; grief was *"nibhrita O pabitra."*[85] *Pabitra* of course can be easily translated as sacred or holy, but *nibhrita* poses a problem. Partha

Chatterjee, in his excellent discussion of this controversy, carefully avoiding "private," has translated *nibhrita* as "seclusion."[86] Clearly both Nabin Chandra and Panchkori Bandyopadhyay, cited earlier, would have liked to see a return to the older ways of expressing grief; but are they urging "private" grieving, or even grieving in solitude, because social organization of sorrow in such a manner, as we saw above, would have been unthought of in precolonial times? Rabindranath's sharp rejoinder to Nabin Chandra Sen further complicates this terrain.

In an article first printed in his own journal *Sadhana*, in an essay titled "Sok Sabha" or "Condolence Meeting," Rabindranath got to the heart of the matter by recognizing the category error that Nabin Chandra had made in this debate about expressing sorrow. Nabin Chandra's argument about how Hindus had traditionally memorialized the dead and how the Western imitators were going about it assumed that the two rituals were working with the same categories: both Hindus of the past and the new English-educated elite, according to Nabin Chandra, were part of the same *samaj*, which is why the new rules of operation seemed so scandalous and "impure." They were being enacted on the same terrain on which Nabin Chandra's idealized Hindus had conducted themselves with sobriety and purity. But Rabindranath made the vital sociological discovery that the current *samaj* was not the same as that of the past. Something had changed, and it was the change in the terrain itself that necessitated changes in ritual social behavior and made new rituals appropriate.

Indian *samaj* had always been, Rabindranath argued, a *samaj* of households (*garhasthyapradhan Samaj*) where filial piety and dependence on the authority of elders were the bases of social bonds. This was why the passing of elders was not simply a matter of personal sorrow but subject to societal regulation. But something had changed in this previous arrangement:

> Recently there has been a transformation (Rupantar) in this samaj of domestic households. A new flood has entered this samaj. Its name is the "public."
>
> The element is new, and its name too is new. It is impossible to translate it into Bengali. Therefore "Public" and its opposite "Private" have now been accepted as Bengali words. . . .
>
> Now that what is illuminated in our samaj is not just the household but also this rising "public" it is inevitable that new public responsibilities will arise in their due course.[87]

Mourning figures who had worked toward the public good was then no longer the responsibility of the family of the deceased alone, but a matter of public mourning. But this novel "public" Rabindranath further identified was not yet fully mature, bearing as it did the signs of childhood. It was incapable of recognizing its benefactors and thus needed education. Public meetings were spaces where, through healthy debate and discussion, such education could be conducted and thereby help in creating a robust and mature "public." Partha Chatterjee's analysis of the kind of public sphere Rabindranath aspired to is astute and deserves to be reproduced in full:

> It was a public sphere consisting of not only books and journals and newspapers but also active literary societies, literary gatherings, an involvement of the public with things literary and cultural, an interest of ordinary people in greatness not as a superhuman gift but as a human achievement. Following Habermas, we can even sense here a hint of that new conception of personhood where the private and the intimate are, as it were, always oriented towards a public.[88]

Let us now return to Nabin Chandra's use of the word *nibhrita* and hold it up against this newly defined "public." Nabin Chandra is not advocating for the sort of solitude that Debendranath craved on his father's death. Instead, he is contesting this new "public" with his own definition of public sociability. Instead of wasteful condolence meetings, the true way to memorialize the great poets of Bengal, according to him, was to hold sacred/religious festivals at the poets' places of birth and turn them into sites of pilgrimage. Religious mendicants had long followed such a path regarding medieval poets such a Vidyapati and Jayadeva, and it was this indigenous "tradition" of memorialization that Nabin Chandra thought was appropriate, as opposed to "laughable condolence and memorial meetings devoid of all true compassion."[89]

Both Nabin Chandra Sen and Panchkori Bandyopadhyay are harking back to a precolonial concept of *samaj*, that which was nonunitary, multiple, and hence multifariously defined through caste, religious observance, family lineage, and other specifically anchored denominations. Sorrow was specific to the grieving community, rather than a universalist concern. Rabindranath, by contrast, is invoking a unitary *civic-public*, whose ideal function was precisely to unify. The country, he lamented, was fragmented into "different samajs, different jatis, different families" and, even within homes, partitioned along gendered lines of the "interior realm [*antahpur*] and the outside." Against such a disintegrated lifeworld, Rabindranath is proposing his view of the civic-public, which would serve two important functions: first, unify people as citizens, and second, through such civic functions as condolence meetings, introduce the general public to great men and their lives in edifying ways. Instead of "banishing" great men to heavenly realms, such secular, civic ceremonies would bring great men close to the public, who could truly then learn from their lives.[90]

By the first decade of the twentieth century, it was clear that Rabindranath's worldview had won over Nabin Chandra Sen's. Literary societies such as the Bangiya Sahita Parishat had made it a habit of acknowledging the death of its members and sending formal condolences to the deceased's family. Allied rituals of installing portraits of the deceased and unveiling them in ceremonious ways became part of the life of such societies.[91] The very Victorian habit of composing poems about a departed loved one became widespread, as print connected the private world of grief to the aestheticized mode of literary expression. When Man Kumari Basu lost her husband at the tender age of nineteen, "maddened with grief" she poured her heart out into the prose poem "Priyo Prashanga" (About My Beloved). A relative read it and recommended it for publication "to provide solace to other young widows." It is interesting to note that the young Man Kumari saw publication as the means to "preserve the memory of my dear husband."[92] Deaths of famous men were marked through a spectrum of public rituals, including the publication of pamphlets that were an odd mix of collected press clippings of obituaries, reminiscences, and private letters of condolence about the deceased.[93] Insurance companies further secularized the business of dying, tying grief to somber market speculation. Although the insurance business was first introduced in India in 1818, it was the Indian Life Assurance Companies Act of 1912 that began to regularize it. The state began publishing returns of such companies from 1914, and in 1928, the Indian Insurance Companies Act was passed, allowing the government to collect statistical information about all life insurance business conducted in India by both Indian and foreign companies. The Bengali Bhadralok threw their support behind such enterprise, and we find liberal journals such as *Somprakash* advocating for life insurance as early as 1863.[94]

If this chapter has etched out practices and spaces that produced, nurtured, and sustained the new spirits that replaced the heterodox premodern ghosts, in conclusion it will be instructive to go back to Rabindranath's notion of the civic-public as the generative context for these new discourses. What we witness in this period is a gradual textualization and secularization of memory, moving the uncertainty of memory firmly into the certainty of history. Memory, in contrast to history, as Pierre Nora has reminded us, necessarily "takes root in the concrete, in spaces, gestures, images, and objects," while history is the guardian of the abstract universal that purportedly "belongs to everyone and to no one."[95] Once more here we encounter the ghost of abstraction that is perpetually suspicious of concrete and plural lifeworlds. A historical sensibility, as opposed to an experience of memory, could be expressed only through a language of the new civic-public and anchored in a form and an institution that could exist only in the abstract—the modern nation. It is to the nation we turn next, to explore and divine its own ghosts.

FIVE

National Ghosts, Ghostly Nations

We have seen, in chapter 3, how British administrators and historians manipulated ghosts to refashion colonial temporality—a trick of ghostly light lending British rule the seal of historical legacy or, more specifically, History. If the British claimed the mantle of History through their ghosts, in this chapter I look at how such European ghostly histories contrasted with and related to Bengali spirits, and to what end. Did Bengali spirits also claim the mantle of History, albeit a different one?

Scholarly accounts of "ghostly" encounters in Bengal rightly focus on the rich history of spirituality and Theosophy in the region. We have already seen (in chapter 2) how deeply immersed the upper caste Bhadralok were in ideas of Theosophy and its adjacent spiritual traditions and how the discourse of Scientific Spiritualism helped fertilize organizational and ideological soil for Theosophy to take root and even flourish for a brief period. Studies of the Indian theosophical movement likewise trace the relationship of the movement, and its leaders, with the emergent nationalist movement. Leading Theosophists, both Indian and European, steadily engaged with Indian nationalism to the extent of holding important positions in the Indian National Congress. History, with a capital "H," then, was one of the products of the encounter between spirits and the nation. But rather than retrace this history, in this chapter I offer a more Kantian proposition: that this history is in fact an *a posteriori* account of the relationship between the two movements. To understand the nature of the relationship, we need to first actualize the *a priori* propositions that served as background conditions to this history. In other words, we do not so much ask *how* Indian spiritualism related to the emergent nation, but *why*.

Consequently, this chapter tracks three distinct, but closely related, developments in this ghost story of the nation. First, I set the stage by exploring the history, and motives, of European ghosts, who began haunting the Indian landscape from the very dawn of colonial contact. Second, I trace these narratives about ghosts of white men against the backdrop of an increasingly beleaguered empire, which used science as its tool to bludgeon superstitions of the colonized, and ask how European ghosts could sit comfortably within a matrix of European Science. Finally, I turn to the Bengali response to the Spiritualist movement and ask two questions: How did the movement, as a global phenomenon, become legible to Bengali spiritualists? and, Why?

"An Unavenged and Unappeased Ghost": British Ghosts, Colonial Projects

"Right at the back of the mind of many an Indian the Mutiny flits as he talks with an Englishman—an unavenged and unappeased ghost," wrote Edward Thompson in his acclaimed *The Other Side of the Medal* (1925), a text that has been seen as exposing the contradictory impulses of liberal imperialism in the interwar period.[1] Thompson may well have been literal in his comment, as Roger Luckhurst locates a peak in British public interest of ghost stories from different parts of the empire from the 1880s. The fate of empire and the fate of colonial ghosts were more intertwined than we give them credit for, as the British Society for Psychical Research (SPR) was established in 1882 while the Berlin Conference and the first meeting of the Indian National Congress both took place in 1885.[2] This is unsurprising, as ghosts of white men and women routinely stalked colonial society. As early as 1654, John Campbell, the "Gunfounder to the Mogul Emperors," left us a testimony of his encounter with the spirit of a colleague. In the best ghostly tradition, the spirit of William Gates, "a rare artist and in the service of the Mogul against King Sivaji," led Campbell to hidden treasure, for, as the deceased Gates put it, "I cannot rest, having hid some money, till I shew you where [sic] it is."[3]

Warren Hasting's return to Hasting's House in search of his lost possession, or the haunting of a house on Free School Street by the murdered wife of Lewis Cooper, a bookkeeper, remain the more famous stories of haunting in Calcutta, but such Saheb ghosts were not limited to the city. "A mysterious light appears every night at the distant signal post of the Chandernagore

Railway station on the Hooghly side," wrote the superintendent of the Imperial Library, E. W. Madge, in his article on "Anglo-Indian ghosts" in 1909. It was the ghost of a guard "killed at this distant signal years ago when the line was first opened, and that from that time . . . has been appearing in various forms."[4] Indigo factories, like slave plantations of the American South, and for similar reasons, were often haunted by ghosts of planters and their victims. In Dinabandhu Mitra's *Nil Darpan*, recall the fear of peasants when they hear a ghost crying in a Nil Kuthi (plantation), or how the violent planters were themselves called "Nil Bhut" and "Nil Mamdo" by the fearful peasants.[5] Why did such stories circulate and survive despite the strong association of Europe with science?

Ghost stories were narrated by Europeans in two dominant modes: anthropologically and fictionally. In the former category we can include reports and surveys of generations of colonial officials such as W. W. Hunter, William Crooke, and Herbert Risley, who dispassionately reported on the myriad "superstitions" of natives. The latter mode, however, was more complex. The framing of such stories had to speak to the Gothic form, so fashionable in Victorian England, and yet also, because they were in the colony, be seen as distinct from native ghost stories and bearing at least some traces of European Science. The result was a unique re-presentation of facticity as the basis of the Gothic. A keen observer of this mode, the Anglo-Indian author Ruskin Bond detected this strain in his remarks about such stories: "The British are a phlegmatic people, not given to displaying much emotion or excitement, with the result that their supernatural experiences are quite convincing when put down on paper. When C.A. Kincaid of the Indian Civil Service described people who turned into panthers (or vice-versa), and mischievous spirits who entered the bodies of straitlaced Englishmen, we have to believe him."[6] Patrick Brantlinger's influential formulation, the Imperial Gothic, reveals the anxieties and ambitions of a declining empire that overlay this form, thus giving European Science a far more urgent hearing in the colonies than in the metropole.[7]

European Science, however, was not dependent on stray references in ghost stories related by British administrators for amusement. It was the backbone of empire and the burgeoning capitalist economy. Because science, as a discipline and "objective" method of enquiry, is able to invisibilize the political projects of its practitioners, as Kris Manjapra's recent work shows, "military operations, seaway engineering, railroad and river canal construction, environmental sciences, and ethnographic surveillance," or the applied sciences, emerged as the most coveted professions under colonial capitalism.[8]

Science was the base seam on which other ideological projects were deposited. The dominant mode in which stories of Indian ghosts, magic, and the supernatural were received by the British, both at home and in India, was thus disbelief. The stories consolidated the image of the cunning "Oriental" who, with the help of tricks and artifices, was out to defraud the honest European.

Indian Magic, British Science

Since Edward Said's classic study, scholars have continued to explore such Orientalist paradigms of the deceitful colonized, and India as the land of dark mysteries and crime.[9] A spate of books, often by retired British administrators, built up this narrative of fraudulent Indian magicians and tricksters. In *Myth of the Mystic East*, Robert Henry Elliot, "Late of the Indian Medical Service" and amateur magician himself, put the case most forcefully. There was, he believed, "widespread belief" in Britain that "the East is the 'Home of Mystery.'" Nothing could have been further from the truth. His task in the book, firmly situated in what can be called the "exposure genre," was to show how absurd it was to believe that "natural laws are habitually altered at the whim of a strolling performer." Elliot's book is sprinkled with a certain roguish universality, which in itself was a hallmark of the Enlightenment. "The fact that a man has a brown, yellow or black skin, and lives in far away parts of the earth little known to the majority of us," he writes, "gives him no claim to mystery. Man is man, wherever you find him. His powers are as limited in China as in Chiswick, in Tibet as in Tooting."[10] As a medical doctor, he was particularly exercised by widespread faith in indigenous medicine and practices of healing: "I studied this subject . . . in connection with drugs for diseases of the eye. It would be difficult to imagine anything more degrading, more ridiculous, and more primitive than the Eastern ideas on the matter. . . . The dung of the sacred cow, human milk and virgin's urine were among the favorite ingredients recommended by the Professors of Indian ophthalmology, who indeed are dirty, ignorant, illiterate and unscientific."[11]

The psychiatrist Lionel Weatherly published a similar broadside against magical fraud in 1891. None other than John Nevil Maskelyne, who had already made a name for himself in the exposure genre, having exposed the spiritism of the Davenport brothers, contributed a long chapter on Indian magics. The chapter, divided into three parts, dealt with "Oriental Jugglery," "Spiritualism," and "Theosophy." Maskelyne claimed for himself a pitiless lens of "clear, cold . . . matter of fact criticism" that allows him to "prove" all such "Oriental" mystics to be the "direst failures, the most transparent frauds."[12] He reserved special opprobrium for Emperor Jahangir, to whose memoir, according to Maskelyne, "may be traced quite fifty per cent of the marvels which are generally quoted in illustration of the powers possessed by Eastern Jugglers." To Jahangir's memoirs Maskelyne traced accounts of magical mango trees growing in a single day from a seed, of food appearing miraculously, and of course the famous rope trick. In other words, all the famous marvels that were supposedly representative of India were, according to him, only so because of the drunken ramblings of a deceitful emperor. Some think, he wrote, "that it is to his superior talent of falsification that we owe his ultra marvellous records," while others claim "that the cup which cheers and also inebriates, entered largely into their composition." From this evidence, Maskelyne piously concluded that what "we may truly say of him . . . [is] that he touched nothing he did not adorn."[13] Maskelyne spiced his exposure narrative, in good measure, with confident comments on the Indian political economy. For instance, while talking about the marvel of food appearing in a cauldron by magic, enough to feed hundreds, he remarked, "and yet we read, at times, of famine in India!"[14]

While the image of the mystical Indian "shaded into the related image of the cunning "Oriental" well into the twentieth century, as Sean Scalmer captures in his study of Gandhian politics, it is however important to note that such racialized "orientalism" was never a monolith.[15] Peter Lamont and Crispin Bates have catalogued the many positive images of India that were part of the panorama of representation and the ways in which such affirmative images created a sense of wonder about India in Britain. Lamont and Bates concur with literary historian Allen J. Greenberger that, when the late nineteenth-century British writers called India mysterious, they were expressing "not only a belief that the East and West were very different, but also that the British were at something of an disadvantage in that India possessed knowledge beyond that of the West."[16]

In Victorian London, where tales of "Oriental" marvels contrasted sharply with racialized exposure narratives, the Society for Psychical Research, established in 1882, tried to carve out a middle ground between belief and derision.[17] The society had evolved from its previous incarnation, the Psychological Society of Great Britain (PSGP), but shared the PSGP's investigative mission to establish the veracity of marvelous phenomena through scientific methods. At its helm was a group of academics from Oxford and Cambridge interested in psychical research, but its membership extended to a wider circle of elite intellectuals in Britain and Europe. As Shane McCorristine has pointed out, its membership resembled a veritable "Who's Who of the fin-de-siècle world" including politicians like William E. Gladstone and Arthur Balfour; writers such as Lord Tennyson, Arthur Conan Doyle, and Robert Louis Stevenson; and scientists and psychologists such as Charles Richet, Sigmund Freud, and Carl Jung.[18] The SPR devoted many pages on Indian magics in its proceedings and journal. The tone was always respectful, investigative, and empirical, but the conclusions were often ambivalent. An account of the phenomenon of fire walking by folklorist Andrew Lang, president of the society in 1911, is a typical example of how the SPR dealt with tales of marvels from "savage" lands.

Lang's article goes through various accounts of fire walking, from Fiji, Sumatra, and Malabar in the east to Hawai'i, Trinidad, and Bulgaria in the west. He makes careful note of his informants to establish the scientific mode of the essay. One such informant was Mr. Tawney, librarian at the India Office, who provided Lang with an account of fire walking, a practice outlawed in British India but still practiced in rural areas. Lang editorializes his frustration about such accounts: "The statements are rather vague. No evidence is adduced as to the actual effect of the fire on the feet of the ministrants. We hear casually of ointments which protect the feet, and of the thickness of the skins of the fire-walkers, and of the unapproachable heat, but we have nothing exact, no trace of scientific precision. The Government 'puts down,' but does not really investigate the rite." Lang's conclusions from these reports mirror the middle-of-the-road positions the SPR took on such matters:

> There is no harm in collecting examples, and the question remains, are all those rites, from those of Virgil's Hirpi to Bulgaria of to-day, based on some actual but obscure and scientifically neglected fact in nature? At all events, . . . philology only supplies her competing etymologies, folk-lore her modern rural parallels, anthropology her savage examples, psychical research her "cases" at first-hand. . . . The performances deserve the study of physiologists and physicians.[19]

A firsthand report from Henry K. Beauchamp, fellow of the University of Madras and editor of a leading daily, the *Madras Mail*, encloses a similar ambivalence. After a discussion of "possible explanations" for this practice, Beauchamp concludes that he must leave his readers to "choose which they like of these explanations; and if they believe that none of them is satisfactory, to account for the phenomenon in their own way."[20]

Race, though muted, was never absent, however. Testimony from Europeans served as the gold standard of veracity for all instances of marvel.

The famous Indian rope trick, over which the society spilled much ink, was investigated by various members, including the veteran psychic researcher W. W. Baggally (1848–1928). One day the society received news that one S. T. Burchett, recently returned from India, had witnessed the rope trick in Ambala in 1900 or 1901. Baggally went to investigate for himself and wrote the following in his report: "Mr. S. T. Burchett is a gentleman about 24 years of age. He gave me the impression of being absolutely truthful. As this is one of those rare cases of an Englishman who has personally witnessed the Indian rope-climbing trick, it is to be regretted that he was unable to give the names of other Europeans who witnessed this performance at the same time."[21]

If investigation into ghostly phenomena was prompted by what some scholars have called the "agnostic malaise" of post-Darwinian Victorian Britain, an imperial impulse simmered as the organizing principle of such projects. It is important to keep this context in place as we turn to the history of the Theosophy movement to understand both its utterances of Indian superiority that explained its appeal to elite Indians, as well as its origins and discursive limits, tied as it was, by many filaments, to empire.

An "Old Irish Peasant Woman with an Air of Humor and Audacious Power"

The Christian Literature Society of Madras was worried. In 1893 it had brought in its most erudite member, Oxbridge-educated Samuel Satthianadhan (1860–1906), to take up arms against Theosophy. In his *Theosophy: An Appeal to My Countrymen*, Satthianadhan had outlined the myriad problems of Theosophy, a stiff competitor to his own religion. Theosophy was, according to Satthianadhan, first and foremost "entirely a foreign movement." Second, it was imprecise: "No two Theosophists are agreed as to what exactly is the teaching for their system." And finally, it was fraudulent in two significant ways: the movement's avowed leader had already been exposed as a fraud, and all of Theosophy's claims about promoting Aryan culture and religion were unsustainable because "not a single individual prominently connected with the society ha[d] attempted to study Sanskrit or any of the oriental classics."[22] But this well-reasoned tract clearly was not enough. So, the following year, the society had to resort to publishing another one, this time with a more specific target/title: *Who Is Mrs. Besant and Why Has She Come to India?* (1894). Although published anonymously, Satthianadhan's authorship is evident. The text carries some of the key themes of *Theosophy: An Appeal*, albeit with a sharper and more personalized focus. It begins, however, with an undeniable nationalist charge:

> A few years ago a white lady, Madame Blavatsky, caused a great sensation in Ceylon by calling herself a Buddhist. The Sinhalese showed her as much honour as if she had been a queen. Now a white lady, Mrs. Besant, has caused equal wonder in India by declaring herself a Hindu, and going about lecturing in favour of her new religion. When she and Colonel Olcott came to Tinnevelly, they attracted great audiences. . . . Hundreds of people who did not know one word of English came pressing and crushing one another, at least to see them, and to hear them pronounce the sacred words "Sri Krishna" and "Arjuna." There is supposed to be great virtue in hearing the name of a god pronounced by a European.[23]

The brilliantly caustic comment gives us an opportunity to examine the theosophical movement and its alliances and antinomies with Indian nationalism. Satthianadhan's anxiety about "hundreds of people" flocking to the Theosophists' cause is as significant as his dark derision about white Europeans teaching Indians about India; both are consubstantial components of this story.

The Theosophical Society (TS) was founded in 1875 in New York by the Russian émigré Helena Petrovna Blavatsky (1831–91) and a retired American colonel, Henry Steel Olcott (1832–1907). In 1879 the founders moved to India, and in 1882, after a brief stint in Bombay followed by a tour of India, the society's global headquarters were established at Adyar, near Madras.

India as the "cradle of civilization" had a special place in theosophical tradition. Already in 1877 Blavatsky's first major published work, the two-volume *Isis Unveiled*, accorded to India and her golden Hindu past the kind of tropes and histories that were very much in keeping with Scientific Spiritualism. For instance, the *Isis* claimed that "Hindu sages and scholars" of the Vedic age were already acquainted with the heliocentric universe, and that Pythagoras and Plato obtained their knowledge from India.[24] Indeed, the move to India was explained by Blavatsky as having been inspired and commanded by the Mahatmas or "Masters of the Great White Lodge," mysterious Beings who lived in Tibet, who selected as their "adepts" from people with high spiritual leanings and who were in fact the true founders of TS. For a few decades the movement was popular and widespread enough for some scholars to claim recently that TS belongs on the "short list of pivotal chapters of religious history," such as the epochal works of the Emperor Constantin, Martin Luther, and the critical voices of the European Enlightenment.[25]

Theosophy's project was to explore occulted knowledge about life and matter, to follow the threads of such knowledge through a study of comparative religions and to promote the universal brotherhood of man. Blavatsky borrowed generously, and sometimes without attribution, from several European occult traditions.[26] I use the terms occultism, Spiritualism, and Theosophy interchangeably because in Bengal the ideologies had a braided existence. As Blavatsky herself argued, occultism related to Spiritualism "as the infinite to the finite, as the cause to the effect, or as the unity to multifariousness,"[27] and occultism embraced "the whole range of psychological, physiological, cosmical, physical, and spiritual phenomena."[28] The history of Theosophy in India, Orientalism's shadow on its doctrines, and the TS' involvement in the Indian nationalist movement have all been studied extensively. In this chapter I have a narrower focus. I try to understand why the newly emergent nation leaned so unproblematically on discourses of Scientific Spiritualism, and I contend that it was the theosophical movement that opened space for that ideological relationship to flourish, by appealing simultaneously to a set of anti-oppression politics and Hindu nationalism. The appeal of Theosophy to people and nations suffering under the yoke of imperialism should be placed within the same interpretive framework as its contribution to a Hindu-ized polity. W. B. Yeats's perception of Blavatsky, with which this section begins, perfectly captures these contradictory currents—on the one hand, Theosophy had the earthiness of peasant life and, on the other, dreams of "audacious power."[29]

A Philosophy for the Oppressed?

That Theosophy was popular among the educated Indian elite has been attested by numerous contemporary sources and scholars alike. The movement's close association with nationalism, especially among the elite, is likewise well documented. What remains underanalyzed is Theosophy's attraction for the oppressed. Its universalist claims about humanity stood out in an imperial landscape shaped and scoured by racialized views about India. Blavatsky was confident that if Theosophy's "real nature" was understood by the world, all prejudices against it would collapse. It was not, as many supposed, a "nursery for forcing a supply of Occultists—as a factory for the manufactory of Adepts," but a project to stem the current of materialism manifest in the world as "brutality, hypocrisy and, above all, selfishness." How was Theosophy going to achieve its goal? By being in full solidarity with the oppressed. In her address to the American chapters of TS, Blavatsky put it thus:

> We are the friends of all those who fight against drunkenness, against cruelty to animals, against injustice to women, against corruption in society or in government, although we do not meddle in politics. We are the friends of those who exercise practical charity, who seek to lift a little of the tremendous weight of misery that is crushing down the poor. But, in our quality of Theosophists, we cannot engage in any one of these great works in particular. As individuals we may do so, but as Theosophists we have a larger, more important, and much more difficult work to do. . . . The function of Theosophists is to open men's hearts and understandings to charity, justice, and generosity, attributes which belong specifically to the human kingdom and are natural to man when he has developed the qualities of a human being.[30]

In 1879, only four years into its history, TS expanded its mission to include "universal brotherhood" as one of its goals. In an editorial in the very first issue of the society's journal, the *Theosophist*, Blavatsky asserted Theosophy's uniqueness from other religions in that "it makes no difference between Gentile, Jew, or Christian, . . . the Society has been established upon the footing of a Universal Brotherhood."[31]

The claim was even stronger when restated by the colonized. "Our work as Theosophists," wrote the polymath Sri Lankan Theosophist C. Jinarajadasa, was "above all things to proclaim this message of Brotherhood." But not proclaim so in any idealist way, "as some beautiful dream born in the imagination of tender-hearted men," but as reality, "as a law of nature." Evoking a familiar language of the natural sciences, Jinarajadasa observed that, "just as by the law of gravity all of us are held to the surface of the earth, . . . so all of us are bound in the chains of one Brotherhood." Jinarajadasa had a very clear vision of how to define this Brotherhood. It was a brotherhood "not only within the nation, but throughout the whole world, excluding none, be he black or white or brown or yellow, including all, the criminal as the law-abiding, the poor as the rich, the peasant as the aristocrat."[32] This expansive notion of humanity allowed for a deeply held belief in solidarity. Soon after A. Phillip Randolph threatened his March on Washington, Jinarajadasa wrote approvingly in the *American Theosophist* about how Brazil had done what "no American statesman ever dreamed of doing, nor . . . dreams of even now" by giving freed slaves "absolute legal equality with the whites" along with "social equality."[33]

If anxieties about white racial purity and racial miscegenation defined the social world of British India, Theosophist men and, especially, women frequently defied racial boundaries.[34] A pioneer in revamping the classical dance form in India, Rukmini Devi Arundale (1904–86) came from Theosophist royalty. Both her parents were prominent Theosophists, and in 1920 she married the English Theosophist George Arundale, causing a scandal due in equal measure to the interracial character of the union as well as the fact that George was twenty-eight years her senior. According to contemporary observer Emily Lutyens, the marriage of Jinarajadasa to Dorothy Graham caused a similar scandal in 1916. Some scholars have speculated on whether there was a discrepancy in the reception of such marriages even in Theosophy circles, whether interracial marriages were deemed more acceptable if the woman in question was not white.[35] Racial boundaries were perceived to be so blurred, at least for Europeans and Americans in the movement, that in 1886 the American lawyer and Theosophist, William Quran Judge, wrote to Olcott from America: "I don't get on here with these . . . Westerners. I am a Hindu in Irish form, and as an apparent foreigner, can do more for the cause in India than I can here."[36]

As with race, Theosophist men and women were equally iconoclastic about women's rights.[37] Joy Dixon's history of Theosophy and feminism is a remarkable study of the movement's complex gender politics. Dixon has shown both how feminism-infused spirituality was "one of the sites at which feminist politics . . . was constituted and transformed" and, more significantly, the ways in which Theosophy, along with other esoteric traditions of its time, provided an important "space for the articulation of . . . unorthodox vision."[38] If crossing racial borders caused scandals in the case of interracial marriages, allegations of homosexuality, sexual deviance, and pedophilia, were added spices to such unorthodoxy. What remains undisputed is the fact that the TS was consistently led by charismatic women, many of whom came to the movement from other radical traditions or left the movement to participate in radical politics. Again, this was not limited to European and American feminists alone, although the overwhelming presence of Irish feminists in the Indian TS, drawn no doubt by a shared history of anti-imperialism, deserves a separate study.

TS' gendered appeal in India is authenticated by Rabindranath's niece, Sarala Devi (1872–1945). "Everyone," writes Sarala Devi breezily in her autobiography, "was into Theosophy in those days."[39] Her nationalist, proto-feminist mother, Swarnakumari Devi (1855–1932), started a specifically women's chapter in their home. Wives and daughters of prominent male Theosophists found their way to Swarnakumari's theosophical club, while

Olcott and Blavatsky were frequent visitors. Sarala Devi fondly remembers the miracles performed by the duo, including the instance where Olcott, using mesmerism, cured a terrible crick in her neck. Theosophic miracles were not the preserve of white women and men alone. Sarala Devi proudly mentions young Dinu, son of Nabin Banerjee of Bhowanipur, who had become a *siddhapurush* of mesmerism. Perhaps even more impressive was the fact that his mother was an expert at it too. Sushila Banerjee was a member of the Theosophical Society and, according to Sarala Devi, "carried within her the power to mesmerize."[40]

An even more impressive history of this chapter of the TS unfolded, ironically, after the retreat of Theosophy. As Madame Blavatsky's popularity receded, and the meetings ceased, Swarnakumari organized all those she had met through the TS to establish a new organization, Sakhi Samiti (Society of Women Friends). Sarala Devi's now-famous uncle came up with the name. In a short time, the Sakhi Samiti became famous for "establishing scholarships for young women and widows to be educated, upon completing such courses finding them salaried employment teaching women in purdah, hiring lawyers and barristers to fight legal battles on behalf of raped women from the districts, collecting Bengali art and crafts from rural areas and exhibiting them in craft fairs in the city and training women to perform/act at these fairs." Rabindranath's dance-drama/opera *Mayar Khela* was first staged for the Sakhi Samiti in 1888.[41]

The TS, under the leadership of Annie Besant, Margaret Cousins, and Dorothy Jinarajadasa, all Irish feminists, deepened its ties with the fledgling Indian women's movement. The establishment of the Women's Indian Association (WIA), one of the first women's organizations on a national level, was mainly the work of these Theosophist women. The WIA's membership was open to Indians and Europeans alike, and its mission was to promote education, sports, and handicrafts for and by women. According to its founding president, Annie Besant, within a few years the association had fifty-one branches, eighteen centers, a membership of 2,700, and was "at the back of the great political movement of Women in India."[42] The WIA set up a Women's Home of Service in Madras, a Theosophist stronghold, where it held educational classes in English and Sanskrit, taught handicrafts in its training schools, and organized various social welfare programs such as relief work during natural disasters. When the viceroy's wife and philanthropist Alice Issacs announced a National Baby Week in 1924 to promote child welfare, the WIA took a lead role in organizing events nationally and had close to twenty thousand infant and child attendants at its Baby Welcome.[43]

As can be imagined from such numbers, the membership of the WIA was not limited to Theosophists alone. But it was precisely this kind of embedded work in these front organizations that strengthened the bridge between TS and the nationalist movement. As early as 1917, members of the WIA were petitioning Secretary of State Edwin Montagu for women to have the vote. It was at the annual convention of the TS, not the WIA, that Besant claimed credit for two of WIA's members becoming the first women admitted to the Indian Bar, with six appointed to municipal councils while three served as bench magistrates.[44]

This cursory survey of TS' critical antiestablishment practices should clarify the appeal of TS to Indian anti-imperialists. As feminist scholar Kumari Jayawardena identified, the Theosophists may have been guilty of orientalism (more on this later), but "they were sharp in their critique of Christianity and 'cultural colonialism.'"[45] Anti-imperialism, however, was not the sole register along which Theosophy consolidated itself in India. The Scottish missionary J. N. Farquhar (1861–1929) found its appeal very understandable as a doctrine that provided "a new defense of Hinduism for the thousands of educated men whose Western education had filled them with shivering doubts about their religion."[46] It is to this compact between social class and Hindu revivalism that we now turn.

Theosophy's Social Milieu

Victorian occultism, of which Theosophy was a part, had a twin charge. One, it was critical of the "West" as understood in terms of industrialization, materialism, and their attendant evils. Two, many strands of this tradition, most importantly Theosophy, privileged Eastern religious traditions over the West, and saw such traditions as key to human upliftment. Specifically, Blavatsky and her followers projected a neo-Hinduism that fitted comfortably into the mosaic of discourses already created by Scientific Spiritualism.

Two leading advocates of the occult and Theosophy in Bengal came to the movement through personal loss. Death of loved ones propelled both Peary Chand Mittra and Shishir Kumar Ghose to seek answers beyond death, and, as we saw in chapter 2, engaging the occult was a way for them to heal themselves. There already existed what has been called "an alternative spiritual subculture" in colonial Bengal, which made their turn to the occult both easy and meaningful.[47] Freemasons had operated in Calcutta since the eighteenth century, and countercultural currents such as animal magnetism, mesmerism, and, more dubiously, phrenology, were already in the groundwater of the city.

James Esdaile received generous donations from the Bhadralok in his efforts to establish his mesmeric hospital. Popularly called the "jadoo hospital" (magic hospital), Esdaile's hospital in Hooghly became wildly popular among working people and the poor. While controversy about the efficacy of such "magic" dogged Esdaile throughout his life, he received enough support from the government of Bengal to set up a second establishment, an experimental hospital in Calcutta, in 1846. Esdaile, trained as a medical surgeon, was also secretary to the Hooghly branch of the Agricultural and Horticultural Society of India. Peary Chand, too, was heavily involved with the society, becoming a member as early as 1847, and even mentioned as the vice president of the Calcutta branch in its proceedings.[48] Given the proximity of the dates of Esdaile's move to Calcutta and Peary Chand's involvement with the society, it is likely that they had some sort of a connection, especially since Peary Chand was a strong believer in mesmerism, claiming that mesmerism and clairvoyance, by rendering the body insensible, freed the soul from "the bondages of flesh . . . [thus enabling] it to reveal startling truths."[49]

In the early 1860s, Peary Chand was corresponding with leading European and American Spiritualists, including with Emma Hardinge Britten, who, with Madame Blavatsky, would go on to become one of the six founding members of the TS in New York in 1875. These theoretical explorations in Spiritualism took concrete shape with the coming of a French homoeopath and Spiritualist, Thiennette de Bérigny, to the city in 1863. This was precisely the period when homeopathy was emerging as a powerful *indigenized* alternative to Western medical systems.[50] In his work as a homeopath and Spiritualist, Bérigny thus expressed a double heterodoxy and challenge to the colonial order. Séance sessions at Bérigny's home soon began to attract the Bhadralok of the city and, according to Shishir Kumar Ghose's nephew, Mrinal Kanti Ghose, it is at one of these sessions that Peary Chand Mittra first manifested "signs of his mediumistic power."[51] Another member of these gatherings observed that Peary Chand was now in frequent communication with his dead wife and could even see his wife with his eyes closed.[52]

Once Bérigny left Calcutta, the séances, now well established, continued in the offices of another European, one J. G. Meugens, who worked for the firm Moran and Company, and it was here that the first Spiritualist organization of India, the United Association of Spiritualists (UAS), held its first meeting on May 30, 1880. Although not much is known about Meugens, he was also a member of the Agricultural and Horticultural Society. He worked closely with Peary Chand Mittra on various committees, proving yet again the importance of these informal social networks that fed into the consolidation of Scientific Spirituality as a discourse in search of institutions.[53]

Given Peary Chand's prominence in Bhadralok society, the séances soon developed into yet another iteration of the Bhadralok social milieu. Consider this report on one of the sessions from a close associate of Peary Chand Mittra's, another homeopath-turned-Spiritualist, Raj Krishna Mitter:

> One of the principal teachers of a Government school, Babu Wooma Churn Das (afterwards Inspector of Schools, Cooch Behar), Babu Girish Chunder Chowdhury, Munsiff, (afterwards Sub-Judge of Chittagong) and Sunjib Chunder Chatterjee, Deputy Collector were one day present at a spiritual circle. The spirit of the English poet, Milton, was present and controlled the Munsiff Babu. None of the above named gentlemen knew Latin, and the spirit of Milton was, therefore, solicited to compose a poem in that language. For fully one hour the right hand of the medium continued violently striking the table without producing any writing. After this period, and in the twinkling of an eye, he wrote fourteen lines of Latin poetry. This composition was submitted to the Civilian Collector of the District, and he was good enough to translate it into English and to send it back with the message that though the poem was certainly in Milton's style, he could not find it among that poet's published writings.[54]

With Milton himself providing imprimatur to the proceedings, it is easy to overlook the other class/caste markers of validation. Just as we observed in Spiritualist journals such as *Hindu Spiritual Magazine* (HSM), the presence of literary celebrities such as Bankim's brother Sanjib Chandra Chattopadhyay, the professional qualifications of the attendants, and their assumed membership in the Bhadralok class/caste nexus, were presuppositions that framed interactions in these gatherings.

The list of figures, important in the sociocultural world of Calcutta, is long and impressive. But rather than catalogue names, I want to turn to the two fields of operation where the Bhadralok were most active and begin to think about how Theosophy and Scientific Spiritualism provided the means of their amalgamation. The two fields I have in mind are cultural/literary production and nationalism. I do not want to rehearse here the largely *explanatory* argument I have made earlier about why and how, from the mid-nineteenth century, "culture" emerged in Bengal as a marker of class, at a time when the colonial economy closed off other avenues of capital accumulation for the Bengal elite.[55] Here, I would like to make a more *descrip-*

tive argument about how these two fields operated in conjunction with the reigning discourse of Scientific Spiritualism and, in the next section, explore its consequences and meaning. I survey the careers of two leading Spiritualists/Theosophists with whom we began this section, Peary Chand Mittra and Shishir Kumar Ghose, as representatives of each field, and follow through on their respective trajectories.

Theosophy and the Bhadralok

Long before his explorations in the occult, Peary Chand Mittra was a well-established literary and cultural figure in Calcutta. He belonged to the radical wave of the 1830s, clustered around the Hindu College, and was a leading member of the Young Bengal student movement. He was known for his involvement with several literary journals, and as editor of *Masik Patrika*, he pioneered a style of written Bengali close to the spoken form. Peary Chand was thus already embedded in the most significant Bhadralok social relations and, as was the norm with this class, connected by marriage or friendship to other prominent members of the class.[56] When he began to think about the occult in an organized way, he brought to his experiments these already-existent social connections. The list of people who arrived at Meugens's office for the first meetings of UAS had thus already been at myriad meetings with each other—socially and institutionally.

Peary Chand Mittra then brought into the movement the cultural capital that he had accumulated both personally and more broadly, which explains the movement's unusual braiding with literary and cultural activism. He was the first Bengali member of the TS, and the third Indian admitted, member #135 in the Adyar membership books, with an entry date of December 9, 1877. Theosophists, for example, were foundational to the establishment of the first, and most enduring, literary academies of Bengal, the Bangiya Sahita Parishat. The idea of such an academy was first proposed in 1872 by the civil servant and grammarian John Beames (1837–1902). But it was under the stewardship of Kshetrapal Chakrabarti and L. Liotard, an official with the Department of Revenue and Agriculture, that the plans for such a society came to fruition in 1893.

Kshetrapal Chakrabarti appears as contributor to the *Theosophist*, wherein, through multiple issues, he tried to reinvigorate a conversation about tantric and yogic philosophy, but reframed tantra in accordance with the dominant Scientific Spiritualist discourse by combining science with séances. Tantra, according to Kshetrapal, was science and "unlike the scientists of the day who separate religion from science, . . . Tantriks sought nature to understand religion."[57] Séances performed within the tantric tradition were of the purest form, for "Indians have not the appliances of civilized countries to either hide or impose," meaning use trickery. Indian séances were thus "always held on the bare ground of a room devoid of furniture, having nothing but an orthodox oil light illuminating the place."[58] Kshetrapal Chakrabarti, like Peary Chand Mittra and other Bhadralok Theosophists, was as adept in pursuing the occult sciences as he was in talking about art and literature. In the journal for the Bengal Academy, Kshetrapal, as secretary, contributed several essays on Bengali drama and the state of the Bengali language. The academy counted among its members Hirendranath Datta, prominent Theosophist, nationalist, and a counsel alike of Annie Besant and Rabindranath. If we sense, in these frequent invocations of Indian superiority and/or uniqueness, the unmistakable shadow of the future nation, then Shishir Kumar Ghose's engagement with the occult and Theosophy is the best instantiation of this historic transition.

In chapter 2 we saw how Shishir Kumar's already existent popularity as a nationalist journalist and intellectual ensured the success of his *Hindu Spiritual Magazine*. Centering "India" and equating "India" with Hinduism was HSM's trademark, which Shishir Kumar continued to develop in his work in the spiritualist movement. Devastated by his brother's suicide in 1865, Shishir Kumar had a crisis of faith. Recollecting that experience later in the HSM, he wrote about how he felt that god must be "the most cruel Being in existence," almost a "monster," for "snatch[ing] a child from the bosom of its mother." Fortunately, he soon learned that Americans had found a way to "get into communication with the departed souls of men and even to carry on conversation with them." Shishir Kumar prepared to travel to America to learn the art but decided first to make a stop at the Calcutta Public Library, to both read up on Spiritualism and also to consult with the one person who had already made his name as a Spiritualist: Peary Chand Mittra. According to his brother Motilal Ghose, "Peary Babu gave him some verbal instructions as how to form circles etc. and some books to read and advised him that it is not necessary for any person to go anywhere but we can succeed if we practise here."[59] His nephew Mrinal Kanti Ghose then continues this biographical account describing Shishir Kumar's journey back to their family home in Amrita Bazar in Jessore, "equipped with these precious volumes," and his subsequent "arrangements for forming a spiritual circle on American lines."[60]

The séance circles at the Ghoses' home became the meeting place of the great and good of Bhadralok society long before the coming of the Theosophists to India. The famous playwright Dinabandhu Mitra; Deputy Magistrate Srish Chandra Vidyaratna, a close associate of Vidyasagar and the first to marry a widow in Bengal; Sanjib Chandra Chatterjee, another deputy magistrate and Bankim's brother; Girish Chandra Roy Chowdhry, subordinate judge; Raj Krishna Mitter, Magistrate's head clerk; and the Raja Baroda Kanto Roy were all frequent visitors, with Dinabandhu Mitra even developing his skills as a medium.

Timelines are of some importance here. Scholars trace the relationship between Spiritualism/Theosophy and Indian nationalism to the 1880s. According to Mark Bevir, Theosophy provided "part of the framework of action of several of those who founded the Indian National Congress [INC]."[61] Bevir argues that the ideas and practices of the Theosophists gave Western-educated elites in India confidence about their past heritage; experience of organization along modern political lines that the Indians lacked; and, finally, a sense of an united "India" due to TS' diverse membership, drawn from Hindu, Parsee, Sikh, Christian, Muslim, and British communities. It is certainly true that, upon their arrival, Blavatsky and Olcott were greeted with great suspicion by the colonial authorities and even elicited police surveillance. Their meetings with prominent nationalists in Bombay and, later, Calcutta, did not help matters. But unlike Bevir, who seems to be arguing for the TS as the tutelary spirit of the INC, I want to trace this relationship between Scientific Spiritualism and nationalism to the crucial decades between the 1840s and the 1860s to show that Blavatsky and her followers actually fitted comfortably into the mosaic of discourses *already* created by Scientific Spiritualism.

While Shishir Kumar's activities in the 1860s strengthens our case for tracing the relationship between the occult and the new nation to well before the 1880s, I would like to push this conjunction farther back in time. By the time Peary Chand Mittra and members of his generation came to occultism, they were already steeped in liberal reformist politics with a critical vision of British rule. Peary Chand's involvement in politically vocal societies such as the Society for Acquisition of General Knowledge in the 1830s and 1840s and as founding member of the British Indian Association in the 1850s is testament to how voluntary associations provided the germinating ground for the future nation, offering assurances and services, as Emmanuel Wallerstein famously put it in the case of colonial Africa, "that the tribe, the family, and the government could not perform."[62]

Shishir Kumar's nationalist credentials were even more burnished. At just nineteen, he was the Jessore correspondent for the *Hindu Patriot*, reporting on the sufferings of peasants at the hands of Indigo planters. How formative this experience was toward his anticolonial politics is attested by Shishir Kumar himself in a later column for the *Amrita Bazar Patrika*:

> It was the indigo disturbance which first taught the natives the value of combination and political agitations. Indeed, that was the first revolution in Bengal after the advent of the English. If there be a second revolution it will be to free the nation from the death gripes of the all-powerful police and district magistrates. . . . It was oppression of half a century by indigo planters which at last roused the half-dead Bengallee and infused a spark in his cold frame.[63]

Shishir Kumar was also—again, before the arrival of Blavatsky and Olcott—the founding member of the Indian League in 1875, which he defined as "the first instance of a political body formed by public announcement and a call upon the nation to attend it and to mould it to their liking."[64]

It was not Shishir Kumar and Peary Chand alone who had such intimations about the future nation, whether directly or indirectly through protonationalist reformist projects. The prominent men listed in Mrinal Kanti Ghose's recollections about family séances were all part of social and political ventures going back decades. Raja Baroda Kanto Roy, for example, is listed as chairing a meeting at Chandra Sekhar Deb's house in 1843 when the abolitionist and parliamentarian George Thompson visited Calcutta. The Society for Acquisition of General Knowledge was heavily involved in Thompson's visit, with Peary Chand as one of its most prominent members.[65] Chandra Sekhar Deb is of course best known for being a close associate of Rammohan Roy and one of the leading spirits in the foundation of the Brahmo Sabha. Pace Bevir, rather than European Theosophists bringing structure and organizational tutelage to Indian spiritualists and occultists, it was the latter who brought their national and proto-national histories to Spiritualism.

As far as Theosophy was concerned, Shishir Kumar claimed to be a pioneer, having had "something to do" with "the introduction of Theosophy in India." Recalling events in the HSM, he observed:

> We were then living in Deoghar, where we heard that a Russian lady and an American colonel, accompanied by European followers, had come . . . to Bombay, and that they possessed occult powers. . . . So we addressed [Colonel Olcott] a letter asking who and what he was.

The reply came promptly. We were told that they had come get each . . . [to] learn *Vidya*. [When he was asked to clarify], . . . in reply, he wrote "Fie, you a Hindu and don't know what *Vidya* is? There is only one *Vidya* in the world worthy of study, and that is yoga *Vidya*.

So our curiosity was aroused, Europeans dealing with *Yoga*![66]

Following this exchange, to see matters for himself, Shishir Kumar traveled to Bombay, where he was introduced to Blavatsky and Olcott, and to two English Theosophists, Edward Wimbridge and Mrs. Rosa Bates. Olcott explained the project to Shishir Kumar thus: "[Olcott] said there were adepts, mainly Hindus, who had acquired almost unlimited powers by the culture of yoga, that Madame [Blavatsky] herself was almost an adept. . . . They had been brought to India by these adepts—*Mahatmas*—to serve a purpose of their own which was to benefit humanity generally and the Hindus particularly, by establishing the Theosophical Society, which would impart the highest knowledge open to man."[67]

Olcott and Blavatsky were practical institution builders. They "initiated" this key figure into the TS for a fee of ten rupees. The payoff was almost instantaneous. Shishir Kumar, as member, immediately brought in some "leading citizens of Bombay" to the TS, among them prominent social reformer Behramji Malabari and the textile mill baron Morarji Gokuldas.[68] He also wrote to some "wealthy men in Bengal who were good Hindus, to help the society with money." Money came flowing in from Maharani Swarnamoyee, Raja Baroda Kanto Roy and many others.

Other members of this trusted circle of elites soon joined in. Narendranath Sen (1843–1911), the first secretary of UAS and later president of the Bengal Theosophical Society, was the grandson of Ram Kamal Sen (1783–1844), *dewan* of the Bank of Bengal and prominent figure in a host of city institutions such as the Asiatic Society, the Agri-Horticultural Society, and the conservative Goudiya Samaj, which opposed William Bentinck's 1829 law abolishing *sati*. It is worth mentioning that the most prominent biography of Ram Kamal Sen was by none other than Peary Chand Mittra. Narendranath, and his more famous cousin Keshab Chandra Sen, took over the English daily the *Indian Mirror*, Narendranath becoming its sole proprietor in 1879. Under the editorship of yet another scion of the Sen family, Krishnabihari Sen, the *Mirror* prepared the ground for Theosophy. What I have called here TS' "critical antiestablishment practices," were captured in a stunning editorial by Krishnabihari in 1879:

We are not so sure about the justness or soundness of the views held by the members of the Theosophical Society; but when they said that they had come to learn and not to teach, there was surely something very touching and attractive in all that they said about their mission. The members, though belonging to superior races, have proclaimed themselves our brethren in every sense of the term, and there can evidently be no question of race antagonism to mar the pleasant re-unions which must necessarily follow such a declaration. The members of the Theosophical Society have done what no Englishmen have ever thought of doing during their more than a century and a half's administration of this country: they have dared openly to mix with us as equals. Here is something to be grateful for.[69]

Annie Besant, writing about Narendranath after his death, paid the greatest compliment to the *Mirror*, calling the paper "always ready to champion them [the founders of Theosophy] through those days of struggle, when the Government suspected them of political objects, and when the timid consequently shrank from their side."[70]

Brahmoism and Vaishnavism, as they emerged in the nineteenth and twentieth centuries, as hybridized theological compacts between the human and the divine, lent important legacies to the Spiritualist movement. Some of the leading Spiritualists and Theosophists such as the Tagores, Keshab Chandra Sen's family, and Shishir Kumar were part of these reformist currents. Already steeped in the experimental vision of these new religious tendencies, whose adherents were encouraged to explore shared ideas among Christianity, strands of Hinduism, and older Sramanic religions, these men found in Spiritualism yet another congenial space to continue their forms of religious bricolage. Brahmoism and neo-Vaishnavism in this context were, however, sedimented in very specific ways. They were first and foremost self-conscious responses to colonialism's myriad claims about Indian inferiority and barbarity. Thus, a sense of "India" was always already a subliminal part of these movements, only consolidated further from the mid-nineteenth century. Theosophy and Spiritualism joined in the foment.

Spiritual and Hindu: The Nation as She Emerged

If "India" was an image awaiting concretion, what were the particular shadows it projected?

Mark Bevir has called Theosophy a "neo-Hindu movement,"[71] while Julian Strube, in his recent work, has explored the close relationship between

Theosophists and the numerous associations at the forefront of consolidating the Hindu voice, such as the Bharatvarshiya Arya Dharma Pracharini Sabha and the Hindu Mela.[72] In similar vein, Amiya Sen has drawn attention to the disconcerting similarity between the Theosophists' views of ritual purity and the Brahmanical concept of *adhikar-bheda*, which "candidly upheld a fairly inflexible hierarchy in social and religious life."[73]

The accepted scholarly narrative about Hinduism as it slowly coalesced as a corporate identity in the nineteenth century goes as follows.[74] The early nineteenth century was dominated by the "reformists," who responded to the pressures of colonialism and sought to reform Hinduism along what they perceived to be "modern" lines. The Brahmo movement initiated by the polymath Rammohan Roy remains the best exemplar of this tendency, trying, to a limited extent, to restore gender and caste equity to Hinduism.[75] The tide turned in the mid-nineteenth century in favor of the "revivalists," who pursued both a purist as well as deeply exclusionary vision of religion. Following the 1857 uprising, contracted economic opportunities and rampant racism against Indians, irrespective of class location, soured the Bhadralok on colonialism more than ever before. Old templates of a reformed Hinduism no longer seemed adequate to an elite who had begun to ideologically experiment with endowing anticolonialism with the furies of an invented Hindu tradition, and, as one scholar recently put it, Hindu revivalism of this period emphasized "conservatism over progress and the nationalization of Hinduism over the Westernization of Hinduism."[76]

While acknowledging the usefulness of this narrative in understanding some of the violent ruptures of this period, I submit that the break between the "reformists" and the "revivalists" should not be exaggerated, and we would be better served in locating the continuities between the two, and in understanding how the first could function as a condition of possibility for the second. The ways in which Theosophy limned a portrait of the nation is instructive in this regard, as it helps illuminate how the movement could be of interest to both "reformist" Brahmos and "revivalists" such as Dayanand Saraswati.

Rammohan's attempt to rid Hinduism of its darker aspects was nonetheless predicated on projecting into the public domain a set of texts—Vedas and the Upanishads—as the defining core of the religion. Intended as reformist, the freighting of religious debate on to public life meant that there was now a new Hindu "public" who could claim commonality of scripture and purpose, even if disagreeing about the details of such a project.[77] If Debendranath, under the influence of Akshaykumar Dutta, challenged the infallibility of the Vedas, later Brahmos wanted to bring the Vedas back into being a source of scriptural authority. Both discourses, while in formal disagreement, nonetheless established the Vedas as a common text for Hindus, thereby creating a community of believers and a public domain for their intellectual engagement.

On May 22, 1878, shortly before their arrival in India, Blavatsky and Olcott were so moved by their correspondence with Dayanand Saraswati that they changed the name of their organization to the Theosophical Society of the Arya Samaj of India. Such a title change spoke to two of Theosophy's foundational doctrines, ones that the founders were eager to project: the superiority of India over the West and the superiority of Vedic Hinduism within India. While it is true that Dayanand eventually broke with the Theosophists—interestingly, because he found them inauthentically Hindu—his initial attraction for these European newcomers can be understood only if we see the Theosophists as creating a particular kind of anticolonial Hindu public sphere that made both, anticolonialism and Hinduism, legible to a wider public. To sustain this public sphere, these intellectuals had to reach—and create—a sphere of influence wider than expected of premodern religious reformers. Modern technologies of print and modern political forms of community representation assisted in its consolidation. When in 1900 a collection of several orthodox Hindu groups joined together to form the Bharat Dharma Mahamaṇḍal, a precursor to the modern-day Vishwa Hindu parishad, it was unsurprising to find Olcott as one of its founding members.

Such a "public" sphere, grounded in a particularist vision, was then the obverse of what political theorists like Charles Taylor had in mind when he imagined civil society to be one that afforded equal rights to everyone to participate in national life.[78] Most importantly, *Theosophy helped to secularize this newly minted Hinduism.* I use secularism here in the sense that Talal Assad has used the category, not as a simple separation of religious and political institutions, but as a category that presupposes "new concepts of 'religion,' 'ethics,' and 'policies,' and new imperatives associated with them."[79]

In Assad's understanding, secularism is a specific enactment by which a political identity—that of the modern individual citizen negotiating with the state—is considered transcendent over all other identities such as those based on gender, caste, religion, or ethnicity. While this sounds like a unifying concept, one that overcomes sectional identities, in practice, there exists several layers of mediation between the assumed monadic individual citizen and their political representatives and, inter alia, their national imagination. National media and national frameworks of education are two such agents that Assad identifies as mediating and shaping national imaginaries. For instance, to use a recent example, the widespread, largely uncontested Islamophobia that erupted in American public discourse in the aftermath of 9/11 can be explained by the mediating representations that defined American "national personality" that were rooted in its racialized, settler-colonial history and transmitted through generations of public pedagogy. Seen in this light, Theosophy and Spiritualism can be seen as having been produced (internally) and arrived at (externally), within an emergent Bengali civil society that had already been tinged Hindu. Further, the institutional practices of the Theosophists—their publications, international conferences—made the doctrine attractive to all shades of self-identified Hindus, from Brahmos like the Tagores to Dayanand Saraswati alike. The processual dynamic of constructing a Hindu-inflected public sphere, developed within regional, or even national, boundaries, however, cannot be understood without inserting it into the broader sphere of global circulation of capital, labor, and ideas. Theosophy and Spirituality provided one such discursive bridge for the internal dynamics to be expressed globally and more generally, thus making this new Hindu public a part of the "interactional history" of modernity.[80]

Gauri Viswanathan first made this important argument about bureaucratic practices and Theosophy. The vast international networks developed by the Theosophists, their numerous published books and journals, sponsored lecture tours and symposia, gave the movement a "reality effect," thus routinizing occultism "as professional knowledge." The class location of the Theosophists, both Indian and European, rooted among doctors, lawyers, and public intellectuals, likewise gave the movement an effortless authority.[81] Gillian McCann has gone as far as to say that the society mimicked the operational logics of established institutions like the Royal Society, and by the late nineteenth century theosophical journals had emerged as "one of the most important and effective platforms for representing the East."[82]

Partha Chatterjee's proposal that the nation first creates its "own domain of sovereignty" as a "spiritual" domain, distinct from a political one, finds literal substantiation in the history of the theosophical movement, as the movement effectively drew on the world of *spirits* (ghosts) with *spiritualism* (theology). While I have some disagreements with Chatterjee's stageist idea of nationalism, I find the argument at its most persuasive when he shows that it is in this "inner" spiritual domain that nationalism crafts its most significant project "a 'modern' national culture that is nevertheless not Western."[83]

Neil Davidson's distinction between national consciousness and nationalism is more analytically productive for our purposes. Davidson distinguishes the former as a "passive expression of collective identification among a social group" and the latter as an "active participation in the political mobilization of a social group for the construction *or* defense of a state."[84] National consciousness, in Davidson's understanding, always seeks to express itself in outward signs of national identity, sometimes leading to political mobilization, sometimes not. The theosophical/Spiritualist movement should be seen as contributing to national consciousness that later found political expression in nationalist organizing. The overlap between early Spiritualists and later Congress activists is better understood in this light.

The theosophical/Spiritualist movement developed through a conceptual grid composed of three distinct but closely related historical tendencies. First, Theosophy's critical antiestablishment charge made it appealing to a colonial intelligentsia looking for creative ways to shape anticolonial politics. Second, Theosophy's neo-Hinduism ensured that the anticolonial challenge stayed contained within dominant class/caste locations and already hegemonic ideas. Third and finally, Theosophy's secular "truth effect" allowed it to etch a powerful portrait of the new nation that could be Hindu, secular, and anticolonial all at once. Through this tripartite discursive format, Theosophists with a proto-feminist and socialist background like Annie Besant could coexist easily in the movement with someone like Shishir Kumar Ghose, who claimed that the spirituality of ancient Hindus allowed them to discover the fat of a jackal as a remedy for insanity.[85] The "imagined community" thus came to acquire a definite, and powerful, lexicon of imagination.

Conclusion

Thinking about Ends and Beginnings

The book began with the Rabindranath's *Brahmadaitya*, and therefore it is only appropriate to end with Kadambini, the luminescent protagonist of Rabindranath's "Jibito O Mrito" (The Living and the Dead).

When we first meet her, the widow Kadambini is painfully solitary. She has no blood relatives left, as she lives out her life in her in-law's home without a husband or any children. Our story begins one dark and stormy night when Kadambini dies suddenly. To avoid the tentacles of colonial death laws, Kadambini's father-in-law, the *zamindar* Sharadashankar, orders the corpse to be removed immediately for cremation. Then follows the requisite, almost formulaic, Gothic language describing the stormy night, the frightful psycho-geography of the cremation ground where the corpse is laid. But before we get too comfortable, in a spectacular move Rabindranath inverts our comfortable apathy: Kadambini is not dead, her heart had merely stopped for a bit. She wakes up to a deserted cremation ground, terrifying memories, and a deep conviction that she is actually dead. And, if dead, she certainly cannot go back home, to that space of warmth, love, and, dare we say, bourgeois safety: "Why should they accept me back home? I am inauspicious. I have been banished from the world of the living. I am my ghost."

With that, Kadambini, again defying our expectations, experiences an overwhelming sense of liberation: "As this realization struck, all ties generated by worldly laws seemed to break. She now had strange powers, boundless freedom—to go anywhere she liked, do whatever she wanted.

With the dawning of this unique new idea, she rushed out, like a sudden gust of wind, across the dark cremation ground, without a shred of shame, fear or worry."[1]

If only we could place the "dead" Kadambini with our precolonial Beings—back to a world of mighty *petnis*, formidable *shankhchunnis*, terrifying *dakinis*! Kadambini could then retain this powerful sense of freedom and, more importantly, use it to change the fates of humans who crossed her path. But Kadambini remains stuck in modernity, in the Gothic form, neither of which accord that kind of power to women.

Kadambini's inability to become a *petni*, the very word now invoking laughter, is why I decided to write a social history of fear. I wanted to understand the relationships among affect, social formation, and the historical process during a moment of transition. Simply put, I wanted to track Raymond Williams' famous "structure of feeling" in the colonial context.

Williams directs us to look at social life in two registers, to discern the dominant social character and the structure of feeling. The social character of an epoch, for example, can be surmised from the laws, the public justification for such laws, "the majority content of public writing and speaking, and the characters of the men most admired."[2] In my account of colonial Bengal, we can detect at least three distinct social characters, each vying for dominance. We have the colonial state apparatus that casts a long shadow, demanding of its subjects compliance, European rationality, and limited liberal politics. The Bengali intelligentsia wrestled with these affective demands, and the most creative ones, like Rammohan Roy, produced a rich, bricolage discourse that rehabilitated different intellectual traditions under the sign of a more generative modern. The second social character of the age was that of a Hindu-inflected nationalism, one that can be seen filtered through numerous novels and religious and political tracts as well as through new civic institutions such as the Bangiya Sahita Parishat. The third—and the most spectral to capture in print—was the lifeworld of ordinary people, their hopes, their fears, their gods, and, yes, their ghosts.

But what of Williams's second concept, his structure of feeling? In mapping this, Williams is clearly at his most Gramscian. He recognizes that the structure of feeling of an age is more complicated than simply corresponding to *a* dominant social character. Instead, it reflects the interactions between distinguishable social characters and, as such, deals "not only with the public ideals but with their omissions and consequences, as lived."[3] In this book I have tried to trace this structure of feeling through an investigation of ghostly Beings and their histories. Methodologically speaking, I have tried to reconstruct the three primary social characters, outlined above, in terms of the stories generated from those ideological collectives about life, death, and the afterlife. But threaded through such historical reconstruction was always my attempt to capture the structure of feeling about the afterlife—how newer ghosts, nested in the discourse of Scientific Spiritualism, differed from older ones; why a new imaginary of death was necessitated by new regimes of labor and capital; and, most importantly, the ways that the fissures and breaches in discursive forms let slip older Beings as shadows of the old world into a world much altered.

Although this book is about shadows in a certain sense, I have tried to write it as a conscious effort in trying *not* to capture shadows. Shadows, both dark and light, pooled beneath trees and around dwellings before electric lamps chased them away. In his memoir *Jindabahar Lane*, the artist Paritosh Sen tells of a mighty Arjun tree that stood watch in the northeast corner of his family's rural, ancestral home. Many Beings, *jeeb*, living and dead, made the tree their home. Multiple species of birds, squirrels, and monkeys shared space with widowed ghosts, dead ancestors. A "dainty silence" enveloped the tree at night, but whenever the artist approached it, he only ever heard the "immutable song of creation," a song that was always a reminder of life.[4]

It was perhaps this cohabitation with shadows that allowed for an appreciation of multiple Beings as our affiliates on this planet, with whom we were tasked to share the earth. The stunning lack of distinction between ghosts and humans in premodern thought is matched by their chilling exile from modernity. In a deeply terrifying cry of alienation, Kadambini exclaims, "But other than being dead, what harm have I done? If I have no place in this world, or in the next world, then where shall I go?'

I have attempted to make space for Kadambini in this book. I have done so in the hope that distinct histories—the geological history of the planet, life-histories of humans, and history as it emerged through capitalist social relations—be reorganized as a life story of mutuality of Beings—that the clean and violent borderlines of the nation-state be replaced by arborescent social structures with their entangled roots in life, meaningful labor, and, perhaps, ghosts.

Notes

INTRODUCTION

1. Jorasanko is a neighborhood in North Calcutta.
2. Parashuram, *Gaddalika* (Calcutta: Gouranga Press, 1924), 124; illustration by Jatindra Kumar Sen.
3. Sigmund Freud, *The Uncanny*, tr. David Mclintock (London: Penguin Books, 2003), 124.
4. Homi Bhabha, *The Location of Culture* (New York: Routledge, 1994), 9, 113. Also see Patrick Brantlinger's classic study of the colonial uncanny or what he calls the "imperial gothic" in his *Rule of Darkness: British Literature and Imperialism 1830–1914* (Ithaca, NY: Cornell University Press, 1988).
5. Peary Chand Mittra, *Spiritual Stray Leaves* (Calcutta: Stanhope Press, 1879), 53.
6. Maitreyi Debi, *Mongpute Rabindranath* (Calcutta: Pragya Prakashani, [1957] 1958), 70.
7. Mittra, *Spiritual Stray Leaves*, 50.
8. Jay Winter, *Sites of Memory, Sites of Mourning: The Great War in European Cultural History* (Cambridge: Cambridge University Press, 1995), 54.
9. Winter, *Sites of Memory*, 73.
10. Heonik Kwon, *Ghosts of War in Vietnam* (Cambridge: Cambridge University Press, 2013). My favorite specter in Kwon's study is "Red Seed," the dedicated Vietnamese communist ghost, "known to be very agile, sympathetic but moralistic" (124).
11. Marshall Sahlins, *The New Science of the Enchanted Universe: An Anthropology of Most of Humanity* (Princeton, NJ: Princeton University Press, 2022), 3.
12. Sahlins, *New Science*, 2.
13. For a beautiful account of Hudum Deo, see Pragya Sen Gupta and Sriparna Das, "Reading Rain, Reading River: An Interpretative Discussion on Rajbanshi Folk Ritual," *Translation Today* 10, no. 2 (2016): 84–92 (Tariq Khan, ed.).
14. E. A. Gait, *Census of India 1891*, Assam, part 1, Report (Shillong: Government Press, 1892), 199.

15 William Crooke, *Religion and Folklore of Northern India* (Oxford: Oxford University Press, 1926), 198–99.
16 Michael Madhusudan Dutta, *Madhusudan Rachanabali* [Collected Works of Madhusudan] (Calcutta: Sahitya Sansad, 1993), 623.
17 S. Mukerji, *Indian Ghost Stories*, 2nd ed. (Allahabad: A. J. Wheeler, 1917).
18 Robert A. Segal, "Tylor's Anthropomorphic Theory of Religion," *Religion* 25 (1995): 23–30.
19 Lucien Febvre, *The Problem of Unbelief in the Sixteenth Century: The Religion of Rabelais*, tr. Beatrice Gottlieb (Cambridge, MA: Harvard University Press, 1985).
20 David McNally, *Monsters of the Market: Zombies, Vampires and Global Capitalism* (Chicago: Haymarket Books, 2012), 13.
21 McNally, *Monsters of the Market*, 14–15. Emphasis in original.
22 In his classic study of devil belief in rural Colombia and Bolivia, Michael Taussig masterfully wields Marx's concept of commodity fetishism to show that while capitalism "enshrouds" its workings in "phantom objectivity," devil beliefs among peasants undergoing proletarianization are examples of resistance to this commodification of their life and labor. Most importantly, as Taussig reminds us, "such beliefs may even stimulate the political action necessary to thwart or transcend it." Taussig, *The Devil and Commodity Fetishism in South America* (Chapel Hill: University of North Carolina Press, [1980] 2010), 17.
23 I owe this idea of magic belonging to modernity to Saurabh Dube, who remarks on the processes by which modernity creates its own forms of "enchantments," such as the "dense magic of money and markets" and the "novel mythologies of nation and empire"; see Saurabh Dube, ed., *Enchantments of Modernity: Empire, Nation, Globalization* (Delhi: Routledge India, 2010), 1.
24 Without resorting to the limited trope of the Bengal renaissance, which I have critically discussed in my previous work, we can certainly acknowledge that Bengal received the full force of British experimentations with modernity and modernization in a colonial context. In that sense it truly was a "bridgehead" for the British. See P. J. Marshall, *Bengal the British Bridgehead: Eastern India 1740–1828* (Cambridge: Cambridge University Press, 1988).
25 The founding editorial by two Bhadralok men for the first women's journal, *Bama Bodhini Patrika*, first published in 1863, can be considered typical of this highly inflected view: "We will attempt to eradicate error and superstition through the radiance of true learning," it read, "so as to nurture the finer qualities of their minds, and we will pay utmost attention to the basic kinds of knowledge which they require." For more detail, see Bharati Ray, ed., *Sekaler Narishiksha: Bamabodhini Patrika 1270–1329* (Calcutta: University of Calcutta Press, 1994), 1–2; Krishna Sen, "Lessons in Self-Fashioning: 'Bamabodhini Patrika' and the Education of Women in Colonial Bengal," *Victorian Periodicals Review* 37, no. 2 (Summer 2004): 176–91.
26 Babu Rashbihari Bose, "Legends and Ballads of the District of Bhagalpur," *Proceedings of the Asiatic Society of Bengal January–December 1871* (Calcutta: Baptist Mission Press, 1871), 138–51 (139).

27 See "*Probasi* Sampadaker Ekti Baktabya," *Probasi* (Poush 1339/December–January 1932), cited in Chandak Sengoopta, *Rays before Satyajit: Creativity and Modernity in Colonial India* (New Delhi: Oxford University Press, 2016).
28 Robert Menzies Fergusson, *Rambles in the Far North*, 2nd ed. (London: Alex. Gardner, Paisley, 1884), 210–11.
29 John Aubrey, cited in Adam Fox, *Oral and Literate Culture in England 1500–1700* (Oxford: Clarendon Press, 2000), 211.
30 Robert Merton, *Social Theory and Social Structure* (Glencoe, IL: The Free Press of Glencoe, 1949), 346.
31 See Reinhart Koselleck, *Futures Past: On the Semantics of Historical Time* (New York: Columbia University Press, 2004); also see Dipesh Chakrabarty, *Provincializing Europe: Postcolonial Thought and Historical Difference* (Princeton, NJ: Princeton University Press, 2000), esp. chap. 2.
32 Johannes Fabian, *Time and the Other: How Anthropology Makes Its Object* (New York: Columbia University Press, 1983), 13.
33 Fabian, *Time*, 11–12.
34 Fabian, *Time*, 27.
35 This scholarship is too vast and varied to reproduce here, so what follows are either key texts from this tradition, or texts representing particular aspects of this tradition. For an early, passionate defense of the category "colonial modernity," see Tani Barlow, ed., *Formations of Colonial Modernity in East Asia* (Durham, NC: Duke University Press, 1997); Timothy Mitchell pushes this argument further by locating the modern in multiple non-European spaces in Timothy Mitchell, ed., *Questions of Modernity* (Minneapolis: University of Minnesota Press, 2000); anthropologists and historians working with this rubric of non-European modernity have presented us with a rich corpus of case studies: see, for example, Jean Comaroff and John Comaroff, eds., *Millennial Capitalism and the Culture of Neoliberalism* (Durham, NC: Duke University Press, 2001); Dilip P. Gaonkar, ed., *Alternative Modernities* (Durham, NC: Duke University Press, 2001); Saurabh Dube and Ishita Banerjee-Dube, eds., *Unbecoming Modern: Colonialism, Modernity, Colonial Modernities* (New Delhi: Social Science Press, 2006). Of course, Dipesh Chakrabarty's *Provincializing Europe* shaped this debate in transformative ways, and both those in agreement and the detractors have had to engage with it as a key text in the field; see Chakrabarty, *Provincializing Europe*, and Dipesh Chakrabarty, *Habitations of Modernity: Essays in the Wake of Subaltern Studies* (Chicago: University of Chicago Press, 2002); for a strong argument against Chakrabarty's position, see Vivek Chibber, *Postcolonial Theory and the Specter of Capital* (London: Verso, 2013).
36 See, for instance, a special issue of *Daedalus*, "Multiple Modernities"; Arjun Appadurai, *Modernity at Large: Cultural Dimensions of Globalization* (Minneapolis: University of Minnesota Press, 1996); Frederick Cooper, *Colonialism in Question: Theory, Knowledge, History* (Berkeley: University of California Press, 2005); S. N. Eisenstadt, *Comparative Civilizations and Multiple Modernities* (Leiden: Boston Brill Academic Publishers, 2003); Andrew Feenberg, *Alternative Modernity: The*

Technical Turn in Philosophy and Social Theory (Berkeley: University of California Press, 1995); Gaonkar, *Alternative Modernities*; Simon Gikandi, "Globalization and the Claims of Postcoloniality," *South Atlantic Quarterly* 100, no. 3 (2001): 627–58.

37 Anwar Shaikh, *Capitalism: Competition, Conflict, Crises* (Oxford: Oxford University Press, 2016), 726.

38 Dipesh Chakrabarty, *Provincializing Europe*, xii.

39 Partha Chatterjee, *The Nation and Its Fragments: Colonial and Postcolonial Histories* (Princeton, NJ: Princeton University Press, 1993), 235.

40 Hildred Geertz, "An Anthropology of Religion and Magic," Journal of Interdisciplinary History 6, no. 1 (1975): 76.

41 E. P. Thompson, "Anthropology and the Discipline of Historical Context," *Midland History* 1, no. 3 (1972): 54.

42 James Walker, "The Exorcism App: Four Apps That Claim to Communicate with Spirits," NS Business, October 31, 2018, https://www.ns-businesshub.com/transport/the-exorcism-app/.

43 Philip Taylor ed., *Modernity and Re-enchantment: Religion in Post-revolutionary Vietnam* (Lanham, Plymouth: Lexington Books, 2007), 206.

44 Paul Clough and Jon P. Mitchell, eds., *Powers of Good and Evil: Social Transformation and Popular Belief* (New York: Berghahn Books, 2001), 123.

45 A near perfect example of this combination is what the colonialists discovered in the pockets of captured slave-revolutionaries during the Haitian Revolution, "pamphlets printed in France, filled with the commonplaces about the Rights of Man and the Sacred Revolution; in his vest pocket was a large packet of tinder and phosphate and lime. On his chest he had a little sack full of hair, herbs, and bits of loone, which they call a fetish"; see Caroline Fick, *The Making of Haiti: The San Domingo Revolution from Below* (Knoxville: University of Tennessee Press, 1990), 111.

46 Sanjay Subrahmanyam makes a similar point about modernity, that it is "historically a global and *conjunctural* phenomenon, not a virus that spreads from one place to another. It is located in a series of historical processes that brought hitherto relatively isolated societies into contact, and we must seek its roots in a set of diverse phenomena"; Sanjay Subrahmanyam, "Hearing Voices: Vignettes of Early Modernity in South Asia, 1400–1750," *Daedalus* 127, no. 3 (1998): 75–104 (99–100).

47 See Joscelyn Godwin, *The Theosophical Enlightenment* (Albany: State University of New York Press, 1994); Peter Van der Veer, *Imperial Encounters: Religion and Modernity in India and Britain* (Princeton, NJ: Princeton University Press, 2001).

48 Some of the best and early analysis of this idea can be found in Pradip Datta, *Carving Blocs: Communal Ideology in Early Twentieth Century Bengal* (New Delhi: Oxford University Press, 1999), and Tanika Sarkar, *Hindu Wife, Hindu Nation: Community, Religion, and Cultural Nationalism* (Bloomington: Indiana University Press, 2001).

49 See, for example, Prachi Deshpande, *Creative Pasts: Historical Memory and Identity in Western India* (New York: Columbia University Press, 2007), and Vinay Lal, *The History of History: Politics and Scholarship in Modern India* (New Delhi: Oxford University Press, 2003).

50   Passage from T. S. Eliot's "Gerontion." The full passage is as follows:

> After such knowledge, what forgiveness? Think now
> History has many cunning passages, contrived corridors
> And issues, deceives with whispering ambitions,
> Guides us by vanities.

See T. S. Eliot, *Collected Poems* (New York: Harcourt, Brace & World, 1965), 29–31 (30).

1. "UNDISCIPLINED, PLAYFUL AND YET *BHADRA*"

1. The uprising of 1857 was commonly referred to as the "mutiny" by Bengali intellectuals, undoubtedly borrowing the British nomenclature.
2. Rajendralal Mitra was the first Indian to be appointed as president to the prestigious Asiatic Society in 1885. He was an active member of several other contemporary organizations such as the Vernacular Literature Society and the Photographic Society of India. He was widely published and had made a significant contribution toward recovering and restoring old manuscripts. For details of his life, see Brajendrnath Bandyopadhyay, ed., *Sahitya Sadhak Charitmala*, vol. 3 (Calcutta: Lakshmibilash Press, 1944).
3. Rajendralal Mitra, "Bhoutik Byapar," *Bibidartha Saṅgraha* (1857): 378–82, reprinted in Pradip Basu, ed. *Samayiki: Purano Samayik Patrer Prabandha Sankalan*, vol. 1 (Calcutta: Ananda Publishers, 1998), 379; my translation.
4. The Bhadralok as a sociological and historical category has been extensively researched and analyzed. For a recent history of the group, see Tithi Bhattacharya, *Sentinels of Culture: Class, Education and the Colonial Intellectual in Bengal 1848–1885* (New Delhi: Oxford University Press, 2005); John McGuire, *Making of a Colonial Mind: A Quantitative Study of the Bhadralok in Calcutta 1857–1885* (Canberra: Australian National University Press, 1983).
5. Mitra, "Bhoutik Byapar," 380.
6. See, for example, Edward Said, *Orientalism* (Harmondsworth: Penguin, 1995 [1978]); Gauri Viswanathan, *Masks of Conquest: Literary Study and British Rule in India* (New York: Columbia University Press, 1989); Carol Breckenridge and Peter van der Veer, eds., *Orientalism and the Postcolonial Predicament: Perspectives on South Asia* (Philadelphia: University of Pennsylvania Press, 1993); Thomas Trautmann, *Aryans and British India* (New Delhi: Vistaar Publication, 1997).
7. Mitra, "Bhoutik Byapar," 381–82.
8. Brajendranath Bandyopadhyay, *Bangla Samayik Patra (1818–68)* (Calcutta: Bangiya Sahita Parishat, BE 1397), 124.
9. *Report of the Transactions of the Vernacular Literature Society from July 1, 1858 to December 31, 1859* (Calcutta: Sanders, Cones and Co., 1860), Appendix A.
10. *Imperial Gazetteer of India: Provincial Series, Bengal*, vol. 1 (Calcutta: Superintendent of Government Printing, 1909), 418.

11   See J. Wenger, "Popular Literature of Bengal," *Calcutta Review* 13, no. 6 (January–June, 1850): 257–84; James Long, *A Descriptive Catalogue of Bengali Works* (Calcutta: Sanders, Cones, 1855).
12   *Report of the Transactions*, 10.
13   *Report of the Transactions*, 6.
14   Mitra, "Bhoutik Byapar," 379.
15   Rev. Lal Behari Day, *Govinda Samanta or the History of a Bengal Raiyat* (London: Macmillan, 1916), 105–7.
16   Sukumar Sen speculates that it was first published in 1895; see Sen, *Galper Bhut* (Calcutta: Ananda Publishers, 1982), 67.
17   The latest edition of this collection was published from Calcutta as late as 1995, of which I own a copy.
18   The only published collection of popular literature prior to 1857 is a collection of proverbs by William Morton, a senior missionary with the Incorporated Society for Propagating the Gospel in Foreign Parts. Morton's text was published in 1832 and contained 873 proverbs, possibly collected from around the suburbs of Calcutta. There are two references to ghosts in proverbs numbers 297 and 490. For details, see Rev. W. Morton, *Drishtantavakya Sangraha: A Collection of Proverbs, Bengali and Sanskrit with Their Translation and Application in English* (Calcutta: Baptist Mission Press, 1832).
19   See McGuire, *Making of a Colonial Mind*; and Bhattacharya, *Sentinels of Culture*.
20   Sumit Sarkar's essay on the present as Kaliyuga remains one of the best renditions of this historical moment. See Sarkar, "Kaliyuga, Chakri and Bhakti: Ramkrishna and His Times," in *Writing Social History* (New Delhi: Oxford University Press, 1998), 282–357.
21   In this the Bengali Bhadralok were following a global tendency. The European romantic movement found expression in the works of Clemens Brentano, his sister Bettina, and her husband Achim von Arnim; the Grimm brothers; and Charles and Mary Lamb, all in search of an authentic *Volk* to soothe the unease of industrialization. See Ruth B. Bottigheimer, *Grimms' Bad Girls & Bold Boys: The Moral & Social Vision of the Tales* (New Haven, CT: Yale University Press, 1987).
22   Dorothy M. Spencer, *Indian Fiction in English* (Philadelphia: University of Pennsylvania Press, 1960), 13.
23   For more details, see Antonio Gramsci, "Observations on Folklore," in *The Antonio Gramsci Reader: Selected Writings 1916–1935*, ed. David Forgacs (New York: New York University Press, 2000), 360–62.
24   These titles were no doubt conceived by the Bhadralok collector and/or his publisher. The tales themselves existed in different variations in the oral tradition of the countryside.
25   The "spirit in a bottle" is indexed as tale type 331 on the Aarne-Thompson-Uther (ATU) registry.
26   All fairy tales abound with this sort of violence, which Coleridge has called "motiveless malignancy" in narrative. Cited in Marina Warner, *Fairy Tale: A Very Short Introduction* (Oxford: Oxford University Press, 2018 [2014]), 35.

27 See for instance, Gyan Prakash, *Bonded Histories: Genealogies of Labor Servitude in Colonial India* (Cambridge: Cambridge University Press, 1990); Binay Bhushan Chaudhuri, *Peasant History of Late Pre-Colonial and Colonial India* (New Delhi: Pearson-Longman, 2008); Alessandro Stanziani, *Labor on the Fringes of Empire: Voice, Exit and the Law*, ebook, accessed June 30, 2022; Harbans Mukhia, "Illegal Extortions from Peasants, Artisans and Menials in Eighteenth Century Eastern Rajasthan," *Indian Economic and Social History Review* 14, no. 2 (1977): 231–45.

28 Walter Benjamin, *Illuminations*, edited with an Introduction by Hannah Arendt (New York: Schocken Books, 1969), 91. K. M. Ashraf (1903–62), who joined the Communist Party in the 1930s and as his doctoral dissertation wrote a popular history of Bengal, had similar views about peasant life and ghost stories. The Bengali peasant, according to Ashraf, "in his leisure hours . . . sings his popular ballads and folk songs in the common village courtyard (choupal). The younger ones gather round in another corner and recite their favourite ghost stories and other lore." K. M. Ashraf, *Life and Conditions of the People of Hindustan* (Delhi: Jiwan Prashan, 1959), 83.

29 Quoted in Sen, *Galper Bhut*, 14.

30 A derivation of the same tale is titled "Pencho" in the Ashutosh Mukhopadhyay collection.

31 Ashutosh Mukhopadhyay, *Bhut Petni* (Calcutta: Modern Book Agency, 1995), 27.

32 K. P. Chattopadhyay, "The Chadak Festival in Bengal," *Letters of the Journal of the Asiatic Society of Bengal*, vol. I (1935): 397–406 (405).

33 This is Captain Richard Carnac Temple (1850–1931), not to be confused with his father, Sir Richard Temple (1826–1902), the lieutenant governor of Bengal from 1874 to 1877.

34 Lal Behari Day, *Bengal Peasant Life; Folk-Tales of Bengal; Recollections of My School-Days*, ed. Mahadevprasad Saha (Calcutta: Editions Indian, 1969), 265.

35 Besides the Brothers Grimm, Day in his preface refers to Dasent's *Norse Tales*, Arnason's *Icelandic Stories*, and Campbell's *Highland Stories*. Day, *Bengal Peasant Life*, 265–66.

36 Day, *Bengal Peasant Life*, 265–66.

37 *Bengal Magazine* 6 (August 1877–July 1878): 190.

38 *Bengal Magazine*, 295, 331.

39 Day, *Bengal Peasant Life*, xvi. The figure of Kailas Chandra Banerjea is of particular note. He was a childhood playmate of Day and ended up as a teacher in Day's school. Day even had the honor of baptizing him and his wife. For more details, see *The Home and Foreign Record of the Free Church of Scotland*, January 1, 1859, 125–26.

40 Nareshchandra Jana et al., eds., *Atmakatha*, vol. 5 (Calcutta: Ananya Prakashan, 1987), 21.

41 Abanindranath Tagore, *Abanindra Rachanabali*, vol. 1 (Calcutta: Prakash Bhaban, 1973), 22.

42 Dinesh Chandra Sen, *Gharer Katha O Juga Sahitya* (Calcutta: Jigansha, BE 1329), 217.

43 Marina Warner again reminds us that the figure of a living narrator has always been an essential part of the wonder tales as a genre. Evidence for this reaches all the way back to Plato talking about "old women going down to the harbor to comfort the victims bound for the Minotaur's table by telling them stories" and Apuleius' "Tale of Cupid and Psyche" being told by an "old and disreputable bawd." Warner, *Fairy Tale*, 41.

44 Dinesh Chandra Sen, *The Folk Literature of Bengal* (Calcutta: The University of Calcutta, 1920), 86.

45 See, for example, Richard M. Eaton, *The Rise of Islam in the Bengal Frontier 1204–1760* (Berkeley: University of California Press, 1993); Asim Roy, *The Islamic Syncretistic Tradition in Bengal* (Princeton, NJ: Princeton University Press, 1983); Neilesh Bose, *Recasting the Region: Language, Culture and Islam in Colonial Bengal* (New Delhi: Oxford University Press, 2014).

46 See Ayesha Irani, "Sacred Biography, Translation, and Conversion: The Nabīvaṃśa of Saiyad Sultān and the Making of Bengali Islam, 1600–Present," unpublished PhD diss. (University of Pennsylvania, 2011).

47 Satyanarayan Bhattacharya, ed., *Kabi Krishnaram Daser Granthabali* (Calcutta: University of Calcutta Press, 1958), 201. The top knot and the dark skin are hallmarks of Krishna.

48 Roy, *Islamic Syncretistic Tradition*, 50–51.

49 Tagore, *Abanindra Rachanabali*, vol. 1 (Calcutta: Prakashbhaban, 1973), 320.

50 H. H. Risley, *The Tribes and Castes of Bengal*.

51 Risley, *Tribes and Castes of Bengal*, vol. 2, 124.

52 Bernard J. Bamberger, "Fear and Love of God in the Old Testament," *Hebrew Union College Annual* 6 (1929): 39–53 (50).

53 Jiantao Ren and Andrew Lambert, "A Sense of Awe: On the Differences between Confucian Thought and Christianity," *Frontiers of Philosophy in China* 5, no. 1 (March 2010): 111–33.

54 Heonik Kwon, *Ghosts of War in Vietnam* (Cambridge: Cambridge University Press, 2013), chap. 6, esp. 118–19.

55 Kshetra Gupta and Bishnu Basu, eds., *Bharatchandra Rachanasamagra* (Calcutta: Bhaumik and Sons, 1974), 299.

56 P. K. Bhowmick, *Occultism in Fringe Bengal* (Calcutta: Subarnarekha, 1978), 137–38.

57 Risley, *Tribes and Castes of Bengal*, vol. 2, 381. The Sheora tree appears again and again in folklore as the home of the female ghost Being, the *petni*. Monier Williams identifies it as the "Trophis-aspera," provides its Sanskrit name, sakhota, and notes it as "Piśecha-dru, Prsacha-briksha or Bhuta-briksha," the tree of ghosts or goblins. Monier Williams, *A Sanskrit English Dictionary* (Oxford: Clarendon Press, 1872), 576.

58 Haliram Dhekial Phukan, *Assam Buranji*, parts 1–4, ed. Jatindra Mohan Bhattacharjee (Gauhati: Mokshada Pustakalaya, 1962), 79.

59 Bani Kanta Kakati, *The Mother Goddess Kamakhya* (Gauhati: Lawyers' Book Stall, 1948), 38.

60 Kunal Chakrabarti, *Religious Process: The Puranas and the Making of a Regional Tradition* (New Delhi: Oxford University Press, 2001), 170–71.
61 Risley, *Tribes and Castes of Bengal*, vol. 2, 115.
62 Jason A. Josephson-Storm, *The Myth of Disenchantment: Magic, Modernity, and the Birth of the Human Sciences* (Chicago: University of Chicago Press, 2017), 136.
63 Michel Foucault, *The Order of Things: An Archaeology of the Human Sciences* (New York: Random House, 1970), xvii.
64 Putnam, quoted in Stanley J. Tambiah, *Magic, Science, Religion, and the Scope of Rationality* (Cambridge: Cambridge University Press, 1990), 125; also see Hilary Putnam, *Reason, Truth and History* (Cambridge: Cambridge University Press, 1981).
65 Sudeshna Basak, *Cultural History of Bengali Proverbs* (Delhi: Gyan. Publishers, 2007), 52. Translation is my own.
66 For details, see S. C. Banerji, *Tantra in Bengal: A Study in Its Origin, Development and Influence* (Calcutta: Naya Prakash, 1978).
67 Risley, *Tribes and Castes of Bengal*, vol. 2, 534.
68 Even Bhadralok texts acknowledge their presence. Durgacharan Ray's comic account of Hindu gods visiting earth in *Debganer Martye Agaman* (1880) has the god Vishnu envisaging Delhi to be full of *mamdo* ghosts, since the city was teeming with graveyards. See D. C. Ray, *Debganer Martya Agaman* (Calcutta: Dey's Publishing, 1984), 53. This is not to paint an idyllic picture of precolonial religious harmony. This was not a world without caste rules or rules of segregation. As we saw, Lal Behari Day designated *mamdos* as "infinitely more mischievous than Hindu ghosts."
69 *Calcutta Review* 66, no. 131 (1878): 190–226 (218).
70 "Bengali Literature," *Calcutta Review* 52, no. 104 (1871): 294–316 (312).
71 John Nicol Farquhar, *An Outline of the Religious Literature of India* (London: Oxford University Press, 1920), 192.
72 This demotion is not unique to Bengal but fairly common across societies confronting modernity. The self-styled Marxist Frelimo government of Mozambique outlawed all indigenous healers, spirit mediums, and diviners in the name of progress. According to Samora Machel, the second president of Frelimo, such practitioners were "taking advantage of superstition . . . to maintain their retrograde rule over society." Quoted in Alcinda Honwana, "Undying Past: Spirit Possession and the Memory of War in Southern Mozambique," in *Magic and Modernity: Interfaces of Revelation and Concealment*, ed. Birgit Meyer and Peter Pels (Stanford, CA: Stanford University Press, 2003), 62–63.
73 Arun Nag, ed., *Sateek Hutom Pyanchar Naksha* (Calcutta: Subarnarekha, 1992), 178–79; my translation.
74 Kartikeya Chandra Roy, *Atmajiban Charit* (Calcutta: Indian Association Publishing Company, 1956), 78; my translation.
75 Sen, *Folk Literature of Bengal*, 87–97.
76 W. W. Hunter, *A Statistical Account of Bengal Vol III Districts of Midnapur and Hugli (Including Howarh)* (London: Trubner, 1876), 77.

77   Walter J. Ong, "Before Textuality: Orality and Interpretation," *Oral Tradition* 3, no. 3 (1988): 259–69 (261).
78   Tambiah suggests that Malinowski had a similar conception of spells when he called them "verbal missiles," thus referring to both John L. Austin's theory of "speech acts" as well as Tambiah's own concept of ritual as "performative." See Tambiah, *Magic, Science, Religion*, 74; also see J. L. Austin, *How to Do Things with Words* (Oxford: Clarendon Press, 1962).
79   Rev. P. Dehon, "Religion and Customs of the Uraons," in *Memoirs of the Asiatic Society of Bengal* 1, no. 9 (Calcutta: Baptist Mission Press, 1906), 121–81 (148–49).
80   Sen, *Folk Literature*, 90.
81   P. K. Bhowmick, *Occultism in Fringe Bengal* (Calcutta: Subarnarekha, 1978), 110.
82   Dinesh Chandra Sen, *History of Bengali Language and Literature* (Calcutta: University of Calcutta Press, 1911), 793.
83   Quoted in P. N. Bhattacharjee, "Folkcustom and Folklore of the Sylhet District of India," *Man in India* 10, no. 1 (January–March 1930), 19–20, referenced in Eaton, *Rise of Islam*, 295, fn87.
84   See for instance, Rev. P. O. Bodding, *Studies in Santal Medicine and Connected Folklore* (Calcutta: Asiatic Society of Bengal, 1925).
85   Bhowmick, *Occultism in Fringe Bengal*, 28–29.
86   For the relationships among print, capitalism, and modernity, see Benedict Anderson's classic text, *Imagined Communities: Reflections on the Origin and Spread of Nationalism* (London: Verso, 2006 [1983]).
87   In 1875, Roy published *Kshitishbangshabalicharit* (1875), an exceptionally well-documented genealogical history of the Nadia royal family. His own autobiography *Atmajiban Charit* (An Account of My Life), in which he candidly described the social milieu of early nineteenth-century Bengal, serves as a distinctive source of information for the present-day social and cultural historian. Likewise, his talents as composer and lyricist are apparent in his *Gitamanjari* (1875), a wonderful collection of popular songs.
88   Sarkar, "Kaliyuga, Chakri and Bhakti."
89   Basu was among the first generation of graduates from the greatest institutions of English education of nineteenth-century Calcutta, the Hindu College (est. 1817). His critique of the modern present was part of a knowing, self-critical rhetoric about contemporary life.
90   A corollary metonymic discourse, for example, existed about the "new" versus the "traditional" woman. Bankimchandra Chattopadhyay (1833–94), Bengal's foremost novelist, wrote a highly influential essay in 1874 contrasting the "traditional" woman (*prachina*) with the new (*nabina*), obviously, mostly at the expense of the latter. See Bankimchandra Chattopadhyay, "Prachina ebang Nabina," in *Bankim Rachanabali*, vol. 2, ed. Jogeshchandra Bagal (Calcutta: Sahitya Samsad, 1965), 249–56.
91   Roy, *Atmajiban Charit*, 56; my translation.
92   Roy, *Atmajiban Charit*, 56; my translation.

93 Roy, *Atmajiban Charit*, 58; my translation.
94 Roy, *Atmajiban Charit*, 58; my translation.
95 "Ramatanu Babu" refers to the famous social reformer and Hindu College graduate Ramtanu Lahiri (1813–98). A teacher by profession and with tremendous influence over generations of pupils, Lahiri headed various reform projects during his lifetime, including rejecting his upper-caste Brahmin legacy entirely. He is perhaps best known for the seminal biography *Ramtanu Lahiri O Tatkalin Banga Samaj* (1904) by his student Shibnath Shastri, which serves as one of the best social commentaries of the nineteenth century.
96 Roy, *Atmajiban Charit*, 79.
97 Roy, *Atmajiban Charit*, 59; my translation.

2. THE NEW SPIRITS

1 *Basantak*, vol. 1, no. 12, 1874, reproduced in Chandi Lahiri, ed., *Basantak Collected Volume* (Calcutta: New Age Publishers, nd), 231.
2 Mrinal Kanti Ghose, *Paroloker Katha* (Calcutta: np, 1933).
3 Peary Chand Mittra, *On the Soul: Its Nature and Development* (Calcutta: Stanhope Press, 1881), i–iii.
4 See, for instance, David Ludden, ed., *Making India Hindu: Religion, Community and the Politics of Democracy in India* (New Delhi: Oxford University Press, 2005); Trilok Nath Madan, *Modern Myths, Locked Minds: Secularism and Fundamentalism in India* (New Delhi: Oxford University Press, 1997); Ashis Nandy, "The Twilight of Certitudes: Secularism, Hindu Nationalism, and Other Masks of Enculturation," *Alternatives* 22, no. 2 (1997): 157–76.
5 Partha Chatterjee, *The Partha Chatterjee Omnibus* (New Delhi: Oxford University Press, 1999); Sudipta Kaviraj, "Religion, Politics and Modernity," in *Crisis and Change in Contemporary India*, ed. Upendra Baxi and Bhikhu Parekh (New Delhi: Sage, 1995); I make a similar argument in "Tracking the Goddess: Religion, Community, and Identity in the Durga Puja Ceremonies of Nineteenth-Century Calcutta," *Journal of Asian Studies* 66, no. 4 (November 2007): 919–62.
6 Gyan Prakash, *Another Reason: Science and the Imagination of Modern India* (Princeton, NJ: Princeton University Press, 1999), 99.
7 I have in mind men such as Damat Ibrahim Pasha (the Ottoman grand vizier of the Tulip period) and Sugita Genpaku of Tokyo, both early enthusiasts of European science and technology. For details, see Giancarlo Casale, *The Ottoman Age of Exploration* (Oxford: Oxford University Press, 2010) and Maki Fukuoka, *The Premise of Fidelity: Science, Fidelity and Representing the Real in Nineteenth-Century Japan* (Stanford, CA: Stanford University Press, 2012).
8 Full text of the "Prospectus" is now online at https://www.midnapore.in/people/rishi_rajnarayan_basu_prospectus_of_society.html; Basu's commitment to "Western" sciences was so widely known that the poet Ishwar Chandra Gupta satirically wrote that he sought to explain the meaning of Vedānta through a

reading of Bacon (Bacon pariyā kare beder siddhānta) See, Basu, *Bangla Bhasha o Sahitya Bisayak Baktrita* (Calcutta: New Bengal Press, 1879), 32.

9   Quoted in Ajitkumar Chakrabarti, *Maharshi Debendranath Thakur* (Calcutta: Jignyasya Press, 1971 [1916]), 143. The comparison with European scientists is not all that fanciful, as Dutta had portraits of both Newton and Darwin in his home; for details, see Mahendranath Bidyanidhi, *Babu Akshaykumar Datter Jibanbrittanto* (Calcutta: New Sanskrit Press, 1885).

10 Bhudev Mukhopadhyay published *Khetra-Tattwa* (Geometry) (1862), a loose rendition of Rev. K. M. Bannerjee's translation of Euclid's *Geometry* and a work on the life sciences titled *Prakritik Vigyan* (Parts I and II, 1858–59). See also his *Samajik Prabhandha* (Chuchura: Budhoday Press, 1892).

11 Translated and quoted in Amiya Sen, *Hindu Revivalism in Bengal* (New Delhi: Oxford University Press, 2001), 198, fn 503.

12 Namely the Vigyan Sebodhi (April 1832), Vigyan Kowmudee (September 1860), Vigyan Chakrabandhab (April 1871), Vigyan Rahasya (September 1871), Vigyan Bikash Oune 1873), and Vigyan Dar-pan (September 1876).

13 Amiya Sen, *Hindu Revivalism in Bengal*, 163.

14 Duff himself was a staunch Anglicist, aligning himself very strongly with the likes of Thomas Babington Macaulay and Charles Trevelyan in the dispute between the "Orientalists" and the Anglicists in the 1830s, eventually leading to a victory of the latter. In 1841, when a new governor general, Lord Auckland, tried to follow a policy that was not quite so divisive but attempted to appease both sides, Duff wrote him an angry letter, stating, "Your lordship proposes to unite the living with the dead—to revive the spirit of the dark ages and cause it to enter into heterogeneous combination with the spirit of modern enlightenment." For more details, see D. H. Emmott, "Alexander Duff and the Foundation of Modern Education in India," *British Journal of Educational Studies* 13, no. 2 (May 1965): 160–69.

15 Limodine advertised in Kshirod Prasad's journal, *Aloukik Rahasya* 5, no. 5 (1913).

16 I say "partly" because the neo-Hindu discourse was making this argument in a more general sense. In his lecture at the Bangiya Sahita Parishat Manmathamohan, Basu, professor at General Assembly's Institution and president of the Fine Arts Society, summed up the zeitgeist by devoting his talk to how the "conflict" between modern Science and the ancient Rishis on the subject of matter was now resolved in favor of the latter. "The more science progresses," he saw "scientists accepting the ancient norms, thereby creating a unique blend of ancient and modern knowledge." All scientific theories, including the theory of atoms and electrons, owed their origins to the ancient Hindu rishis. Manmathamohan Basu, "Nutan O Puratan Bigyan," *Brahma Bidya* 11, no. 4 (1913): 193–207.

17 *Aloukik Rahasya* 3, no. 3 (1911): 97–106.

18 Bidyabinod, *Aloukik Rahasya*, vol. 1. no. 1 (Calcutta: Universal Library Press, 1909 [baishakh, 1316]), 3.

19 Bidyabinod, *Aloukik Rahasya* 1, no. 1: 4–5.

20 Girijaprasanna Sen Kaviraj, "Bhuter Sange Dwandyajudhdha," *Aloukik Rahasya* 4, no. 2: 65–73 (73).

21 Dwarkanath Basu, "Atmik Anayan," *Aloukik Rahasya* 3, no. 7: 311–15 (314).
22 Kartikchandra Bandyopadhyay, "Dibyadrishti," *Aloukik Rahasya* 2, no. 5: 203–9 (203).
23 "I once heard a methor [lower caste manual scavenger] discuss philosophy with another of his kind with great wisdom." *Aloukik Rahasya* 2, no. 1: 41 ff.
24 Malayneel Sharma, "Dadamashiyer Jhuli," *Aloukik Rahasya* 1, no. 2: 89–90.
25 Hirendranath Datta, "Suksha Sharirer Proman," *Aloukik Rahasya* 3, no. 2: 49–54 (50). Datta was one of the first adherents of Theosophy in India, having joined the society as early as 1894. He was a prominent advocate of nationalist education and one of the vice presidents of the National Council of Education in Calcutta. He also served as a trustee of Rabindranath Tagore's university, Visva-Bharati, and was a much-published author.
26 Peter Harrison, *The Territories of Science and Religion* (Chicago: University of Chicago Press, 2015), 108.
27 For details, see Robert Kirk, *The Secret Commonwealth of Elves, Fauns and Fairies*, introduction by Marina Warner (New York: New York Review of Books, 2007).
28 Richard J. Noakes, "'Instruments to Lay Hold of Spirits': Technologizing the Bodies of Victorian Spiritualism," in *Bodies/Machines*, ed. Iwan Rhys Morus (London: Bloomsbury, 2002), 125–63 (125). Also see Richard J. Noakes, "Telegraphy Is an Occult Art: Cromwell Fleetwood Varley and the Diffusion of Electricity to the Other World," *British Journal for the History of Science* 32 (1999): 421–59; Klaus Staubermann, "Tying the Knot: Skill, Judgement, and Authority in the 1870s Leipzig Spiritistic Experiments," *British Journal for the History of Science* 34 (2001): 67–80; Bret E. Carroll, *Spiritualism in Antebellum America* (Bloomington: Indiana University Press, 1997), 65–71; Steven Connor, *Dumbstruck: A Cultural History of Ventriloquism* (Oxford: Oxford University Press, 2000), 362–93; Pamela Thurschwell, *Literature, Technology and Magical Thinking, 1880-1920* (Cambridge: Cambridge University Press, 2001).
29 Walter J. Kilner, *The Human Atmosphere or the Aura Made Visible by the Aid of Chemical Screens* (London: Rebman Company, 1911), 1–2.
30 *Hindu Spiritual Magazine* 1, no. 1 (March 1903): 1–2.
31 See Anath Nath Basu, *Mahatma Sisir Kumar Ghosh*, 2nd ed. (Calcutta: Tushar Kanti Ghosh, 1976).
32 Shishir Kumar Ghose, *Indian Sketches* (Calcutta: Patrika Offices, 1923), Appendix.
33 *Hindu Spiritual Magazine* 1, no. 1 (March 1903): 2–3.
34 Letter to the editor from subscriber #1021 from Gaya, *Aloukik Rahasya*, May 29, 1909 (no. 4): 151–52.
35 *Aloukik Rahasya* 4, no. 2: 77.
36 *Aloukik Rahasya* 5, no. 7: 323–24.
37 Monier Williams, "Sraddha Ceremonies at Gaya," *Indian Antiquary* 5 (1876): 201.
38 Wendy Doniger, *On Hinduism* (New York: Oxford University Press, 2014), 205.
39 Gananath Obeyesekere, "The Rebirth Eschatology and Its Transformations: A Contribution to the Sociology of Early Buddhism," in *Karma and Rebirth in Classical Indian Traditions*, ed. Wendy Doniger O'Flaherty (Berkeley: University of California Press, 1980), 137–64.

40 *Hindu Spiritual Magazine* 2, part I (August 1907): 78.
41 *Hindu Spiritual Magazine* 2, no. 1 (March 1907): 1–2.
42 Akshay Chandra Sarkar, "Bol Dekhi Bhai ki hoi Mole," *Nabajiban* 1, no. 4 (1884): 474.
43 Sarkar, "Bol Dekhi," 476.
44 *Hindu Spiritual Magazine* 2, no. 6: 241–42.
45 *Aloukik Rahasya* 1, no. 1: 7.
46 Binod Bihari Gupta, "A Letter," *Aloukik Rahasya* 1, no. 6: 241–46 (243).
47 Priyanath Shastri, ed., *Pujyapad Srimaharshi Debendranath Thakurer Swarachit Jiban Charit* (Calcutta: Banerjee Press, 1898), 66–67.
48 Ghose, "Dedication," in *Paroloker Katha* (Calcutta, 1933).
49 See Dinabandhu Mitra, *Paralok Tattva* (Dhaka: Shanti Press, 1924), 169–73.
50 Ghose, "Dedication," in *Paroloker Katha*, 13.
51 Mitra, *Paralok Tattva*, 209.
52 See, for example, the case of the spirit who came to listen to the Ramayana being read, in Nalinaksha Ray, "Bhuter Ramayana Sraban," *Aloukik Rahasya* 2, no. 2: 59–62.
53 Advertisement in *Pandit* 1, no. 3. The journal was an organ of the Brahmanic "Pandit Samiti," edited by Akshaykumar Bidyabinod.
54 Akshay Chandra Sarkar, "Planchetter Prolap," *Sadharani*, February 28, 1875, pp. 211–12.
55 Yeats was a member of the Hermetic Order of the Golden Dawn—an elite and significant magical order of the Victorian period. See Alex Owen, *The Place of Enchantment: British Occultism and the Culture of the Modern* (Chicago: University of Chicago Press, 2004).
56 Sarala Devi Chaudhurani, *Jibaner Jharapata* (Calcutta: Sahitya Samsad, 1879), 59.
57 See, for example, Uma Dasgupta, "The Indian Press 1870–1880: A Small World of Journalism," *Modern Asian Studies* 2, no. 2 (1977): 213–35.
58 Margaret C. Jacob, "The Enlightenment Redefined: The Formation of Modern Civil Society," *Social Research* 58, no. 2 (Summer 1991): 475–95 (477).
59 Dipesh Chakrabarty, "Adda: A History of Sociality," in *Provincializing Europe: Postcolonial Thought and Historical Difference* (Princeton, NJ: Princeton University Press, 2000), 180–213.
60 Chaudhurani, *Jibaner Jharapata*, 57.
61 Tithi Bhattacharya, *The Sentinels of Culture: Class, Education and the Colonial Intellectual in Bengal 1848–1885* (New Delhi: Oxford University Press, 2005), 60.
62 Bhattacharya, *Sentinels*, 104.
63 Quoted in Prakash, *Another Reason*, 69.
64 See, for instance, "Ki Ki kusanskar tirohito hoile edesher sribiddhi hote pare" [Superstitions that must be removed for the betterment of our country] (1861), by Bamasundari Debi, in which she criticizes a range of oppressive social practices. Reproduced in Malini Bhattacharya and Abhijit Sen, eds., *Talking of Power: Early Writings by Bengali Women from the Mid-Nineteenth Century to the Beginning of the Twentieth Century* (Calcutta: Stree, 2003), 17–24.

65 Sircar, quoted in C. Mackenzie Brown, *Hindu Perspectives on Evolution: Darwin, Dharma, and Design* (New York: Routledge, 2012), 169.
66 For example, the Mesmeric Hospital established in 1846.
67 See Pratik Chakrabarty, *Western Science in Modern India: Metropolitan Methods, Colonial Practices* (New Delhi: Permanent Black, 2004).
68 *Indian Mirror*, January 7, 1870.
69 Dr. Mout's Introduction to *Record of Cases Treated in the Mesmeric Hospital, from November 1846 to May 1847: With Reports of the Official Visitors* (Calcutta: Military Orphan Press, 1847), xxxi–xxxii.
70 Letter to the editor, *Somprakash*, August 10, 1863.
71 *Somprakash*, September 28, 1863.
72 Prakash, *Another Reason*, 41.
73 Lahiri, ed., *Basantak*, vol. 2, no. 5, p. 82.
74 Letter to the editor, *Somprakash*, August 31, 1863.
75 Dinesh Chandra Sen, *Gharer Katha O Jugsahitya* (Calcutta: Jignyasya, 1969), 2–3.
76 Rasikmohan Chattopadhyay, ed., *Arunodaya*, 1890–91.
77 Anon., *Sachitra Bibhuti Vidya* (Calcutta: Basak Press, 1900), 256.
78 Manmohan Ghosh records one such relative in his extended family, while authors such as Barodakanta Majumdar presented Tantra as "science" and saw it as a means of national regeneration. See Julian Strube, *Global Tantra: Religion, Science, and Nationalism in Colonial Modernity* (New York: Oxford University Press, 2022).
79 Sumit Sarkar, *Writing Social History* (New Delhi: Oxford University Press, 1998), 53. Art historian Pratapaditya Pal recalls stories about his mother's childhood when "she watched through a keyhole her paternal uncle during meditation levitating himself several inches from the ground and remaining suspended." Pratapaditya Pal, *Hindu Religion and Iconology According to the Tantrasara* (Los Angeles: Vichitra Press, 1981), 21.
80 Panchkori Bandyopadhyay, *Banglar Tantra*, ed. Bimalendu Chakrabarty (Calcutta: Bengal Publishers Private Limited, 1942), 133.
81 Kalimohan Bidyaratna, perhaps a *purohit* himself, published a book of Hindu rituals, *Hindu Sarbashya* (1922), as well as a book of spells, *Indrajal Shiksha* (1919), both from Battala presses.

3. DEADLY SPACES

1 Abanindranath Tagore, *Abanindra Rachanabali*, vol. 1 (Calcutta: Prakash Bhaban, 1973), 57.
2 H. E. A. Cotton, *Calcutta, Old and New: A Historical and Descriptive Handbook to the City* (Calcutta: General Printers and Publishers, 1980), 894.
3 S. Mukerji, *Indian Ghost Stories* (Allahabad: A. H. Wheeler, 1917), 111–12.
4 Sigmund Freud, *The Uncanny* (New York: Penguin Books, 2003).

5   In 1903, Ashutosh Mukhopadhyay published an entire collection of ghost stories, titled *Bhut Petni*. This collection of established fables about "traditional" ghosts proved to be immensely successful. Originally intended for children, the book was approved by the director of public instructions as a suitable book for school awards and libraries in 1939, and it earned several "gold and silver medals and First Class Certificates" from various exhibitions and nationalist enterprises. It had not lost its popularity even by the 1950s; its impressive twelfth edition was published in 1955. Almost all the ghosts in Mukhopadhyay's collected fables reside in the wild. See Ashutosh Mukhopadhyay, *Bhut Petni* (Calcutta: Modern Book Agency, 1995 [1903]).
6   Suchitra Samanta, ed., *Hauntings: Bangla Ghost Stories* (New Delhi: Katha, 2000), 52.
7   Samanta, *Hauntings*, 61.
8   Samanta, *Hauntings*, 65.
9   The reference here is to Georg Lukacs's concept of reification, whereby he defines it as a process in which "a relation between people takes on the character of a thing and . . . acquires a 'phantom-objectivity,' an autonomy that seems so strictly rational and all-embracing as to conceal every trace of its fundamental nature—the relation between people." See Georg Lukacs, *History and Class Consciousness* (London: Merlin, 1971), 83.
10 John Beecroft and Richard M. Powers, eds., *Kipling: A Selection of His Stories and Poems* (Garden City, NY: Doubleday, 1956), 47.
11 See, for instance, Bhabanicharan Bandyopadhyay, *Kalikata Kamalalaya and Kalikata Kalpalata*, ed. Bishnu Basu (Calcutta: Pratibhash, 1986).
12 For details, see Sumit Sarkar, *Writing Social History* (New Delhi: Oxford University Press, 1998), 177.
13 H. E. Busteed, *Echoes from Old Calcutta, Being Chiefly Reminiscences of the Days of Warren Hastings, Francis and Impey* (London: W. Thacker, 1908), 23.
14 Busteed, *Echoes*, 25.
15 Proceedings no. 242, From O. Toogood, Sessions Judge of Cuttack, to the Registrar of the High Court of Judicature at Fort William in Bengal. No. 34, dated 9th February, 1864, Fort William Judicial Department Proceedings, March 1864, West Bengal State Archives (hereafter WBSA).
16 Warren Hastings set up provincial courts in each district divided along civil and criminal lines. District civil courts (Mofussil Diwani Adalats) had their highest court of appeal in the Sadr Diwani Adalat in Calcutta whereas the criminal courts (Faujdari Adalats) had a similar one in the Sadr Nizamat Adalat.
17 Proceedings no. 243, From J. Geoghegan, Under Secretary to the Government of Bengal, to the Superintendent and Remembrancer of Legal Affairs. No. 1627, dated 11th March 1864, Fort William Judicial Department Proceedings, March 1864, WBSA.
18 Proceedings no. 244, From E. G. Birch, Officiating Superintendent and Remembrancer of Legal Affairs, to the Under Secretary to the Government of Bengal,

No. 467, dated 18th March 1864, Fort William Judicial Department Proceedings, March 1864, WBSA.

19   Proceedings no. 245, From F. R. Cockerell, Officiating Secretary to the Government of Bengal to the Registrar of the High Court, No. 2076, dated 31st March 1864, Fort William Judicial Department Proceedings, March 1864, WBSA.

20   There was a history to this kind of response to the British version of legality. According to J. M. Derrett, "The British judicial system, with its disregard for social distinctions, its dependence on pleading and evidence . . . and its harsh and rapid methods of execution," when first introduced, caused such panic that defendants often migrated to princely territories to escape "the abnormal times." J. M. Derrett, "British Administration of Hindu Law," *Comparative Studies in Society and History* 4, no. 1 (November 1961): 52.

21   Reginald Heber, *Narrative of a Journey through the Upper Provinces of India, from Calcutta to Bombay: 1824–1825*, vol. 1 (London: np, 1843), 155; quoted in Radhika Singha, *A Despotism of Law: Crime and Justice in Early Colonial India* (New Delhi: Oxford University Press, 1998), 91. Singha also cites the case of one Ballo Sewak, who killed his own infant daughter and buried her in a disputed plot of land, and of one Mohun Brahmin's widow, who took her deceased husband's corpse and buried it at the door of his enemy. Singha, *Despotism*, 91.

22   David Harvey, *Spaces of Hope* (Berkeley: University of California Press, 2000), 54. Also see Harvey, *Limits to Capital* (Oxford: Basil Blackwell, 1982).

23   Henri Lefebvre, *The Production of Space* (Boston: Blackwell Press, 1991), 73.

24   Lefebvre, *Production of Space*, 73–75.

25   Lefebvre, *Production of Space*, 77.

26   Lefebvre, *Production of Space*, 74.

27   This is particularly true of a new city such as Calcutta, whose very foundation was prompted by the business needs of the East India Company.

28   Proceedings Judicial Department, November 1864, WBSA.

29   Proceedings Judicial Department, June 1864, WBSA.

30   Veena Oldenburg, *The Making of Colonial Lucknow: 1856–1877* (New Delhi: Oxford University Press, 1989).

31   Scholars such as Anthony King, Narayani Gupta, and Mariam Dossal have shown how landscape, topography, and everyday civic life of cities such as Bombay and Delhi were foundationally restructured to promote the imperial agenda of the British state. See Anthony D. King, *Colonial Urban Development: Culture, Social Power and Environment* (London: Routledge and Kegan Paul, 1976); Narayani Gupta, *Delhi between Two Empires 1803–1931: Society, Government and Urban Growth* (Delhi: Oxford University Press, 1981); Mariam Dossal, *Imperial Designs and Indian Realities: The Planning of Bombay City, 1845–1875* (New York: Oxford University Press, 1991).

32   *Somprakash*, March 14, 1864.

33   1 krosh was approximately 4000 yards or 2 ¼ miles.

34   *Somprakash*, March 14, 1864.

35 For more details, see Philippe Aries and Bernard Murchland, "Death Inside Out," *Hastings Center Studies* 2, no. 2 (May 1974): 3–18 (4). Also see Philippe Aries, *The Hour of Our Death* (New York: Oxford University Press, 1991).
36 Shibnath Shastri, *Atmacharit* (Calcutta: Signet Press, BE 1359), 47.
37 Abanindranath Tagore, *Abanindra Rachanabali*, 236–37.
38 Bangachandra Roy, "Amar Kshudra Jibanalekhya," in *Atma Katha*, vol. 4, ed. Naresh Jana, Manu Jana, and Kamalkumar Sanyal (Calcutta: Ananya, 1986), 9.
39 Quoted in George K. Behlmer, "Grave Doubts: Victorian Medicine, Moral Panic and the Signs of Death," *Journal of British Studies* 42, no. 2 (2003): 206.
40 Proceedings of the Judicial Department, March 1865, WBSA.
41 P. R. Hay Jagganadham, *Cremation and Burial or Extracts from a Paper Read at the Indian Medical Congress* (Lahore: Arorbans Press, 1895), 10.
42 Rudyard Kipling, "My Own True Ghost Story," in *The Phantom Rickshaw and Other Ghost Stories* (New York: R. F. Fenno, 1899), 53–54.
43 Henri Lefebvre, *The Production of Space* (Boston: Blackwell Press, 1991 [Paris: Editions Anthropos, 1974]), 95.
44 Lefebvre, *Production of Space*, 96.
45 According to Hutchins, the British during the early days of the Raj were happy to contemplate an eventual dissolution of their rule and an eventual withdrawal from India. In the aftermath of the mutiny, however, when the queen was declared the Empress of India, it seemed almost disloyal to suggest that her rule could ever come to an end, thus strengthening discourses of continuity and permanence. For details, see Francis G. Hutchins, *The Illusion of Permanence: British Imperialism in India* (Princeton, NJ: Princeton University Press, 1967).
46 Hiren Chakrabarty, "The Victoria Memorial," in *Calcutta: The Living City*, vol. 1, ed. Sukanta Chaudhuri (Calcutta: Oxford University Press, 1990), 256.

4. ENACTING GHOSTS

1 Doreen Massey, *Space, Place and Gender* (Minneapolis: University of Minnesota Press/Cambridge: Polity Press, 1994), 4.
2 Sarah Nuttall, *Entanglement: Literary and Cultural Reflections on Postapartheid* (Johannesburg: Wits University Press, 2009).
3 Massey, *Space, Place and Gender*, 5.
4 Leslie Salzinger, *Genders in Production: Making Workers in Mexico's Global Factories* (Berkeley: University of California Press, 2003), 15.
5 Biren Bonnerjea, *A Dictionary of Superstitions and Mythology* (London: Folk Press Limited, 1927), 105.
6 For Black Death ghosts in Europe, see Kathryn A. Edwards, "Medieval Ghost Stories: An Anthology of Miracles, Marvels and Prodigies," *History Compass* 10, no. 4 (April 2012): 353–66; for a similar story in Japan, see Lafcadio Hearn, *Kwaidan: Stories and Studies of Strange Things* (Boston: Houghton and Mifflin, 1904).
7 Edward Said, *Orientalism* (New York: Pantheon Books, 1978), 72.

8   For more details on Petty, see Margaret T. Hodgen, *Early Anthropology in the Sixteenth and Seventeenth Centuries* (Philadelphia: University of Pennsylvania Press, 1964); for an epistemology and history of statistics, see Ian Hacking, *The Taming of Chance* (Cambridge: Cambridge University Press, 1990); for the specific context of British India, see David Ludden, "Orientalist Empiricisms and the Transformations of Colonial Knowledge," in *Orientalism and the Post-Colonial Predicament*, ed. C. A. Breckenridge and Peter Van der Veer (Philadelphia: University of Pennsylvania Press, 1993), 250–78.
9   Gopaul Chunder Roy, *The Causes, Symptoms and Treatment of Burdwan Fever, or The Epidemic Fever of Lower Bengal* (Calcutta: Thacker, Spink and Co., 1876), 1.
10 *The Proceedings of the Second All India Sanitary Conference Vol II* (Simla: Government Central Branch Press, 1913), 542.
11 Paramananda Dutt, *Moti Lal Ghose* (Calcutta: Amrita Bazar Patrika Office, 1935), 7.
12 Rohan Deb Roy, *Malarial Subjects: Empire, Medicine and Nonhumans in British India, 1820–1909* (Cambridge: Cambridge University Press, 2017), 121.
13 The findings of the 1864–65 Sanitary Commission for Bengal, quoted in Hemendra Prasad Ghose, "Decay of Villages in Bengal," *Calcutta Review* 124 (July 1907): 397.
14 Michel Foucault, *The History of Sexuality Vol. 1*, ed. Robert Hurley (New York: Pantheon Books, 1978), 25. Bernard Cohn in his seminal essay on the census has shown how, in addition to the "estimates made in the 1820s for the total population of India, the British continued in the 1830s and 1840s to try to determine the population of India." Much of such efforts were predicated on "revenue surveys and were a by-product of attempts to map villages and lands." Bernard Cohn, "The Census, Social Structure and Objectification in South Asia," in *An Anthropologist among the Historians and Other Essays* (New Delhi: Oxford University Press, 1987), 233.
15 Government of Bengal Legislative Department, *Bengal Act IV of 1873* (Calcutta: Bengal Secretariat Press, 1915), 2.
16 Government of Bengal Legislative Department, *Bengal Act IV of 1873*, 4.
17 W. W. Hunter, *A Statistical Account of Bengal Vol. 8* (London: Trubner, 1876), 199.
18 *The Calcutta Gazette Part I*, November 8, 1922, pp. 2041–42.
19 *Sixteenth Annual Report of the Sanitary Commissioner with the Government of India 1879, With Appendices and Returns of Sickness and Mortality among British Troops, Native Troops and Prisoners, in India* (Calcutta: Office of the Superintendent of Government Printing, 1881), 69.
20 *Supplement to the Annual General Administration Report for 1885–86* (Calcutta: Bengal Secretariat Press, 1887).
21 George Toynbee, "The Village Police of Bengal," *Calcutta Review* 7, no. 174 (October 1888): 209.
22 Hunter, *Statistical Account of Bengal*, 177, 274.
23 Norman Chevers, *Manual of Medical Jurisprudence* (Calcutta: Bengal Military Orphan Press, 1856), 33.
24 *The Proceedings of the Second All-India Sanitary Conference Madras Vol. 2* (Simla: Government Central Branch Press, 1913), 3.

25 Bertell Ollman, *Dance of the Dialectic: Steps in Marx's Method* (Urbana: University of Illinois Press, 2003), 60.
26 Karl Marx and Frederick Engels, *Selected Correspondence*, trans. and ed. Dona Torr (London: Lawrence and Wishart, 1941), 12.
27 Karl Marx, *Economic and Philosophical Manuscripts 1844* (Moscow: Progress Publishers, 1977 [1959]), 132.
28 For more details, see M. C. Buer, *Health, Wealth and Population in the Early Days of the Industrial Revolution* (London: G. Routledge and Sons, 1926).
29 William Radice, introduction to *Selected Short Stories by Rabindranath Tagore* (London: Penguin Books, [1991] 1994), 27.
30 See W. W. Hunter, *A Statistical Account of Bengal* (Delhi: Concept Publishing Company, 1976 [1877]), 205.
31 Sabyasachi Bhattacharya, *Rabindranath Tagore: An Interpretation* (New Delhi: Penguin Books India, 2011), 84. In that last decade, Tagore wrote more than half the stories of the three-volume, eighty-four-story collection, *Galpaguchcha*. *Galpaguchcha* was first published in two parts, in 1900–1901, and was followed in 1908–1909 by an enlarged edition in five parts. A complete list of his published works is available at the website of the Rabindra Bharati Museum at http://museum.rbu.ac.in/rabindranath_tagore/list_works7.htm.
32 Radice, introduction to *Selected Short Stories by Rabindranath Tagore*, 26.
33 For a detailed analysis of this wild/home divide, see chapter 3 of this book.
34 Rabindranath Tagore, "Kankal," *Sadhana* 1, no. 1 (Falgun 1892): 287–88; translation mine.
35 For a vivid description of the skeleton from his childhood, see Rabindranath Tagore, *My Boyhood Days*, trans. Marjorie Sykes (Calcutta: Visva Bharati, 1940), 40.
36 E. J. Clery, *The Rise of Supernatural Fiction 1762–1800* (Cambridge: Cambridge University Press, 1995), 9.
37 Clery, *Rise of Supernatural Fiction*, 8–9.
38 Radice, "Nishithe," 263, iBook.
39 Radice, "Nishithe," 266, iBook.
40 Rabindranath Tagore, "Manihara," in *Galpaguchcha Vol. 2* (Calcutta: Visva Bharati, 1975), 402–3. Digital Library of India Item 2015.338597; translations are my own.
41 Troilakyanath Mukhopadhyay, "Damaru Charit," in *Akhando Troilakyanath*, ed. Prafulla Kumar Patra (Calcutta: Patra's Publication, 1957), 306. All subsequent quotations are from this edition; translation is mine.
42 *Ananda Bazar Patrika* 18 (April 28, 1880): 5. Quoted in Anindita Mukhopadhyay, *Behind the Mask: The Cultural Definition of the Legal Subject in Colonial Bengal 1715–1911* (New Delhi: Oxford University Press, 2006), 119.
43 Rabindranath Tagore, "Kankabati," *Sadhana* 1, no. 2, 1892; reprinted in Troilakyanath Mukhopadhyay, *Kankabati*, ed. Bijanbihari Bhattacharya (Calcutta: Orient Books, BE 1367), 77–80.
44 There is word play on Lullu's moniker in the original Bangla: Lullu was a "shabhya, bhabya, nabya" bhut! Figure 4.01 from Troilakyanath Mukhopadhyay, "Lullu," 29–49.

45 Troilakyanath Mukhopadhyay, "Lullu," in *Troilokyanather Granthabali Vol. 2* (Calcutta: Basumati Sahitya Mandir, nd), 29–49.
46 Sisir Kumar Das, *A History of Indian Literature 1800–1919: Western Impact, Indian Response* (New Delhi: Sahiya Akademi, 1991), 308.
47 Buddhu-Bhutum, Manimala, and the Lal Kamal-Neel Kamal stories are all part of Dakshinaranjan Mitra Majumdar's *Thakurmar Jhuli* (Calcutta: Mitra O Ghosh Publisher, BE 1412).
48 Foucault, *History of Sexuality*, 27.
49 Partha Chatterjee, "Five Hundred Years of Fear and Love," *Economic and Political Weekly* 33, no. 22 (May 30–June 5, 1998): 1334; Tapodhir Bhattacharjee, *Makers of Indian Literature: Trailokyanath Mukhopadhyay* (New Delhi: Sahitya Akademi, 2001), 50.
50 Bodhisattva Chattopadhyay calls his Damarudhar series "science-fantasy tall tales," while William Radice calls his work "highly original fantasy fiction." Chattopadhyay, "Kalpavigyan and Imperial Technoscience: Three Nodes of an Argument," *Journal of the Fantastic in the Arts* 28, no. 1 (98) (2017): 116; Radice, "Review of *Travels to Europe: Self and Other in Bengali Travel Narratives 1870–1910* by Simonti Sen," *Bulletin of the School of Oriental and African Studies, University of London* 69, no. 1 (2006): 159.
51 Troilakyanath Mukhopadhyay, "Lullu," 31.
52 Troilakyanath Mukhopadhyay, *Kankabati*, 115–26.
53 Troilakyanath Mukhopadhyay, "Birbala," in *Troilokyanather Granthabali Vol. 2* (Calcutta: Basumati Sahitya Mandir, nd), 25–27.
54 Troilakyanath Mukhopadhyay, *Kankabati*, 129–30.
55 Troilakyanath Mukhopadhyay, "Damaru Charit," 339.
56 Robert Darnton, "Peasants Tell Tales: The Meaning of Mother Goose," in *The Great Cat Massacre and Other Episodes in French Cultural History* (New York: Basic Books, 1984), 53.
57 Troilakyanath Mukhopadhyay, "Lullu," 34.
58 Troilakyanath Mukhopadhyay, *Kankabati*, 116.
59 Pramathanath Bishi, Introduction to *Troilakyanath Mukhopadhayer Sreshtho Galpa* (Calcutta: Mitra O Ghosh, nd), xii; translation mine.
60 Mikhail Bakhtin, *Rabelais and His World* (Bloomington: Indiana University Press, 1984), 12.
61 T. N. Mukharji, *A Visit to Europe* (Calcutta: W. Newman), 151.
62 Mukharji, *Visit to Europe*, 150.
63 See Tapodhir Bhattacharjee, *Makers of Indian Literature*, 73.
64 Sudhirkumar Mukhopadhyay, "Pitrismriti," in *Trailokya Rachanasamagra Vol. 1*, ed. Satyanarayan Bhattacharya, Nirmal Das, and Shyamal Sengupta (Calcutta: Granthamela, 1973), 18.
65 Bakhtin, *Rabelais*, 109.
66 Puck's final speech in *A Midsummer Night's Dream*. See William Shakespeare, *A Midsummer Night's Dream*, ed. Henry Cuningham (London: Methuen, 1905), 159.

67 Panchkori Bandyopadhyay, "Smriti Sabha," in *Panchkori Rachanbali Vol. 2*, ed. Brajendranth Bandyopadhya and Sajantikanta Das (Calcutta: Bangiya Sahita Parishat, nd), 135–36.

68 *Mookerjee's Magazine*, April 1861, pp. 166–69; quoted in N. N. Ghose, *Memoirs of Maharaja Nubkisssen Bahadur* (Calcutta: K. B. Basu, 1901), 182–83.

69 With differing emphases, historians note this shift from around 1500, or what I would identify as the beginnings for the constitution of a capitalist modernity; see Eamon Duffy, *The Stripping of the Altars: Traditional Religion in England c.1400–c.1580* (New Haven, CT: Yale University Press, 1992), esp. 301–76, 474–75, and 577–78; Ralph Houlbrooke, "Death, Church, and Family in England between the Late Fifteenth and Early Eighteenth Centuries," in *Death, Ritual, and Bereavement*, ed. Ralph Houlbrooke (London: Routledge Press, 1989), 25–42; Clare Gittings, *Death, Burial and the Individual in Early Modern England* (Dover, NH: Croom Helm, 1984); and the classic study by Keith Thomas, *Religion and the Decline of Magic* (New York: Scribner Press, 1971).

70 Debendranath Tagore, *Atmajiboni*, ed. Satishchandra Chakrabarty (Calcutta: Viswabharati Press, 1927), 114.

71 Debendranath Tagore, *The Autobiography of Maharshi Devendranath Tagore*, trans. Satyendranath Tagore and Indira Devi (London: Macmillan, 1914), 117–18.

72 See Brian Hatcher, *Bourgeois Hinduism, or The Faith of the Modern Vedantists: Rare Discourses from Early Colonial Bengal* (New York: Oxford University Press, 2008).

73 Rajnarayan Basu, *Atmacharit* (Calcutta: Kuntalin Press, 1909), 59.

74 Tagore, *Atmajiboni*, 125.

75 Akshay Chandra Sarkar, "Pita Putra," in *Atmakatha Vol. 5*, ed. Naresh Jana, Manu Jana, and Kamalkumar Sanyal (Calcutta: Ananya Prakashan), 117.

76 Minoru Hara, "Sraddha in the Sense of Desire," *Asiatische Studien* 46 (1992): 191.

77 Matthew R. Sayers, *Feeding the Dead: Ancestor Worship in Ancient India* (New York: Oxford University Press, 2013), 88. Emphasis added.

78 See Stephanie W. Jamison, *Sacrificed Wife, Sacrificer's Wife: Women, Ritual and Hospitality in Ancient India* (New York: Oxford University Press, 1996).

79 Prathama Banerjee, *Elementary Aspects of the Political: Histories of the Global South* (Durham, NC: Duke University Press, 2020), 222.

80 Sugata Bose and Ayesha Jalal, *Modern South Asia: History, Culture, Political Economy* (New York: Taylor and Francis, 2006), 20.

81 Marx, in *German Ideology*. See Karl Marx and Frederick Engels, *Selected Works*, vol. 1 (Moscow: Progress Publishers, 1969), 77.

82 Eugene Pashukanis, "The General Theory of Law and Marxism," in *Soviet Legal Philosophy*, ed. J. Hazard, vol. 5 of *20th Century Legal Philosophy* (Cambridge, MA: Harvard University Press, 1951), 185.

83 Partha Chatterjee, "On Civil and Political Society in Postcolonial Democracies," in *Civil Society: History and Possibility*, ed. Sudipta Kaviraj and Sunil Khilnani (Cambridge: Cambridge University Press, 2001), 169.

84 Romesh C. Dutt "The Late Bankim Chandra Chatterjee C.I.E," *Journal of the Royal Asiatic Society of Great Britain and Ireland* (1897): 702.

85 Nabin Chandra Sen, "Sahitya Parishat o Shiksha Pranali," in *Amar Jiban Vol. 5* (Calcutta: Sanyal and Co, 1913), 71–72.
86 Chatterjee, "On Civil and Political Society," 165–78.
87 Rabindranath Tagore, "Sok Sabha," in *Rabindra Rachanbali Vol. 9* (Calcutta: Visva Bharati Press, 1958), 532.
88 Chatterjee, "On Civil and Political Society," 168–69.
89 Nabin Chandra Sen, quoted in Chatterjee, "On Civil and Political Society," 169.
90 Tagore, "Sok Sabha," 536.
91 See, for example, the discussion about unveiling a portrait of the late Raja Benoykrishna Deb in *Sahitya Parishat Patrika* 23 (1916): 102–12.
92 Man Kumari Basu, "Amar Atit Jiban," in *Sekele Katha: Satak Suchanai Meyeder Smritikatha*, ed. Abhijit Bhattacharya and Abhijit Sen (Calcutta: Naya Udyog, 1997), 111.
93 See *A Few Facts Regarding the Life and Career of the Late Roy Obhoy Chandra Das Bahadur* (Calcutta: The University Press, 1893) and *The Press on the Death of the Late Nawab Bahadur Abdool Luteef with Proceedings of the Public Meetings Held in Honour of his Memory* (Calcutta: The Mahomedan Literary Society of Calcutta, 1893).
94 *Somprakash*, December 21, 1863.
95 Pierre Nora, "Between Memory and History: Les Lieux de Memoire," *Representations* 29 (1989): 9.

5. NATIONAL GHOSTS, GHOSTLY NATIONS

1 Edward Thompson, *The Other Side of the Medal*, 3rd ed. (London: Hogarth Press, 1930), 30.
2 Roger Luckhurst, "Knowledge, Belief and the Supernatural at the Imperial Margin," in *The Victorian Supernatural*, ed. Nicola Bown, Carolyn Burdett, and P. Thurschwell (Cambridge: Cambridge University Press, 2004), 202, 204.
3 The story "The Wondrous Narrative of John Campbell Gunfounder to the Mogul Emperors 1654–1670" was reproduced in Richard Temple's essay, "The Travels of Richard Bell (and John Campbell)," published serially in *The Indian Antiquary*. Temple found the manuscript at the British Museum catalogued as Sloane 811 and wrote in his introduction that it "contained 128 folio pages, written in a somewhat illiterate 17th. Century hand. . . . The natural assumption is the Bell wrote down, John Campbell's wonderful stories, which record facts strangely distorted in the telling." See Richard Temple, "The Travels of Richard Bell (and John Campbell) in the East Indies, Persia, and Palestine 1654–1670," pt. 1, *Indian Antiquary* 37 (May 1906): 131–42; Temple, "Travels," pt. 2, *Indian Antiquary* 38 (June 1906): 168–78.
4 E. W. Madge, "Anglo-Indian Ghost Stories," *Bengal Past and Present* 3, no. 1 (January–March 1909): 6.
5 Dinabandhu Mitra, *Dinabandhu Granthabali Vol. 1*, ed. Brajendranath Bandyopadhyay and Sajanikanta Das (Calcutta: Bangiya Sahita Parishat, 1943); see especially,

pp. 34 and 79 for references to ghosts. The Nil Kuthi continued to be the Gothic presence in literature well into the twentieth century. See for instance, Satyajit Ray's famous ghost story "Nil Atanka" (Indigo Terror), first published in *Sharadiya Sandesh* in 1968. See Ray, "Nil Atanka," in *Galpa 101* (Calcutta: Ananda Publishers, 2001), 99–107.

6   Ruskin Bond, ed., *Ghost Stories from the Raj* (New Delhi: Rupa and Co., 2002), x.
7   Patrick Brantlinger, *Rule of Darkness: British Literature and Imperialism 1830–1914* (Ithaca, NY: Cornell University Press, 1988).
8   Kris Manjapra, *Colonialism in Global Perspective* (Cambridge: Cambridge University Press, 2020), 131.
9   See for example, Ronald Inden, *Imagining India* (Bloomington: Indiana University Press, 1990); Carol Breckenridge and Peter Van der Veer, eds., *Postcolonial Predicament: Perspectives on South Asia* (Philadelphia: University of Pennsylvania Press, 1993); Bernard S. Cohn, *Colonialism and Its Forms of Knowledge* (Princeton, NJ: Princeton University Press, 1996); Amal Chatterjee, *Representations of India 1740–1840: The Creation of India in the Colonial Imaginations* (London: Macmillan Press, 1998); Richard King, *Orientalism and Religion: Postcolonial Theory, India and the Mystic East* (London: Routledge, 1999).
10 Robert Henry Elliot, *The Myth of the Mystic East* (Edinburgh: Wm. Blackwood and Sons, 1935), 3, 57, 5.
11 Elliot, *Myth*, 27–28.
12 John Nevil Maskelyne, "Oriental Jugglery," in *The Supernatural?*, ed. Lionel Weatherly (Bristol, UK: J. W. Arrowsmith, 1891), 158.
13 Maskelyne, "Oriental Jugglery," 165.
14 Maskelyne, "Oriental Jugglery," 166.
15 Sean Scalmer, *Gandhi in the West: The Mahatma and the Rise of Radical Protest* (Cambridge: Cambridge University Press, 2011), 52.
16 Greenberger, quoted in Peter Lamont and Crispin Bates, "Conjuring Images of India in Nineteenth-Century Britain," *Social History* 32, no. 3 (August 2007): 310.
17 The SPR, however, had its own exposure moment, when it investigated Madame Blavatsky, as we will see.
18 Shane McCorristine, *Spectres of the Self: Thinking about Ghosts and Ghost-Seeing in England, 1750–1920* (Cambridge: Cambridge University Press, 2010), 104.
19 Andrew Lang, *Magic and Religion* (London: Longmans, Green, and Co., 1901), 294.
20 "Fire Walking Ceremony," *Journal of the Society for Psychical Research* 9, no. 173 (November 1900): 315.
21 "The Indian Rope Trick," *Journal of the Society for Psychical Research* 11, no. 213 (1904–5): 301.
22 S. Satthianadhan, *Theosophy: An Appeal to My Countrymen* (Madras: Christian Literature Society, 1893), 6–8.
23 Anon., *Who Is Mrs. Besant and Why Has She Come to India?* (Madras: Christian Literature Society, 1894).
24 Helena Petrovna Blavatsky, *Isis Unveiled Vol. 1* (Point Loma, CA: The Aryan Theosophical Press, 1919), 9–10.

25 Olav Hammer and Mikael Rothstein, "Introduction," in *Handbook of the Theosophical Current*, ed. Olav Hammer and Mikael Rothstein (Leiden: Brill, 2013), 1.
26 For a detailed discussion, see Robert S. Ellwood, *Alternative Altars: Unconventional and Eastern Spirituality in America* (Chicago: University of Chicago Press, 1979).
27 Blavatsky, quoted in Mark Bevir, "Theosophy and the Origins of the Indian National Congress," *International Journal of Hindu Studies* 7, no. 1/3 (February 2003): 100.
28 Blavatsky, *Isis Unveiled*, xxxvii.
29 W. B. Yeats on first meeting Helena Blavatsky, quoted in Seamus Heaney, "All Ireland's Bard," *Atlantic Monthly* 280, no. 5 (November 1997): 156.
30 H. P. Blavatsky, *Five Messages* (Bombay: The Theosophical Company, 1930), 8–9. The messages were collected addresses of Blavatsky to the American Theosophists Convention between 1888 and 1891.
31 H. P. Blavatsky, "What Are the Theosophists?" *The Theosophist* 1, no. 1 (October 1879): 5–7.
32 C. Jinarajadasa, "The Future of Brotherhood," *American Theosophist* 31, no. 3 (March 1943): 65.
33 C. Jinarajadasa, "The Negro and South America," *American Theosophist* 31, no. 3 (March 1943): 66.
34 For an important study on the construction of whiteness and history of anti-miscegenation ideas in British India, see Satoshi Mizutani, *The Meaning of White Race, Class, and the "Domiciled Community" in British India 1858–1930* (Oxford: Oxford University Press, 2011).
35 See Emily Lutyens, *Candles in the Sun* (London: Rupert Hart-Davis, 1957); Joy Dixon, *Divine Feminine: Theosophy and Feminism in England* (Baltimore, MD: Johns Hopkins University Press, 2001).
36 H. S. Olcott, *A Historical Retrospect of the Theosophical Society 1875–1896* (Madras: Theosophical Society, 1896), 21.
37 This was by no means unique to the Theosophists, as Spiritualists, generally, had a history of holding radical views about women's rights. The British National Association of Spiritualists, for example, were against existing divorce and lunacy laws and believed in the equality between the sexes. See Alex Owen, *The Darkened Room: Women, Power, and Spiritualism in Late Victorian England* (Chicago: University of Chicago Press, 1989).
38 Dixon, *Divine Feminine*, 3.
39 Sarala Devi Chaudhurani, *Jibaner Jharapata* (Calcutta: Sahitya Samsad, 1957), 57.
40 Chaudhurani, *Jibaner*, 57–58.
41 Chaudhurani, *Jibaner*, 59.
42 *Presidential Address of Annie Besant to the Forty-Ninth Annual Convention of the Theosophical Society* (Madras: Theosophical Publishing House, 1925), 25. For more details on the WIA, see Geraldine Forbes, *Women in Modern India* (Cambridge: Cambridge University Press, 1996).
43 *Presidential Address*, 25.
44 *Presidential Address*, 25.
45 Kumari Jayawardena, *The White Woman's Other Burden* (London: Routledge, 1995), 11.

46 J. N. Farquhar, *Modern Religious Movements in India* (New Delhi: Munshiram Manoharlal, 1977 [1914]), 233.
47 Mriganka Mukhopadhyay, "Occult's First Foot Soldier in Bengal: Peary Chand Mittra," in *The Occult Nineteenth Century: Roots, Development and Impact in the Modern World*, ed. Lukas Pokorny and Franz Winter (London: Palgrave Macmillan, 2021), 273.
48 For a brief report on Peary Chand's work with the society, see his obituary in *Journal of the Agricultural and Horticultural Society* 6 (1882): xxxix.
49 Peary Chand Mittra, *Spiritual Stray Leaves* (Calcutta: Stanhope Press, 1879), 72.
50 Shinjini Das, *Vernacular Medicine in Colonial India: Family, Market and Homeopathy* (Cambridge: Cambridge University Press, 2019).
51 M. K. Ghose, *Life beyond Death* (New Delhi: Cosmo Publications, 1987 [1934]), 117.
52 Ghose, *Life beyond Death*, 117.
53 Meugens is listed as a "Calcutta merchant" in the membership lists of the society, and his affiliation is recorded as having started in 1865. See, for example, *Journal of the Agricultural and Horticultural Society* 6 (1882).
54 S. M., "Spiritualism in Calcutta," *National Magazine* 28, no. 4 (April 1916): 170–71.
55 Tithi Bhattacharya, *Sentinels of Culture* (New Delhi: Oxford University Press, 2005).
56 Peary Chand Mittra and Vidyasagar were close friends. On the former's death, the latter treated his family with the same tenderness and affection. Peary Chand's first son, Babu Khetra Nath Mittra, is at present a Munsiff, and his youngest son, Avinas Chandra Mittra, is Serishtadar of the Judge's Court at Burdwan. His son-in-law, Babu Giris Chandra Basu, is the managing proprietor of the Bangabasi College at Calcutta. Vidyasagar loved Giris Chandra most dearly. The two families are still on very good terms of friendship. Subal Chandra Mitra, *Isvar Chandra Vidyasagar: A Study of His Life and Works* (Calcutta: New Bengal Press, 1902).
57 Kshetrapal Chakrabarti, *Lectures on Hindu Religion, Philosophy and Yoga* (Calcutta: New Britannia Press, 1893), 56.
58 Kshetrapal Chakrabarti, "Religious Aspects of the Early Tantras," *The Theosophist* 12, no. 1 (October 1890): 27.
59 Quoted in Mrinal Kanti Ghose, *Paroloker Katha* (Calcutta: np, 1933), 6.
60 M. K. Ghose, *Life beyond Death*, 4.
61 Bevir, "Theosophy," 106.
62 Emmanuel Wallerstein, "Voluntary Associations," in *Political Parties and National Integration in Tropical Africa*, ed. Carl G. Rosberg and James S. Coleman (Berkeley: African Studies Center, University of California, 1964), 320. While Partha Chatterjee has famously argued that the nation was first imagined in these nonstate spaces, this argument about voluntary associations as midwives to the nation have been made before by other scholars of the global south. See, for example, Thomas Hodgkin, *Nationalism in Colonial Africa* (London: Frederick Mueller, 1956); Timothy P. Daniels, *Building Cultural Nationalism in Malaysia: Identity, Representation and Citizenship* (New York: Routledge, 2005); Keith David Watenpaugh, *Being Modern in the Middle East: Revolution, Nationalism, Colonialism, and the Arab Middle Class* (Princeton, NJ: Princeton University Press, 2014), among others.

63 *Amrita Bazar Patrika*, May 21, 1874, 4.
64 *Amrita Bazar Patrika*, September 30, 1875.
65 *Calcutta Review* 128, no. 255 (January 1909): 114.
66 Shishir Kumar Ghose, "The Origin of Theosophy in India," *Hindu Spiritual Magazine* 3, no. 12, (February 1909): 422–23.
67 Ghose, "Origin of Theosopy," 424.
68 "Thanks are also due to Byramji M. Malabari, a well-known journalist and public citizen, for enriching our Library with a set of Emmanuel Swedenborg's books in 1895."
69 *Indian Mirror*, March 30, 1879.
70 Annie Besant, "Theosophical Worthies: Norendranath Sen," *The Theosophist* 32, no. 3 (January 1911): 694–96.
71 Bevir, "Theosophy," 105.
72 Julian Strube, *Global Tantra* (New York: Oxford University Press, 2022).
73 Amiya Sen, *Hindu Revivalism in Bengal* (New Delhi: Oxford University Press, 2001), 17.
74 See Amiya Sen's comment about how "an influential class of Hindus increasingly came to believe that 'Hinduism' was a name that could justly be given to a readily identifiable religion common to all Hindus," in *Hindu Revivalism*, 68.
75 Rammohan, for instance, insisted that all the Vedic texts ought to be available to women and low castes (*shudras*).
76 Jason D. Fuller, "Colonial Devotional Paths," in *Hinduism in the Modern World*, ed. Brian A. Hatcher (New York: Routledge, 2016), 92.
77 Lata Mani makes this point very powerfully in her discussion of *sati*. See Lata Mani, *Contentious Traditions: The Debate on Sati in Colonial India* (Berkeley: University of California Press, 1998).
78 Charles Taylor, "Modes of Secularism," in *Secularism and Its Critics*, ed. Rajeev Bhargava (Delhi: Oxford University Press, 1998), 31–53.
79 Talal Assad, *Formations of the Secular: Christianity, Islam, and Modernity* (Stanford, CA: Stanford University Press, 2003), 2.
80 This is Peter Van der Veer's term; see Van der Veer, *Imperial Encounters: Religion and Modernity in India and Britain* (Princeton, NJ: Princeton University Press, 2001).
81 Gauri Viswanathan, "Ordinary Business of Occult," *Critical Enquiry* 27 (Autumn 2000): 6–7.
82 Gillian McCann, "Emergent Representations of the East: The Role of Theosophical Periodicals, 1879–1900," in *Imagining the East: The Early Theosophical Society*, ed. Tim Rudbog and Erik Sand (New York: Oxford University Press, 2020).
83 Partha Chatterjee, *Nation and Its Fragments: Colonial and Postcolonial Histories* (Princeton, NJ: Princeton University Press, 1993), 6.
84 Neil Davidson, *Nation-States: Consciousness and Competition* (Chicago: Haymarket Books, 2016), 104.
85 Ghose, *Life beyond Death*, 16.

CONCLUSION

1. Rabindranath Tagore, "Jibito O Mrito," TagoreWeb; my translation. The story was first published in *Sadhana* in 1892.
2. Raymond Williams, *The Long Revolution* (Peterborough, Canada: Broadview Press, 2001 [1961]), 78.
3. Williams, *Long Revolution*, 80.
4. Paritosh Sen, *Jindabahar Lane* (Calcutta: Papyrus, BE 1366), 114.

Bibliography

JOURNALS

Aloukik Rahasya
Amrita Bazar Patrika, September 30, 1875
Amrita Bazar Patrika, May 21, 1874, 4
Arunodaya, 1890–91, Rasikmohan Chattopadhyay, ed.
Calcutta Review 128, no. 255 (January 1909): 114
Hindu Spiritual Magazine
Indian Mirror, January 7, 1870
Indian Mirror, March 30, 1879
Sahitya Parishat Patrika 23 (1916)
Somprakash

OFFICIAL

Calcutta Gazette Part I. November 8. Calcutta: Bengal Secretariat Office, 1922.
Fort William Judicial Proceedings. West Bengal State Archives, 1850–1900.
Gait, E. A. *Census of India, 1891*, Assam, part 1, Report. Shillong: Government Press, 1892.
Government of Bengal Legislative Department. *Bengal Act IV of 1873*. Calcutta: Bengal Secretariat Press, 1915.
The Home and Foreign Record of the Free Church of Scotland. Vol. 3. Edinburgh: James Nichol, 1859.
Imperial Gazetteer of India: Provincial Series, Bengal. Vol. 1. Calcutta: Superintendent of Government Printing, 1909.
Journal of the Agricultural and Horticultural Society 6 (1882).
Presidential Address of Annie Besant to the Forty-Ninth Annual Convention of the Theosophical Society. Madras: Theosophical Publishing House, 1925.

Proceedings of the Second All-India Sanitary Conference Madras Vol. 2. Simla: Government Central Brach Press, 1913.

Proceedings of the Second All India Sanitary Conference Vol. 2. Simla: Government Central Branch Press, 1913.

Record of Cases Treated in the Mesmeric Hospital, from November 1846 to May 1847: With Reports of the Official Visitors. Calcutta: Military Orphan Press, 1847.

Report of the Transactions of the Vernacular Literature Society from July 1, 1858 to December 31, 1859. Calcutta: Sanders, Cones and Co., 1860.

Sixteenth Annual Report of the Sanitary Commissioner with the Government of India 1879, with Appendices and Returns of Sickness and Mortality among British Troops, Native Troops and Prisoners, in India. Calcutta: Office of the Superintendent of Government Printing, 1881.

Supplement to the Annual General Administration Report for 1885–86. Calcutta: Bengal Secretariat Press, 1887.

PRIMARY SOURCES, BANGLA

Anon. *Sachitra Bibhuti Vidya.* Calcutta: Basak Press, 1900.

Bandyopadhyay, Bhabanicharan. *Kalikata Kamalalaya and Kalikata Kalpalata.* Edited by Bishnu Basu. Calcutta: Pratibhash, 1986.

Bandyopadhyay, Brajendranath. *Bangla Samayik Patra (1818–68).* Calcutta: Bangiya Sahita Parishat, BE 1397.

Bandyopadhyay, Brajendranath, ed. *Sahitya Sadhak Charitmala.* Vol. 3. Calcutta: Lakshmibilash Press, 1944.

Bandyopadhyay, Panchkori. *Banglar Tantra.* Edited by Bimalendu Chakrabarty. Calcutta: Bengal Publishers Private Limited, 1942.

Bandyopadhyay, Panchkori. "Smriti Sabha." In *Panchkori Rachanbali*, vol. 2, edited by Brajendranath Bandyopadhya and Sajantikanta Das, 135–37. Calcutta: Bangiya Sahita Parishat, nd.

Basu, Anath Nath. *Mahatma Sisir Kumar Ghosh.* 2nd ed. Calcutta: Tushar Kanti Ghosh, 1976.

Basu, Man Kumari. "Amar Atit Jiban." In *Sekele Katha: Satak Suchanai Meyeder Smritikatha*, edited by Abhijit Bhattacharya and Abhijit Sen, 99–116. Calcutta: Naya Udyog, 1997.

Basu, Manmathamohan. "Nutan O Puratan Bigyan." *Brahma Bidya* 11, no. 4 (1913): 193–207.

Basu, Rajnarayan. *Atmacharit.* Calcutta: Kuntalin Press, 1909.

Basu, Rajnarayan. *Bangla Bhasha o Sahitya Bisayak Baktrita.* Calcutta: New Bengal Press, 1879.

Basu, Rajnarayan. *The Prospectus of a Society for the Promotion National Feeling among the Educated Natives of Bengal.* 1866. https://www.midnapore.in/people/rishi_rajnarayan_basu_prospectus_of_society.html.

Bhattacharya, Satyanarayan, ed. *Kabi Krishnaram Daser Granthabali.* Calcutta: University of Calcutta Press, 1958.

Bidyanidhi, Mahendranath. *Babu Akshaykumar Datter Jibanbrittanto.* Calcutta: New Sanskrit Press, 1885.

Bidyaratna, Kalimohan. *Hindu Sarbashya*. Calcutta: Narayan Printing and Publishing House, 1922.
Bishi, Pramathanath. Introduction to *Troilakyanath Mukhopadhayer Sreshtho Galpa*, xii. Calcutta: Mitra O Ghosh, nd.
Chakrabarti, Ajitkumar. *Maharshi Debendranath Thakur*. Calcutta: Jignyasya Press, 1971 [1916].
Chattopadhyay, Bankimchandra. *Bankim Rachanabali*. Vol. 2. Edited by Jogeshchandra Bagal. Calcutta: Sahitya Samsad, 1965.
Chaudhurani, Sarala Devi. *Jibaner Jharapata*. Calcutta: Sahitya Samsad, 1957 [1879].
Debi, Maitreyi. *Mongpute Rabindranath*. Calcutta: Pragya Prakashani, 1958 [1957].
Dutta, Michael Madhusudan. *Madhusudan Rachanabali* [Collected Works of Madhusudan]. Calcutta: Sahitya Sansad, 1993.
Ghose, Mrinal Kanti. *Paroloker Katha*. Calcutta: np, 1933.
Gupta, Kshetra, and Bishnu Basu, eds. *Bharatchandra Rachanasamagra*. Calcutta: Bhaumik and Sons, 1974.
Jana, Nareshchandra, Manu Jana, and Kamalkumar Sanyal, eds. *Atmakatha*. Vol. 5. Calcutta: Ananya Prakashan, 1987.
Lahiri, Chandi, ed. *Basantak Samagra*. Calcutta: New Age Publishers, nd.
Mitra, Dinabandhu. *Dinabandhu Granthabali*, vol. 1, edited by Brajendranath Bandyopadhyay and Sajanikanta Das. Calcutta: Bangiya Sahita Parishat, 1943.
Mitra, Dinabandhu. *Paralok Tattva*. Dhaka: Shanti Press, 1924.
Mitra, Rajendralal. "Bhoutik Byapar." *Bibidartha Saṅgraha* (1857): 378–82. Reprinted in Pradip Basu, ed., *Samayiki: Purano Samayik Patrer Prabandha Sankalan*, vol. 1 (Calcutta: Ananda Publishers, 1998).
Mitra, Rajendralal. *Samayiki: Purano Samayik Patrer Prabandha Sankalan*, vol. 1. Calcutta: Ananda Publishers, 1998.
Mitra Majumdar, Dakshinaranjan. *Thakurmar Jhuli*. Calcutta: Mitra O Ghosh Publisher, BE 1412.
Mukhopadhyay, Ashutosh. *Bhut Petni*. Calcutta: Modern Book Agency, 1995 [1903].
Mukhopadhyay, Bhudev. *Bhudeb prabandha samagra*. Calcutta: Charchapada, 2010.
Mukhopadhyay, Sudhirkumar. "Pitrismriti." In *Trailokya Rachanasamagra*, vol. 1, edited by Satyanarayan Bhattacharya, Nirmal Das, Shyamal Sengupta, Dibyajyoti Majumdar, and Nepalpada Das, 15–24. Calcutta: Granthamela, 1973.
Mukhopadhyay, Troilakyanath. "Birbala." In *Troilokyanather Granthabali*, vol. 2, 18–28. Calcutta: Basumati Sahitya Mandir, nd.
Mukhopadhyay, Troilakyanath. "Damaru Charit." In *Akhando Troilakyanath*, edited by Prafulla Kumar Patra, 261–362. Calcutta: Patra's Publication, 1957.
Mukhopadhyay, Troilakyanath. *Kankabati*. Edited by Bijanbihari Bhattacharya. Calcutta: Orient Books, BE 1367.
Mukhopadhyay, Troilakyanath. "Lullu." In *Troilokyanather Granthabali*, vol. 2, 29–49. Calcutta: Basumati Sahitya Mandir, nd.
Nag, Arun, ed. *Sateek Hutom Pyanchar Naksha*. Calcutta: Subarnarekha, 1992.
Parashuram. "Bhushundir Mathe." In *Gaddalika*. Calcutta: Brajendranath Bandyopadhyay, 1924.
Parashuram. *Gaddalika*. Calcutta: Gouranga Press, 1924.

Phukan, Haliram Dhekial. *Assam Buranji*. Edited by Jatindra Mohan Bhattacharjee. Gauhati: Mokshada Pustakalaya, 1962 [1829].

Ray, Bharati, ed. *Sekaler Narishiksha: Bamabodhini Patrika 1270–1329*. Calcutta: University of Calcutta Press, 1994.

Ray, D. C. *Debganer Martye Agaman*. Calcutta: Dey's Publishing, 1984.

Ray, Kartekeya Chandra Dewan. *Kartekeya Chandra Rayer AtmaJiban Charit*. Calcutta: Indian Associated Publishing Company, BE 1363.

Roy, Kartikeya Chandra. *Atmajiban Charit*. Calcutta: Indian Association Publishing Company, 1956.

Ray, Satyajit. "Nil Atanka." In *Galpa 101*, 99–107. Calcutta: Ananda Publishers, 2001.

Roy, Bangachandra. "Amar Kshudra Jibanalekhya." In *Atma Katha*, vol. 4, edited by Naresh Jana, Manu Jana, and Kamalkumar Sanyal. Calcutta: Ananya, 1986.

Sarkar, Akshay Chandra. "Bol Dekhi Bhai ki hoi Mole." *Nabajiban* 1, no. 4 (1884): 474–76.

Sarkar, Akshay Chandra. "Pita Putra." In *Atmakatha*, vol. 5, edited by Naresh Jana, Manu Jana and Kamalkumar Sanyal, 3–119. Calcutta: Ananya Prakashan, 1987.

Sarkar, Akshay Chandra. "Planchetter Prolap." *Sadharani* (February 28, 1875): 211–12.

Sen, Dinesh Chandra. *Gharer Katha O Juga Sahitya*. Calcutta: Jigansha, BE 1329.

Sen, Dinesh Chandra. *Gharer Katha O Jugsahitya*. Calcutta: Jignyasya Press, 1969.

Sen, Nabin Chandra. "Sahitya Parishat o Shiksha Pranali." In *Amar Jiban*, vol. 5, 71–98. Calcutta: Sanyal and Co., 1913.

Sen, Paritosh. *Jindabahar Lane*. Calcutta: Papyrus, BE 1366.

Sen, Sukumar. *Galper Bhut*. Calcutta: Ananda Publishers, 1982.

Shastri, Priyanath, ed. *The Autobiography of Maharshi Devendranath Tagore*. Translated by Satyendranath Tagore and Indira Devi. London: Macmillan, 1914.

Shastri, Shibnath. *Atmacharit*. Calcutta: Signet Press, BE 1359.

Shastri, Shibnath. "Atmacharit." In *Atma Katha*, vol. 5, edited by Naresh Jana, Manu Jana, and Kamalkumar Sanyal. Calcutta: Ananya, 1987.

Tagore, Abanindranath. *Abanindra Rachanabali*, vol. 1. Calcutta: Prakash Bhaban, 1973.

Tagore, Debendranath. *Atmajiboni*. Edited by Satishchandra Chakrabarty. Calcutta: Viswabharati Press, 1927.

Tagore, Debendranath. *Pujyapad Srimaharshi Debendranath Thakurer Swarachit Jiban Charit*. Calcutta: Banerjee Press, 1898.

Tagore, Rabindranath. "Kankal." *Sadhana* 1, no. 1. (Falgun 1892): 287–98.

Tagore, Rabindranath. "Manihara." In *Galpaguchcha*, vol. 2, 394–406. Calcutta: Visva Bharati, 1975.

Tagore, Rabindranath. "Sok Sabha." In *Rabindra Rachanbali*, vol. 9, 529–36. Calcutta: Visva Bharati Press, 1958.

PRIMARY SOURCES, ENGLISH

Anon. "Bengali Literature." *Calcutta Review* 52, no. 104 (1871): 294–316.

Anon. *A Few Facts Regarding the Life and Career of the Late Roy Obhoy Chandra Das Bahadur*. Calcutta: The University Press, 1893.

Anon. "Fire Walking Ceremony." *Journal of the Society for Psychical Research* 9, no. 173 (November 1900): 312–21.

Anon. "The Indian Rope Trick." *Journal of the Society for Psychical Research* 11, no. 213 (1904–5): 299–308.

Anon. "Pearychand Mittra Obituary." *Journal of the Agricultural and Horticultural Society* 6 (1882): xxxix.

Anon. *The Press on the Death of the Late Nawab Bahadur Abdool Luteef with Proceedings of the Public Meetings Held in Honour of His Memory*. Calcutta: The Mahomedan Literary Society of Calcutta, 1893.

Anon. "Religions in India." *Calcutta Review* 66, no. 131 (1878): 190–226.

Anon. *Who Is Mrs. Besant and Why Has She Come to India?* Madras: Christian Literature Society, 1894.

Bengal Magazine 6 (August 1877–July 1878).

Besant, Annie. "Theosophical Worthies: Norendranath Sen." *The Theosophist* 32, no. 3 (January 1911): 694–96.

Blavatsky, Helena Petrovna. *Five Messages*. Bombay: The Theosophical Company, 1930.

Blavatsky, Helena Petrovna. *Isis Unveiled Vol. 1*. Point Loma, CA: The Aryan Theosophical Press, 1919.

Blavatsky, Helena Petrovna. "What Are the Theosophists." *The Theosophist* 1, no. 1 (October 1879): 5–7.

Bodding, Rev. P. O. *Studies in Santal Medicine and Connected Folklore*. Calcutta: Asiatic Society of Bengal, 1925.

Bond, Ruskin, ed. *Ghost Stories from the Raj*. New Delhi: Rupa and Co., 2002.

Bonnerjea, Biren. *A Dictionary of Superstitions and Mythology*. London: Folk Press Limited, 1927.

Busteed, H. E. *Echoes from Old Calcutta, Being Chiefly Reminiscences of the Days of Warren Hastings, Francis and Impey*. London: W. Thacker, 1908.

Chakrabarti, Kshetrapal. *Lectures on Hindu Religion, Philosophy and Yoga*. Calcutta: New Britannia Press, 1893.

Chakrabarti, Kshetrapal. "Religious Aspects of the Early Tantras." *The Theosophist* 12, no. 1 (October 1890): 23–29.

Chevers, Norman. *Manual of Medical Jurisprudence*. Calcutta: Bengal Military Orphan Press, 1856.

Cotton, H. E. A. *Calcutta, Old and New: A Historical and Descriptive Handbook to the City*. 1907. Calcutta: General Printers and Publishers, 1980.

Crooke, William. *Religion and Folklore of Northern India*. Oxford: Oxford University Press, 1926.

Day, Rev. Lal Behari. *Bengal Peasant Life; Folk-Tales of Bengal; Recollections of My School-Days*. Edited by Mahadevprasad Saha. Calcutta: Editions Indian, 1969.

Day, Rev. Lal Behari. *Govinda Samanta or the History of a Bengal Raiyat*. London: Macmillan, 1916.

Dehon, Rev. P. "Religion and Customs of the Uraons." In *Memoirs of the Asiatic Society of Bengal* 1, no. 9, 121–81. Calcutta: Baptist Mission Press, 1906.

Dutt, Paramananda. *Moti Lal Ghose*. Calcutta: Amrita Bazar Patrika Office, 1935.

Dutt, Romesh C. "The Late Bankim Chandra Chatterjee C.I.E." *Journal of the Royal Asiatic Society of Great Britain and Ireland* (1897): 700–702.

Elliot, Robert Henry. *The Myth of the Mystic East*. Edinburgh: Wm. Blackwood and Sons, 1935.

Farquhar, J. N. *Modern Religious Movements in India*. 1914. New Delhi: Munshiram Manoharlal, 1977.

Fergusson, Robert Menzies. *Rambles in the Far North*. 2nd ed. London: Alex. Gardner, Paisley, 1884.

Ghose, Hemendra Prasad. "Decay of Villages in Bengal." *Calcutta Review* 194 (July 1907): 394–408.

Ghose, M. K. *Life beyond Death*. 1934. New Delhi: Cosmo Publications, 1987.

Ghose, N. N. *Memoirs of Maharaja Nubkisssen Bahadur*. Calcutta: K. B. Basu, 1901.

Ghose, Shishir Kumar. *Indian Sketches*. Calcutta: Patrika Offices, 1923.

Ghose, Shishir Kumar. "The Origin of Theosophy in India." *Hindu Spiritual Magazine* 3, no. 12 (February 1909): 422–28.

Hearn, Lafcadio. *Kwaidan: Stories and Studies of Strange Things*. Boston: Houghton and Mifflin, 1904.

Hunter, W. W. *A Statistical Account of Bengal*. Delhi: Concept Publishing Company, 1976 [1877].

Hunter, W. W. *A Statistical Account of Bengal Vol. 8*. London: Trubner, 1876.

Jinarajadasa, C. "The Future of Brotherhood." *American Theosophist* 31, no. 3 (March 1943): 65.

Jinarajadasa, C. "The Negro and South America." *American Theosophist* 31, no. 3 (March 1943): 66.

Kilner, Walter J. *The Human Atmosphere or the Aura Made Visible by the Aid of Chemical Screens*. London: Rebman Company, 1911.

Kipling, Rudyard. "My Own True Ghost Story." In *The Phantom Rickshaw and Other Ghost Stories*, 51–66. New York: R. F. Fenno, 1899.

Lang, Andrew. *Magic and Religion*. London: Longmans, Green, and Co., 1901.

Long, James. *A Descriptive Catalogue of Bengali Works*. Calcutta: Sanders, Cones, 1855.

Lutyens, Emily. *Candles in the Sun*. London: Rupert Hart-Davis, 1957.

Madge, E. W. "Anglo-Indian Ghost Stories." *Bengal Past and Present* 3, no. 1 (January–March 1909): 1–6.

Maskelyne, John Nevil. "Oriental Jugglery." In *The Supernatural?*, edited by Lionel Weatherly, 153–81. Bristol: J. W. Arrowsmith, 1891.

Mitra, Subal Chandra. *Isvar Chandra Vidyasagar: A Study of His Life and Works*. Calcutta: New Bengal Press, 1902.

Mittra, Peary Chand. *On the Soul: Its Nature and Development*. Calcutta: Stanhope Press, 1881.

Mittra, Peary Chand. *Spiritual Stray Leaves*. Calcutta: Stanhope Press, 1879.

Morton, Rev. W. *Drishtantavakya Sangraha: A Collection of Proverbs, Bengali and Sanskrit with Their Translation and Application in English*. Calcutta: Baptist Mission Press, 1832.

Mukerji, S. *Indian Ghost Stories*. 2nd ed. Allahabad: A. J. Wheeler, 1917.

Olcott, H. S. *A Historical Retrospect of the Theosophical Society 1875–1896*. Madras: Theosophical Society, 1896.

Radice, William, ed. *Selected Short Stories by Rabindranath Tagore*. London: Penguin Books, 1991.

Risley, H. H. *The Tribes and Castes of Bengal*. Vol 2. Calcutta: Bengal Secretariat Press, 1892.

Roy, Gopaul Chunder. *The Causes, Symptoms and Treatment of Burdwan Fever, or The Epidemic Fever of Lower Bengal*. Calcutta: Thacker, Spink, 1876.

S. M. "Spiritualism in Calcutta." *National Magazine* 28, no. 4 (April 1916): 170–71.

Samanta, Suchitra, ed. *Hauntings: Bangla Ghost Stories*. New Delhi: Katha, 2000.

Satthianadhan, S. *Theosophy: An Appeal to My Countrymen*. Madras: Christian Literature Society, 1893.

Sen, Dinesh Chandra. *The Folk Literature of Bengal*. Calcutta: University of Calcutta Press, 1920.

Sen, Dinesh Chandra. *History of Bengali Language and Literature*. Calcutta: University of Calcutta Press, 1911.

Tagore, Rabindranath. *My Boyhood Days*. Translated by Marjorie Sykes. Calcutta: Visva Bharati, 1940.

Temple, Richard. "The Travels of Richard Bell (and John Campbell) in the East Indies, Persia, and Palestine 1654–1670." Pts. 1 and 2. *Indian Antiquary* 37 (May 1906): 131–42 (38) (June 1906): 168–78.

Toynbee, George. "The Village Police of Bengal." *Calcutta Review* 7, no. 174 (October 1888): 203–12.

Wenger, J. "Popular Literature of Bengal." *Calcutta Review* 13, no. 26 (January–June 1850): 257–84.

Williams, Monier. *A Sanskrit English Dictionary*. Oxford: Clarendon Press, 1872.

Williams, Monier. "Sraddha Ceremonies at Gaya." *Indian Antiquary* 5 (1876): 200–204.

SECONDARY SOURCES, ENGLISH

Anderson, Benedict. *Imagined Communities: Reflections on the Origin and Spread of Nationalism*. 1983. London: Verso, 2006.

Appadurai, Arjun. *Modernity at Large: Cultural Dimensions of Globalization*. Minneapolis: University of Minnesota Press, 1996.

Aries, Philippe. "Death Inside Out." Translated by Bernard Murchland. *Hastings Center Studies* 2 (1974): 3–18.

Aries, Philippe. *The Hour of Our Death*. New York: Oxford University Press, 1991.

Ashraf, K. M. *Life and Conditions of the People of Hindustan*. Delhi: Jiwan Prashan, 1959.

Assad, Talal. *Formations of the Secular: Christianity, Islam, and Modernity*. Stanford, CA: Stanford University Press, 2003.

Austin, J. L. *How to Do Things with Words*. Oxford: Clarendon Press, 1962.

Bakhtin, Mikhail. *Rabelais and His World*. Bloomington: Indiana University Press, 1984.

Bamberger, Bernard J. "Fear and Love of God in the Old Testament." *Hebrew Union College Annual* 6 (1929): 39–53.

Banerjee, Prathama. *Elementary Aspects of the Political: Histories of the Global South*. Durham, NC: Duke University Press, 2020.

Banerji, S. C. *Tantra in Bengal: A Study in Its Origin, Development and Influence*. Calcutta: Naya Prakash, 1978.

Barlow, Tani, ed. *Formations of Colonial Modernity in East Asia*. Durham, NC: Duke University Press, 1997.

Basak, Sudeshna. *Cultural History of Bengali Proverbs*. Delhi: Gyan Publishers, 2007.

Beecroft, John, and Richard M. Powers, eds. *Kipling: A Selection of His Stories and Poems*. Garden City, NY: Doubleday, 1956.

Behlmer, George K. "Grave Doubts: Victorian Medicine, Moral Panic and the Signs of Death." *Journal of British Studies* 42, no. 2 (2003): 206–35.

Benjamin, Walter. *Illuminations*. Edited with an introduction by Hannah Arendt. New York: Schocken Books, 1969.

Bevir, Mark. "Theosophy and the Origins of the Indian National Congress." *International Journal of Hindu Studies* 7, no. 1/3 (February 2003): 99–115.

Bhabha, Homi. *The Location of Culture*. New York: Routledge, 1994.

Bhattacharjee, Tapodhir. *Makers of Indian Literature: Trailokyanath Mukhopadhyay*. New Delhi: Sahitya Akademi, 2001.

Bhattacharya, Malini, and Abhijit Sen, eds. *Talking of Power: Early Writings by Bengali Women from the Mid-Nineteenth Century to the Beginning of the Twentieth Century*. Calcutta: Stree, 2003.

Bhattacharya, Sabyasachi. *Rabindranath Tagore: An Interpretation*. New Delhi: Penguin Books India, 2011.

Bhattacharya, Tithi. *Sentinels of Culture: Class, Education and the Colonial Intellectual in Bengal 1848–1885*. New Delhi: Oxford University Press, 2005.

Bhattacharya, Tithi. "Tracking the Goddess: Religion, Community, and Identity in the Durga Puja Ceremonies of Nineteenth-Century Calcutta." *Journal of Asian Studies* 66, no. 4 (2007): 919–62.

Bhowmick, P. K. *Occultism in Fringe Bengal*. Calcutta: Subarnarekha, 1978.

Bose, Babu Rashbihari. "Legends and Ballads of the District of Bhagalpur." *Proceedings of the Asiatic Society of Bengal January–December 1871*, 138–51. Calcutta: Baptist Mission Press, 1871.

Bose, Neilesh. *Recasting the Region: Language, Culture and Islam in Colonial Bengal*. New Delhi: Oxford University Press, 2014.

Bose, Sugata, and Ayesha Jalal. *Modern South Asia: History, Culture, Political Economy*. New York: Taylor and Francis, 2006.

Bottigheimer, Ruth B. *Grimms' Bad Girls & Bold Boys: The Moral & Social Vision of the Tales*. New Haven, CT: Yale University Press, 1987.

Brantlinger, Patrick. *Rule of Darkness: British Literature and Imperialism 1830–1914*. Ithaca, NY: Cornell University Press, 1988.

Breckenridge, Carol, and Peter van der Veer, eds. *Orientalism and the Postcolonial Predicament: Perspectives on South Asia*. Philadelphia: University of Pennsylvania Press, 1993.

Brown, C. Mackenzie. *Hindu Perspectives on Evolution: Darwin, Dharma, and Design*. New York: Routledge, 2012.

Buer, M. C. *Health, Wealth and Population in the Early Days of the Industrial Revolution*. London: G. Routledge and Sons, 1926.

Carroll, Bret E. *Spiritualism in Antebellum America*. Bloomington: Indiana University Press, 1997.

Casale, Giancarlo. *The Ottoman Age of Exploration*. Oxford: Oxford University Press, 2010.

Chakrabarti, Kunal. *Religious Process: The Puranas and the Making of a Regional Tradition.* New Delhi: Oxford University Press, 2001.

Chakrabarty, Dipesh. *Habitations of Modernity: Essays in the Wake of Subaltern Studies.* Chicago: University of Chicago Press, 2002.

Chakrabarty, Dipesh. *Provincializing Europe: Postcolonial Thought and Historical Difference.* Princeton, NJ: Princeton University Press, 2000.

Chakrabarty, Hiren. "The Victoria Memorial." In *Calcutta: The Living City*, edited by Sukanta Chaudhuri, 256–60, vol. 1 of *Calcutta: The Living City*. Calcutta: Oxford University Press, 1990.

Chakrabarty, Pratik. *Western Science in Modern India: Metropolitan Methods, Colonial Practices.* New Delhi: Permanent Black, 2004.

Chatterjee, Amal. *Representations of India 1740–1840: The Creation of India in the Colonial Imaginations.* London: Macmillan Press, 1998.

Chatterjee, Partha. "Five Hundred Years of Fear and Love." *Economic and Political Weekly* 33, no. 22 (May 30–June 5, 1998): 1330–36.

Chatterjee, Partha. *The Nation and Its Fragments: Colonial and Postcolonial Histories.* Princeton, NJ: Princeton University Press, 1993.

Chatterjee, Partha. "On Civil and Political Society in Postcolonial Democracies." In *Civil Society: History and Possibility*, edited by Sudipta Kaviraj and Sunil Khilnani, 165–78. Cambridge: Cambridge University Press, 2001.

Chatterjee, Partha. *The Partha Chatterjee Omnibus.* New Delhi: Oxford University Press, 1999.

Chattopadhyay, Bodhisattva. "Kalpavigyan and Imperial Technoscience: Three Nodes of an Argument." *Journal of the Fantastic in the Arts* 28, no. 1 (2017): 102–22.

Chattopadhyay, K. P. "The Chadak Festival in Bengal." *Letters of the Journal of the Asiatic Society of Bengal* 1 (1935): 397–406.

Chaudhuri, Binay Bhushan. *Peasant History of Late Pre-Colonial and Colonial India.* New Delhi: Pearson-Longman, 2008.

Chibber, Vivek. *Postcolonial Theory and the Specter of Capital.* London: Verso, 2013.

Clery, E. J. *The Rise of Supernatural Fiction 1762–1800.* Cambridge: Cambridge University Press, 1995.

Clough, Paul, and Jon P. Mitchell, eds. *Powers of Good and Evil: Social Transformation and Popular Belief.* New York: Berghahn Books, 2001.

Cohn, Bernard S. "The Census, Social Structure and Objectification in South Asia." In *An Anthropologist among the Historians and Other Essays*, 224–54. New Delhi: Oxford University Press, 1987.

Cohn, Bernard S. *Colonialism and Its Forms of Knowledge.* Princeton, NJ: Princeton University Press, 1996.

Comaroff, Jean, and John Comaroff, eds. *Millennial Capitalism and the Culture of Neoliberalism.* Durham, NC: Duke University Press, 2001.

Connor, Steven. *Dumbstruck: A Cultural History of Ventriloquism.* Oxford: Oxford University Press, 2000.

Cooper, Frederick. *Colonialism in Question: Theory, Knowledge, History.* Berkeley: University of California Press, 2005.

Daniels, Timothy P. *Building Cultural Nationalism in Malaysia: Identity, Representation and Citizenship*. New York: Routledge, 2005.

Darnton, Robert. "Peasants Tell Tales: The Meaning of Mother Goose." In *The Great Cat Massacre and Other Episodes in French Cultural History*, 9–74. New York: Basic Books, 1984.

Das, Shinjini. *Vernacular Medicine in Colonial India: Family, Market and Homeopathy*. Cambridge: Cambridge University Press, 2019.

Das, Sisir Kumar. *A History of Indian Literature 1800–1919: Western Impact, Indian Response*. New Delhi: Sahiya Akademi, 1991.

Dasgupta, Uma. "The Indian Press 1870–1880: A Small World of Journalism." *Modern Asian Studies* 2, no. 2 (1977): 213–35.

Datta, Pradip. *Carving Blocs: Communal Ideology in Early Twentieth Century Bengal*. New Delhi: Oxford University Press, 1999.

Davidson, Neil. *Nation-States: Consciousness and Competition*. Chicago: Haymarket Books, 2016.

Deb Roy, Rohan. *Malarial Subjects: Empire, Medicine and Nonhumans in British India, 1820–1909*. Cambridge: Cambridge University Press, 2017.

Derrett, J. M. "British Administration of Hindu Law." *Comparative Studies in Society and History* 4, no. 1 (1961): 10–52.

Deshpande, Prachi. *Creative Pasts: Historical Memory and Identity in Western India*. New York: Columbia University Press, 2007.

Dixon, Joy. *Divine Feminine: Theosophy and Feminism in England*. Baltimore, MD: Johns Hopkins University Press, 2001.

Doniger, Wendy. *On Hinduism*. New York: Oxford University Press, 2014.

Dossal, Mariam. *Imperial Designs and Indian Realities: The Planning of Bombay City, 1845–1875*. New York: Oxford University Press, 1991.

Dube, Saurabh, ed. *Enchantments of Modernity: Empire, Nation, Globalization*. Delhi: Routledge India, 2010.

Dube, Saurabh, and Ishita Banerjee-Dube, eds. *Unbecoming Modern: Colonialism, Modernity, Colonial Modernities*. New Delhi: Social Science Press, 2006.

Duffy, Eamon. *The Stripping of the Altars: Traditional Religion in England c.1400–c.1580*. New Haven, CT: Yale University Press, 1992.

Eaton, Richard M. *The Rise of Islam in the Bengal Frontier 1204–1760*. Berkeley: University of California Press, 1993.

Edwards, Kathryn A. "Medieval Ghost Stories: An Anthology of Miracles, Marvels and Prodigies." *History Compass* 10, no. 4 (April 2012): 353–66.

Eisenstadt, S. N. *Comparative Civilizations and Multiple Modernities*. Leiden: Brill, 2003.

Eliot, T. S. *Collected Poems*. New York: Harcourt, Brace & World, 1965.

Ellwood, Robert S. *Alternative Altars: Unconventional and Eastern Spirituality in America*. Chicago: University of Chicago Press, 1979.

Emmott, D. H. "Alexander Duff and the Foundation of Modern Education in India." *British Journal of Educational Studies* 13, no. 2 (1965): 160–69.

Enright, D. J., ed. *The Oxford Book of the Supernatural*. New York: Oxford University Press, 1994.

Fabian, Johannes. *Time and the Other: How Anthropology Makes Its Object*. New York: Columbia University Press, 1983.
Farquhar, John Nicol. *An Outline of the Religious Literature of India*. London: Oxford University Press, 1920.
Febvre, Lucien. *The Problem of Unbelief in the Sixteenth Century: The Religion of Rabelais*. Translated by Beatrice Gottlieb. Cambridge, MA: Harvard University Press, 1985.
Feenberg, Andrew. *Alternative Modernity: The Technical Turn in Philosophy and Social Theory*. Berkeley: University of California Press, 1995.
Fick, Caroline. *The Making of Haiti: The San Domingo Revolution from Below*. Knoxville: University of Tennessee Press, 1990.
Forbes, Geraldine. *Women in Modern India*. Cambridge: Cambridge University Press, 1996.
Foucault, Michel. *The History of Sexuality, Volume 1: An Introduction*. Translated by Robert Hurley. New York: Pantheon Books, 1978.
Foucault, Michel. *The Order of Things: An Archaeology of the Human Sciences*. New York: Random House, 1970.
Fox, Adam. *Oral and Literate Culture in England 1500–1700*. Oxford: Clarendon Press, 2000.
Freud, Sigmund. *The Uncanny*. Translated by David Mclintock. London: Penguin Books, 2003.
Fukuoka, Maki. *The Premise of Fidelity: Science, Fidelity and Representing the Real in Nineteenth-Century Japan*. Stanford, CA: Stanford University Press, 2012.
Fuller, Jason D. "Colonial Devotional Paths." In *Hinduism in the Modern World*, edited by Brian A. Hatcher, 80–95. New York: Routledge, 2016.
Gaonkar, Dilip P., ed. *Alternative Modernities*. Durham, NC: Duke University Press, 2001.
Geertz, Hildred. "An Anthropology of Religion and Magic, I." *Journal of Interdisciplinary History* 6, no. 1 (1975): 71–89.
Gikandi, Simon. "Globalization and the Claims of Postcoloniality." *South Atlantic Quarterly* 100, no. 3 (2001): 627–58.
Gittings, Clare. *Death, Burial and the Individual in Early Modern England*. Dover, NH: Croom Helm, 1984.
Godwin, Joscelyn. *The Theosophical Enlightenment*. Albany: State University of New York Press, 1994.
Gramsci, Antonio. "Observations on Folklore." In *The Antonio Gramsci Reader: Selected Writings 1916–1935*, edited by David Forgacs, 360–62. New York: New York University Press, 2000.
Gupta, Narayani. *Delhi between Two Empires 1803–1931: Society, Government and Urban Growth*. Delhi: Oxford University Press, 1981.
Hacking, Ian. *The Taming of Chance*. Cambridge: Cambridge University Press, 1990.
Hammer, Olav, and Mikael Rothstein, eds. *Handbook of the Theosophical Current*. Leiden: Brill, 2013.
Hara, Minoru. "Sraddha in the Sense of Desire." *Asiatische Studien* 46 (1992): 180–94.
Harrison, Peter. *The Territories of Science and Religion*. Chicago: University of Chicago Press, 2015.
Harvey, David. *The Limits to Capital*. Oxford: Basil Blackwell, 1982.
Harvey, David. *Spaces of Hope*. Berkeley: University of California Press, 2000.

Hatcher, Brian. *Bourgeois Hinduism, or The Faith of the Modern Vedantists: Rare Discourses from Early Colonial Bengal.* New York: Oxford University Press, 2008.
Heaney, Seamus. "All Ireland's Bard." *Atlantic Monthly* 280, no. 5 (November 1997): 155–60.
Hodgen, Margaret T. *Early Anthropology in the Sixteenth and Seventeenth Centuries.* Philadelphia: University of Pennsylvania Press, 1964.
Hodgkin, Thomas. *Nationalism in Colonial Africa.* London: Frederick Mueller, 1956.
Houlbrooke, Ralph. "Death, Church, and Family in England between the Late Fifteenth and Early Eighteenth Centuries." In *Death, Ritual, and Bereavement,* edited by Ralph Houlbrooke, 25–42. London: Routledge Press, 1989.
Hutchins, Francis G. *The Illusion of Permanence: British Imperialism in India.* Princeton, NJ: Princeton University Press, 1967.
Inden, Ronald. *Imagining India.* Bloomington: Indiana University Press, 1990.
Irani, Ayesha. "Sacred Biography, Translation, and Conversion: The Nabīvaṃśa of Saiyad Sultān and the Making of Bengali Islam, 1600–Present," PhD dissertation, University of Pennsylvania, 2011.
Jacob, Margaret C. "The Enlightenment Redefined: The Formation of Modern Civil Society." *Social Research* 58, no. 2 (1991): 475–95.
Jagganadham, P. R. Hay. *Cremation and Burial or Extracts from a Paper Read at the Indian Medical Congress.* Lahore: Arorbans Press, 1895.
Jamison, Stephanie W. *Sacrificed Wife, Sacrificer's Wife: Women, Ritual and Hospitality in Ancient India.* New York: Oxford University Press, 1996.
Jayawardena, Kumari. *The White Woman's Other Burden.* London: Routledge, 1995.
Josephson-Storm, Jason A. *The Myth of Disenchantment: Magic, Modernity, and the Birth of the Human Sciences.* Chicago: University of Chicago Press, 2017.
Kakati, Bani Kanta. *The Mother Goddess Kamakhya.* Gauhati: Lawyers' Book Stall, 1948.
Kaviraj, Sudipta. "Religion, Politics and Modernity." In *Crisis and Change in Contemporary India,* edited by Upendra Baxi and Bhikhu Parekh, 295–316. New Delhi: Sage, 1995.
King, Anthony D. *Colonial Urban Development: Culture, Social Power and Environment.* London: Routledge and Kegan Paul, 1976.
King, Richard. *Orientalism and Religion: Postcolonial Theory, India and the Mystic East.* London: Routledge, 1999.
Kirk, Robert. *The Secret Commonwealth of Elves, Fauns and Fairies.* Introduction by Marina Warner. New York: New York Review of Books, 2007.
Koselleck, Reinhart. *Futures Past: On the Semantics of Historical Time.* New York: Columbia University Press, 2004.
Kwon, Heonik. *Ghosts of War in Vietnam.* Cambridge: Cambridge University Press, 2013.
Lal, Vinay. *The History of History: Politics and Scholarship in Modern India.* New Delhi: Oxford University Press, 2003.
Lamont, Peter, and Crispin Bates. "Conjuring Images of India in Nineteenth-Century Britain." *Social History* 32, no. 3 (August 2007): 308–24.
Lefebvre, Henri. *The Production of Space.* Boston: Blackwell Press, 1991.
Luckhurst, Roger. "Knowledge, Belief and the Supernatural at the Imperial Margin." In *The Victorian Supernatural,* edited by Nicola Bown, Carolyn Burdett, and P. Thurschwell, 197–216. Cambridge: Cambridge University Press, 2004.

Ludden, David, ed. *Making India Hindu: Religion, Community and the Politics of Democracy in India*. New Delhi: Oxford University Press, 2005.

Ludden, David. "Orientalist Empiricisms and the Transformations of Colonial Knowledge." In *Orientalism and the Post-Colonial Predicament*, edited by C. A. Breckenridge and Peter Van der Veer, 250–78. Philadelphia: University of Pennsylvania Press, 1993.

Lukacs, Georg. *History and Class Consciousness*. London: Merlin, 1971.

Madan, T. N. *Modern Myths, Locked Minds: Secularism and Fundamentalism in India*. New Delhi: Oxford University Press, 1997.

Mani, Lata. *Contentious Traditions: The Debate on Sati in Colonial India*. Berkeley: University of California Press, 1998.

Manjapra, Kris. *Colonialism in Global Perspective*. Cambridge: Cambridge University Press, 2020.

Marshall, P. J. *Bengal the British Bridgehead: Eastern India 1740–1828*. Cambridge: Cambridge University Press, 1988.

Marx, Karl. *Economic and Philosophical Manuscripts 1844*. Moscow: Progress Publishers, 1977 [1959].

Marx, Karl, and Frederick Engels. *Selected Correspondence*. Translated and edited by Dona Torr. London: Lawrence and Wishart, 1941.

Marx, Karl, and Frederick Engels. *Selected Works*. Vol. 1. Moscow: Progress Publishers, 1969.

Massey, Doreen. *Space, Place and Gender*. Minneapolis: University of Minnesota Press, 1994.

McCann, Gillian. "Emergent Representations of the East: The Role of Theosophical Periodicals, 1879–1900." In *Imagining the East: The Early Theosophical Society*, edited by Tim Rudbog and Erik Sand, 165–86. New York: Oxford University Press, 2020.

McCorristine, Shane. *Spectres of the Self: Thinking about Ghosts and Ghost-Seeing in England, 1750–1920*. Cambridge: Cambridge University Press, 2010.

McGuire, John. *Making of a Colonial Mind: A Quantitative Study of the Bhadralok in Calcutta 1857–1885*. Canberra: Australian National University Press, 1983.

McNally, David. *Monsters of the Market: Zombies, Vampires and Global Capitalism*. Chicago: Haymarket Books, 2012.

Merton, Robert. *Social Theory and Social Structure*. Glencoe, IL: The Free Press of Glencoe, 1949.

Meyer, Birgit, and Peter Pels, eds. *Magic and Modernity: Interfaces of Revelation and Concealment*. Stanford, CA: Stanford University Press, 2003.

Mitchell, Timothy, ed. *Questions of Modernity*. Minneapolis: University of Minnesota Press, 2000.

Mizutani, Satoshi. *The Meaning of White Race, Class, and the "Domiciled Community" in British India 1858–1930*. Oxford: Oxford University Press, 2011.

Mukhia, Harbans. "Illegal Extortions from Peasants, Artisans and Menials in Eighteenth Century Eastern Rajasthan." *Indian Economic and Social History Review* 14, no. 2 (1977): 231–45.

Mukhopadhyay, Anindita. *Behind the Mask: The Cultural Definition of the Legal Subject in Colonial Bengal 1715–1911*. New Delhi: Oxford University Press, 2006.

Mukhopadhyay, Mriganka. "Occult's First Foot Soldier in Bengal: Peary Chand Mittra." In *The Occult Nineteenth Century: Roots, Development and Impact in the Modern World*, edited by Lukas Pokorny and Franz Winter. London: Palgrave Macmillan, 2021.

Nandy, Ashis. "The Twilight of Certitudes: Secularism, Hindu Nationalism, and Other Masks of Enculturation." *Alternatives* 22, no. 2 (1997): 157–76.

Noakes, Richard J. "'Instruments to Lay Hold of Spirits': Technologizing the Bodies of Victorian Spiritualism." In *Bodies/Machines*, edited by Iwan Rhys Morus, 125–63. London: Bloomsbury, 2002.

Noakes, Richard J. "Telegraphy Is an Occult Art: Cromwell Fleetwood Varley and the Diffusion of Electricity to the Other World." *British Journal for the History of Science* 32, no. 4 (1999): 421–59.

Nora, Pierre. "Between Memory and History: Les Lieux de Memoire." *Representations* 29 (1989): 7–24.

Nuttall, Sarah. *Entanglement: Literary and Cultural Reflections on Postapartheid*. Johannesburg: Wits University Press, 2009.

Obeyesekere, Gananath. "The Rebirth Eschatology and Its Transformations: A Contribution to the Sociology of Early Buddhism." In *Karma and Rebirth in Classical Indian Traditions*, edited by Wendy Doniger O'Flaherty, 137–64. Berkeley: University of California Press, 1980.

Oldenburg, Veena. *The Making of Colonial Lucknow: 1856–1877*. New Delhi: Oxford University Press, 1989.

Ollman, Bertell. *Dance of the Dialectic: Steps in Marx's Method*. Urbana: University of Illinois Press, 2003.

Ong, Walter J. "Before Textuality: Orality and Interpretation." *Oral Tradition* 3/3 (1988): 259–69.

Owen, Alex. *The Darkened Room: Women, Power, and Spiritualism in Late Victorian England*. Chicago: University of Chicago Press, 1989.

Owen, Alex. *The Place of Enchantment: British Occultism and the Culture of the Modern*. Chicago: University of Chicago Press, 2004.

Pal, Pratapaditya. *Hindu Religion and Iconology According to the Tantrasara*. Los Angeles: Vichitra Press, 1981.

Pashukanis, Eugene. "General Theory of Law and Marxism." In *Soviet Legal Philosophy*, translated by Hugh W. Babb, vol. 5 of *20th Century Legal Philosophy*. Cambridge, MA: Harvard University Press, 1968 [1951].

Prakash, Gyan. *Bonded Histories: Genealogies of Labor Servitude in Colonial India*. Cambridge: Cambridge University Press, 1990.

Prakash, Gyan. *Another Reason: Science and the Imagination of Modern India*. Princeton, NJ: Princeton University Press, 1999.

Putnam, Hilary. *Reason, Truth and History*. Cambridge: Cambridge University Press, 1981.

Radice, William. "Review of 'Travels to Europe: Self and Other in Bengali Travel Narratives 1870–1910' by Simonti Sen." *Bulletin of the School of Oriental and African Studies, University of London* 69, no. 1 (2006): 158–60.

Ren, Jiantao, and Andrew Lambert. "A Sense of Awe: On the Differences between Confucian Thought and Christianity." *Frontiers of Philosophy in China* 5, no. 1 (2010): 111–33.

Roy, Asim. *The Islamic Syncretistic Tradition in Bengal*. Princeton, NJ: Princeton University Press, 1983.
Sahlins, Marshall. *The New Science of the Enchanted Universe: An Anthropology of Most of Humanity*. Princeton, NJ: Princeton University Press, 2022.
Said, Edward. *Orientalism*. New York: Pantheon Books, 1978.
Said, Edward. *Orientalism*. Harmondsworth: Penguin, 1995 [1978].
Salzinger, Leslie. *Genders in Production: Making Workers in Mexico's Global Factories*. Berkeley: University of California Press, 2003.
Sarkar, Sumit. *Writing Social History*. New Delhi: Oxford University Press, 1998.
Sarkar, Tanika. *Hindu Wife, Hindu Nation: Community, Religion, and Cultural Nationalism*. Bloomington: Indiana University Press, 2001.
Sayers, Matthew R. *Feeding the Dead: Ancestor Worship in Ancient India*. New York: Oxford University Press, 2013.
Scalmer, Sean. *Gandhi in the West: The Mahatma and the Rise of Radical Protest*. Cambridge: Cambridge University Press, 2011.
Segal, Robert A. "Tylor's Anthropomorphic Theory of Religion." *Religion* 25 (1995): 23–30.
Sen, Amiya. *Hindu Revivalism in Bengal*. New Delhi: Oxford University Press, 2001.
Sen, Krishna. "Lessons in Self-Fashioning: 'Bamabodhini Patrika' and the Education of Women in Colonial Bengal." *Victorian Periodicals Review* 37, no. 2 (Summer 2004): 176–91.
Sengoopta, Chandak. *Rays before Satyajit: Creativity and Modernity in Colonial India*. New Delhi: Oxford University Press, 2016.
Sen Gupta, Pragya, and Sriparna Das. "Reading Rain, Reading River: An Interpretative Discussion on Rajbanshi Folk Ritual." *Translation Today* 10, no. 2 (2016): 84–92.
Shaikh, Anwar. *Capitalism: Competition, Conflict, Crises*. Oxford: Oxford University Press, 2016.
Shakespeare, William. *A Midsummer Night's Dream*. Edited by Henry Cuningham. London: Methuen, 1905.
Singha, Radhika. *A Despotism of Law: Crime and Justice in Early Colonial India*. New Delhi: Oxford University Press, 1998.
Spencer, Dorothy M. *Indian Fiction in English*. Philadelphia: University of Pennsylvania Press, 1960.
Stanziani, Alessandro. *Labor on the Fringes of Empire: Voice, Exit and the Law* (ebook). Accessed June 30, 2022.
Staubermann, Klaus. "Tying the Knot: Skill, Judgement, and Authority in the 1870s Leipzig Spiritistic Experiments." *British Journal for the History of Science* 34 (2001): 67–80.
Strube, Julian. *Global Tantra: Religion, Science, and Nationalism in Colonial Modernity*. New York: Oxford University Press, 2022.
Subrahmanyam, Sanjay. "Hearing Voices: Vignettes of Early Modernity in South Asia, 1400–1750." *Daedalus* 127, no. 3 (1998): 75–104.
Tambiah, Stanley J. *Magic, Science, Religion, and the Scope of Rationality*. Cambridge: Cambridge University Press, 1990.

Taussig, Michael. *The Devil and Commodity Fetishism in South America*. Chapel Hill: University of North Carolina Press, 2010 [1980].

Taylor, Charles. "Modes of Secularism." In *Secularism and Its Critics*, edited by Rajeev Bhargava, 31–53. Delhi: Oxford University Press, 1998.

Taylor, Philip, ed. *Modernity and Re-enchantment: Religion in Post-revolutionary Vietnam*. Lanham, Plymouth: Lexington Books, 2007.

Thomas, Keith. *Religion and the Decline of Magic*. New York: Scribner Press, 1971.

Thompson, E. P. "Anthropology and the Discipline of Historical Context." *Midland History* 1, no. 3 (1972): 41–55.

Thompson, Edward. *The Other Side of the Medal*. 3rd ed. London: Hogarth Press, 1930.

Thurschwell, Pamela. *Literature, Technology and Magical Thinking, 1880–1920*. Cambridge: Cambridge University Press, 2001.

Trautmann, Thomas. *Aryans and British India*. New Delhi: Vistaar Publication, 1997.

Van der Veer, Peter. *Imperial Encounters: Religion and Modernity in India and Britain*. Princeton, NJ: Princeton University Press, 2001.

Viswanathan, Gauri. *Masks of Conquest: Literary Study and British Rule in India*. New York: Columbia University Press, 1989.

Viswanathan, Gauri. "Ordinary Business of Occult." *Critical Enquiry* 27 (Autumn 2000): 1–20.

Wallerstein, Emmanuel. "Voluntary Associations." In *Political Parties and National Integration in Tropical Africa*, edited by Carl G Rosberg, James S. Coleman, 318–39. Berkeley: African Studies Center, University of California, 1964.

Walker, James. "The Exorcism App: Four Apps That Claim to Communicate with Spirits." NS Business, October 31, 2018. https://www.ns-businesshub.com/transport/the-exorcism-app/.

Warner, Marina. *Fairy Tale: A Very Short Introduction*. Oxford: Oxford University Press, 2018 [2014].

Watenpaugh, Keith David. *Being Modern in the Middle East: Revolution, Nationalism, Colonialism, and the Arab Middle Class*. Princeton, NJ: Princeton University Press, 2014.

Williams, Raymond. 1961. *The Long Revolution*. Peterborough, Canada: Broadview Press, 2001.

Winter, Jay. *Sites of Memory, Sites of Mourning: The Great War in European Cultural History*. Cambridge: Cambridge University Press, 1995.

WEBSITES

Tagore, Rabindranath. *Collected Works*. http://museum.rbu.ac.in/rabindranath_tagore/list_works7.htm.

Index

abstract labor, 10–11
abwabs, extraction from poor of, 32
adda, 74, 172n59
adhikar-bheda, 151
afterlife, Bengali ideas about, 6
Agricultural and Horticultural Society of India, 143–44, 149
Ahmed, Humayun, 22
Ajavikas, 68
Albert Temple of Science, 64–65
Ali, Mir Khoram, 47–48, 50–51
Aloukik Rahasya, 19, 60–62, 66–67
American Theosophist, 139
Amrita Bazar Patrika, 56, 65, 148
Anderson, J. D., 37
Andrews, C. F., 105
animal magnetism, 142–43
anticolonial movement: Scientific Spiritualism and, 72–73; Theosophy and, 142, 146–50, 152–54. *See also* nationalism
Aries, Philippe, 93–94
Arundale, George, 140
Arundale, Rukmini Devi, 140
Arunodaya, 79–80
Aryadarshan, 59
Aryans: Hindu nationalism and, 72; pre-Aryan goddesses and, 42–45; scientific education and, 59–60
Asiatic Society of Bengal, 11, 149

Assad, Talal, 152–53
Assam, religion and gods in, 42
atheism, in Indian literature, 117–18
atmas (soul), 69–71, 119
Aubrey, John, 13–14, 18
Auckland (Lord), 170n14

Baggally, W. W., 136
Balfour, Arthur, 135
Balluka Sagara (Buddhist shrine), 47
Bama Bodhini Patrika, 160n25
Bamberger, Bernard J., 40
Banabibi, 38
Bandyopadhyay, Panchkori, 80, 126–27
Bandyopadhyay, Rangalal, 75
Banerjea, Kailas Chandra, 36
Banerjee, Dinu, 141
Banerjee, Sushila, 141
Bangabasi, 118
Bangadarshan, 59
Bangiya Sahita Parishat, 30, 71, 128, 145, 156–57, 170n16
Baptist Mission Press, 25
Basantak, 56, 78
Basu, Man Kumari, 128
Basu, Rajnarayan, 51, 58, 122–23, 169n8, 170n16
Basu, Rajshekhar, 112
Bates, Rosa, 149

Beadon, Cecil, 93
Beames, John, 145
Beauchamp, Henry K., 135
begar/beth-begar, 32
Beings: capitalist modernity and, 7–8; in children's literature, 8; fairies as, 43; ghosts as, 35
belief: English education and, 9; Roy's discussion of, 53–54; in Tagore's stories, 107–8; in Victorian literature, 108
Bell, Richard, 181n3
Bengal Academy, 146
Bengali culture: *adda* (social gatherings) in, 74; Bhadralok elite influence on, 144–45; Bhadralok in, 5–6; colonialism and, 11–18, 160n24; death and afterlife in, 18–21; ethnography of, 29–30; fear in, 156–57; folklore and ethnographic literature of, 30; ghosts in, 84–88, 130–31; Hindu nationalism and, 58; Islam in, 37–45; mortality and morality in, 95–96; mother goddess worship in, 42–43; occultism in, 57–64, 142–43; science in, 5, 12–13, 20–21; *tantrik* and *roja* figures in, 45–51; Theosophy and, 145–46; uncanny in, 3–4
Bengal Magazine, 29, 36
Bengal Peasant Life (Day), 28
Bengal Theosophical Society, 149
Benjamin, Walter, 32
bereavement. *See* mourning
Bérigny, Thiennette de, 143
Besant, Annie, 141–42, 146, 150, 154
bhadra: class, caste and Western education of, 24; ghosts and, 24; meaning of, 23–24; traditional (premodern) ghosts and, 26–29
Bhadralok elite: authentic and indigenous traditions of, 29–30; Bengali culture and, 5–6, 160n25; bhut in, 7–9; in children's literature, 36–37, 116–17; class and caste structure in, 37–38, 74–77; colonialism and, 28–29, 112–13; folklore classifications by, 43; Ghose family and, 147; ghost of Gadkhali and, 98; goddesses and, 42; Hindu revivalism and, 151–54; life insurance adopted by, 128; magic and superstition in, 11; mesmerism and, 143; occult practices in, 56–64; past and present and, 51–54; political activism and, 72–74; science vs. occult in, 12, 55–57, 59–64; Scientific Spiritualism and, 70–72, 78–81, 130; social identity of, 23–26; storytellers and, 35–37; superstition criticized in, 76–81; Tantric Buddhism and, 78–79; Theosophy and, 5, 19, 64, 72, 74, 130, 144–45

Bharat Dharma Mahamaṇḍal, 152
Bharati (Tagore family journal), 30, 105
Bharatvarshiya Arya Dharma Pracharini Sabha, 151
Bhattacharya, Krishnakamal, 104
"Bhushundir Mathe" (Parashuram), 2
bhut (ghost): Beings as, 7–8; marriage of, 32; Roy's discussion of, 53–54; Scientific Spiritualism rejection of, 69–71, 78, 79–81; subaltern framing of, 43
bhutchcharan (bhut exorcism), 79–80
Bhut Petni (Mukhopadhyay), ii, 27–28, 33, 174n5
Bibhuti Vidya, 80
Bibidartha Ṣaṅgraha (1851), 22–26
Bidyabinod, Kshirod Prasad, 19, 59–63, 66–68, 70–71
birth: colonial statistics on, 101; of ghosts, 34–35
Birth and Death Registration Act of 1873, 94, 101
Bishi, Pramathanath, 117
Blavatsky, Helena Petrovna, 137–39, 141–42, 147–49, 152
Bose, Bhupendranath, 71
Bose, Rashbihari, 11
Boyle, Robert, 63
Brahmadaitya: in Bengali folk tales, 45; Bhadralok criticism of, 78; Mitra's description of, 27; in Mukhopadhyay's ghost tales, 34–35; Roy's discussion of, 53–54; in Tagore's writing, 1–4, 6, 11–13, 23, 37, 106; tree as home of, 84

Brahmanic Hinduism: Bengal multireligious culture and, 38–45; death and afterlife in, 67–69, 89–90; execution exemptions and, 88–89; goddesses in, 44–45; science and, 60–61, 66–67; *sraddha* (bereavement) ceremonies and, 124; supernatural and, 19–21, 59–64
Brahmo movement, 12, 55, 57–58, 76–77, 122–23, 148, 150–51. *See also* Hinduism, revivalist movement in
Bandyopadhyay, Panchkori, 119–20
Brantlinger, Patrick, 132, 159n4
British folklore: classification of, 43; fairies in, 43
British Indian Association, 23, 147
British National Association of Spiritualists, 183n37
Britten, Emma Hardinge, 143
Buddhism: afterlife in, 68; in Bengal, 38
Burdwan fever, 100
bureaucratic practices, Theosophy and, 153–54
Burning Ghat Committee, 94
Burra Bazar Literary Club, 76
business: ghosts' involvement in, 33–35; Scientific Spiritualism and, 71–72

Calcutta: British and Bengali accounts of, 84–88; colonial sanitation reforms in, 91–93, 175n28; Victoria Memorial in, 96
Calcutta Psychical Society, 5
Campbell, John, 131
capitalism: British colonialism and, 29; labor and, 10–11, 103–4; modernity and, 13–17, 161n35; Protestantism and, 13; science and, 132–33; spatiality and, 90; spiritualism and, 10–11; supernatural literature and, 108–9; uncanny and, 9–10
caste: in Bengali culture, 11, 26; Scientific Spiritualism and, 62–64, 70–71, 79–81, 171n23; Theosophy and, 144–45
Chakrabarti, Kshetrapal, 145–46
Chakrabarti, Kunal, 42–43
Chakrabarty, Dipesh, 17, 74
Chandimangal, 33

charak festival, 35
Chatterjee, Partha, 58, 114, 125–27, 153–54
Chatterjee, Sanjib Chandra, 147
Chatterji, Ramananda, 12
Chattopadhyay, Bankimchandra, 46, 55, 58, 69–70, 75–77, 125, 144, 147
Chattopadhyay, Ramankrishna, 79
Chattopadhyay, Rasikmohan, 79–80
Chattopadhyay, Sanjib Chandra, 144
Chaudhurani, Sarala Devi, 72–74, 140–41
Chaukidars, 101–4
Chelebela (Tagore), 1–2, 84
Chevers, Norman, 102–3
children's literature: banning of ghosts in, 11–12; Beings in, 9; ghosts in, 36–37; supernatural in, 111–19
Chowdhury, Girish Chandra Roy, 147
Chowdhury, Upendrakishore Roy, 112
Christian Literature Society of Madras, 136
civic-public, colonial concept of, 124–28
civil courts, colonial-Hindu controversy over, 88–89, 174n17
class: in Bengali culture, 11, 26; Bhadralok elite and role of, 145–46; British colonialism and, 28–29; formation in Bengal of, 74–75; Scientific Spiritualism and, 62–64, 70–71, 74–77, 79–81; storytellers and, 36–37; Theosophy and, 144–45
Clery, E. J., 9, 108
Cockrell, F. R., 92
Cohn, Bernard, 177n14
colonialism: Bengali culture and, 11–18; bereavement and impact of, 125–29; British ghosts and, 83–84, 131–33; capitalism and, 17; census taking under, 99–104, 177n14; childhood and, 35–37; death regulations and mortuary practices under, 88–95, 98–104, 175n21; epidemic policies under, 98–104; fear and, 156–57; Hindu nationalism and, 65; Hindu reformism and, 151; illusion of permanence and, 96, 176n45; Indian literature and, 28–29; magic and, 133–36; multifaith culture of Bengal and, 39–40; Orientalism and, 133; reason and unreason and, 9–10;

INDEX   205

colonialism (continued)
  rojas and, 50–51; Scientific Spiritualism and, 58–59, 71–72, 75–77; spatiality and, 82–83, 175n32; spiritualism and, 19–21; state structure and, 124–29; statistical data under, 98–104; Tantric Buddhism and, 80–81; temporality and, 14–16; Theosophy and, 139–42, 147–50
commodity fetishism, capitalism and, 160n22
common sense, folklore linked to, 30
Cooper, Lewis, 131
Cotton, H. E. A., 83
Cousins, Margaret, 141
criminal courts, colonial-Hindu controversy over, 88–89, 174n17, 175n21
Crooke, William, 8, 28, 132

dakini, 36–37, 43–45, 84
Darwinian evolution, Hinduism and, 76–77
Das, Krishna Ram, 38
Das, Manik Chandra, 36
Das, Sisir Kumar, 113
Datta, Hirendranath, 63, 66, 146, 171n25
Davidson, Neil, 153–54
Day, Lal Behari, 26–27, 29–30, 36
death: Brahmanic afterlife and, 67–68; colonial governance of, 88–95, 98–104; communication with dead, 55–56; of ghosts, 34–35; history and spatiality and, 82–83; indigenous cartographies of, 91; modernization of, 93–94; mourning and, 119–23; science and, 5–6; spectacularization of, 120–21, 124–29; statistical enumeration of, 100–104; Victorian mortuary practices and, 94–95
Deb, Chandra Sekhar, 148
Deb, Nabakrishna, 120–22
Deb, Shibchandra, 75
Debi, Gourmoni, 78
Debi, Maitreyi, 5
decline thesis of magic, 17–18
demons: ghosts and, 40–45; goddesses as, 44–45
Derrett, J. M., 175n20

Devi, Swarnakumari, 72–73, 140–41
Dhaka Gazette, 65
Dictionary of Superstitions, 98
Dixon, Joy, 140
domestic space, ghosts in, 84–88
Doyle, Arthur Conan, 135
Dube, Saurabh, 160n23
Duff, Alexander, 29, 60, 170n14
Durga, 47; ghosts and, 40–41
Durkheim, Emile, 12
Dutt, R. C., 125
Dutta, Akshaykumar, 58–59, 151–52
Dutta, Michael Madhusudan, 9

Edmonds, John W., 57
education: Bengali campaign for, 64–65; caste/class exclusions in, 74; English-educated Bhadralok elite and, 26, 76–77, 125–29; impact on spiritualism of, 9; science education campaign, 59–60, 170n14
Education Gazette, 59
ekal (present), 51–54
ekanore (ghost), 109
electrotherapy, 63–64
Elliot, Robert Henry, 133
English children in India, ghost stories and, 37
English literature: supernatural in, 108–9; Victorian Gothic literature, 6, 84–85
Englishman newspaper, 65
Enlightenment: Bhadralok identity with, 23–24; Brahmanic Hinduism and, 61
Epidemic Fevers Commission, 100
epidemics, colonial statistics on, 99–104, 177n14
Esdaile, James, 143
European ghosts: colonialism in India and, 131–33; Indian ghosts vs., 24; modernity and nostalgia and, 12–13; Supernatural Science and, 63–64
executions, Hindu-colonial controversy over, 88–89
exorcism: *rojas* and, 47–51; Scientific Spiritualism and, 79–80

Fabian, Johannes, 14–15
fairies: in British literature, 43; supernatural Beings and, 63
Farquhar, John N., 46, 142
fear: aestheticization of, in Tagore's stories, 108, 156; structure of feeling and, 156–57
Febvre, Lucien, 9
female sexuality, ghosts and fear of, 42
Fergusson, Robert, 13
fire walking, 135
First World War, memory-making about, 6–7
folk belief: Indian culture and, 28–29; Scientific Spiritualism and, 69–70
Folk Literature of Bengal (Sen), 47
Folk-Lore Society (London), 28
Folk Tales of Bengal (Day), 30
Foucault, Michel, 43, 100–101, 114, 123
fraud: Bengali ghosts and, 46–47; magic linked to, 133–34
Frazer, James, 11–12
freemasonry, 73–74, 142–43
Freud, Sigmund, 3, 84, 135
funeral rituals: in Brahmanic Hinduism, 89–90; for ghosts, 34

Gadkhali ghost, 98, 100
Gate, Williams, 131
Geertz, Hildred, 17
gender: in ghost stories, 119; Theosophy and, 139–42, 183n37
General Theory of Magic, A (Mauss), 12
General Assembly's Institution, 29, 60, 170n16
Ghose, Motilal, 71, 100, 146
Ghose, Mrinal Kanti, 56, 71, 143, 146, 148
Ghose, Shishir Kumar, 56, 64–71, 74, 142–50, 154
Ghosh, Kaliprasanna, 70
Ghosh, Kallimohan, 72
Ghosh, Manmathanath, 62
Ghosh, Motilal, 100
Ghosh, Nagendranath, 121
Ghosh, Ramgopal, 92–93

ghosts: Beings as, 7–8; in Bengali literature, 6, 84–88, 130–31; British colonialism and, 83–84, 87, 131–33; caste and class hierarchies for, 70–71; colonial governance of death and, 98–104, 130; gods' interchangeability with, 39–45; harmlessness of, 31–35; history of, 10; literary worlds of, 104–6; Mitra's discussion of, 22–24; modern vs. premodern distinction, 6–7, 23–29, 55–56, 108–11; old and new, 51–54, 79–81, 105–9, 117–19; science and, 18–21; sociality of fear and, 156–57; in Tagore's short stories, 105–6; traditional (premodern) ghosts, 26–29
Gladstone, William, 135
goddesses, ghosts and, 43–45
Golden Bough, The (Frazer), 12
Gothic literature, ghosts and, 84–85, 119, 132–33
Goudiya Samaj, 149
Govinda Samanta or the History of a Bengal Raiyat (Day), 26–27, 29
Gramsci, Antonio, 30
Great Britain: agnostic malaise, in post-Darwinian period, 136; Bhadralok elite and influence of, 23–24; birth and death records in, 104; ghosts in, 131–33; Gothic literature in, 6, 84–85, 132–33; images of India in, 133–36; mortuary practices in, 94–95; Scientific Spiritualism in, 63–64
Greenberger, Allen J., 134
grief. *See* mourning
Grierson, George, 28
Gunfounder, John Campbell, 64, 181n3
gunins, 39, 45–46, 48–51, 78
Gupta, Binodbihari, 71
Gupta, Ishwar Chandra, 169n8

Hacking, Ian, 99
Haitian Revolution, 162n43
hakini, 43–45
Harvey, David, 90
Hastings, Warren, ghost of, 83, 131–32, 174n16

haunting: history and spatiality and, 82–83; spatiality and, 10
Heber, Reginald (Bishop), 89
heimlich, spectralization of, 84
Hinduism: Bengali multifaith culture and, 38–45; colonial sanitation reforms and, 92–93; nationalism and, 58–59, 65, 72; revivalist movement in, 58–64, 116–23, 151–54, 170n16; Scientific Spiritualism and, 58–64, 69–70; Theosophy and, 137–38. *See also* neo-Hinduism
Hindu Mela, 29–30, 151
Hindu Patriot, 148
Hindu Spiritual Magazine (HSM), 55, 65–66, 79–80, 144, 146, 148–49
history: British colonialism and, 29; capitalism and, 17; memory vs., 128–29; sanitation of death and erasure of, 95; Scientific Spiritualism and, 130–31; spatiality and, 82–83
Hitabadi, 105
homeopathy, spiritualism and, 143–44
Hudum Deo, 7
Human Atmosphere or the Aura Made Visible by the Aid of Chemical Screens, The (Kilner), 63–64
human world, ghosts and, 23, 31–35
humor, in Indian ghost stories, 114–15, 117–19
Hunter, William W., 48, 78, 102, 112, 132
Hutchins, Francis, 96, 176n45
Hutom Penchar Naksha, 46

Ilbert Bill controversy, 65
incantations, multifaith roots of, 49–51
Indian Association for the Cultivation of Science (IACS), 76–77
Indian High Court Act of 1861, 89
Indian Insurance Companies Act (1928), 128
Indian League, 148
Indian Life Assurance Companies Act (1912), 128
Indian literature: children's literature, 8–9, 11–12, 36–37; colonialism in, 28–29;

colonial policies and, 28–29; colonial policies in, 28–29; fairies in, 43; ghosts in, 6, 84–88, 104–6; listening to, 25; supernatural in, 106–11. *See also specific stories and authors*
Indian Mirror, 77, 149–50
Indian National Congress (INC), 23, 130–31, 147
indigenous cultures: magic and supernatural practices in, 20–21; spiritualism in, 9
Indo-European language family, 39–40
insurance business, in India, 128
Isaacs, Alice, 141
Isis Unveiled (Blavatsky), 137–38
Islam, Bengali storytelling and, 38–45

Jacob, Margaret, 73–74
Jainism, 68
Janmabhoomi, 118
Jarasura (Fever Demon), 47
Jayadeva (medieval poet), 127
Jayawardena, Kumari, 142
Jinarajadasa, C., 139–40
Jinarajadasa Graham, Dorothy, 140–41
Josephson-Storm, Jason A., 43
Judge, William Quran, 140
Jugini, 41
Jung, Carl, 135

Kali, 40–41, 44
Kaliyug, 51
Kamakhya (goddess), 42, 47
Kankabati, 112–14, 116–77
"Kankal" (The Skeleton) (Tagore), 105–10
kapalik sect, 46, 78
kapal-kriya (rite of the skull), 94
Kapalkundala (Chattopadhyay), 46
Kandhakata, 7
Kaviraj, Girijaprasanna Sen, 61–62
Kaviraj, Sudipta, 58
Kavyavisharad, Kaliprasanna, 105
Kedarnath De, Mrs., 36
Khan, Dayab, 80

Kilner, Walter J., 63–64
Kincaid, C. A., 132
kinship, of ghosts, 3, 24, 32–34
Kipling, Rudyard, 87, 95–96
Kirk, Robert, 63
Koselleck, Reinhart, 14–15
Krishna, 47
Ksemananda, 49
Kurmis, 44–45
Kwon, Heonik, 7, 40, 159n10

labor: in Bengali culture, 32–33; capitalism and, 10–11, 103–4
Lahiri, Ramtanu, 169n95
Lambert, Andrew, 40
Lamont, Peter, 134
Lang, Andrew, 135
language, Bengali ghost stories and role of, 39–40
Lefebvre, Henri, 90–91, 96
Limodine chemical, 60
Liotard, L., 145
literacy rates, in colonial Bengal, 25
literature: Bhadralok elite and production of, 144–45. *See* children's literature; English literature; Indian literature
location, history and, 82–83, 90–95
London Association for the Prevention of Premature Burials (LAPPB), 94–95
London Spiritualist, 4
Luckhurst, Roger, 1
Lukacs, Georg, 174n9
Lutyens, Emily, 140

Madge, E. W., 132
Madras Mail, 135
magic: in Bengali culture, 76–77; ghosts and, 12; modernity and, 18, 160n23; science and, 12, 133–36; secular decline of, 17–18
Magic, Science and Religion (Malinowski), 12
Majumdar, Barodakanta, 173n78
Majumdar, Dakshinaranjan Mitra, 115
Majumdar, Lila, 112
Malabari, Behramji, 149

Malinowski, Bronislaw, 12
mamdo and *mamdi*, 45
Manasa, 47
Manasa Mangal, 49
Mangal Kavyas, 40–41
marriage, by ghosts, 34
Marx, Karl, 10–11, 123, 127, 160n22
Masik Patrika, 145
Maskelyne, John Nevil, 133–34
Masonic Lodge. *See* freemasonry
Massey, Doreen, 97
Mauss, Marcel, 12
McCorristine, Shane, 134–35
McNally, David, 10–11
memories and memorialization, mourning and, 119–23, 128–29
Merton, Robert, 13–14
mesmerism, 141, 143
Meugens, J. G., 143–45, 184n53
Milton, John, 144
Mitra, Dinabandhu, 132, 147, 181n5
Mitra, Raja Digambar, 56
Mitra, Rajendralal: on European vs. Indian ghosts, 24; on humans and ghosts, 34–35; literary production and political activism of, 22–23; on supernatural and ghosts, 22–26; on traditional ghosts and authentic roots, 26–29
Mitra, Sarat Chandra, 50
Mitter, Raj Krishna, 144, 147
Mittra, Peary Chand: Bhadralok elite and, 97, 145–46; family and friends of, 147, 184n56; Indian nationalism and, 147–48; occultism and, 56–57; Scientific Spiritualism and, 4–6, 75, 142–46; Theosophy and, 145–46; writing by, 149
modernity: Bengali culture and, 11–12, 160n24; capitalism and, 13–17, 161n35; death and, 93–94; European nostalgia and, 12–13; neo-Hinduism and, 153–54; non-Western forms of, 15–16; science and, 5; Scientific Spiritualism and, 71–72; sources of, 162n44; temporality and, 14–15; uncanny and, 84; Weber on, 13
Montagu, Edwin, 142

mortality: Bengali rate of, 95–96; colonial statistics on, 99–104
mortuary practices: Hindu rituals, 90–94; in Victorian Britain, 94–95
mother goddess worship, 42–43
mourning: in colonial public sphere, 125–29; festivals and, 124–29; Hindu revivalism and, 119–23
Mukherjee, Purna, 94
Mukerji, S. C., 83
Mukhopadhyay, Ashutosh, 27–28, 30–35, 174n5
Mukhopadhyay, Bhudev, 59–60, 75, 170n10
Mukhopadhyay, Troilakyanath, 111–19
Mukul, 12
Mullick, Gosto Behary, 76
multifaith culture, Bengali ghost stories and, 37–45, 49–51
Muslims: Bhadralok Islamophobia and, 76; British colonialism and, 76–77; as cultural mediators, 38–39, 47–48; as *ojhas*, 47; as publishers and editors, 47; Tantric practices and, 80; uprising of 1857 and, 28. *See also* Islam
Myth of the Mystic East (Elliot), 133

Nabi Vamsa, 38
Nabajiban, 59, 70
National Baby Week (1924), 141
nationalism: fear in, 156–57; Hindu revival of, 58–59, 65; Scientific Spiritualism and, 71–72, 130–31, 147–54, 171n25; Theosophy in India and, 136–37, 146–54. *See also* anticolonial movement
nature: premodern spiritualism and concepts of, 9; spiritualism and, 58–59
Nayalankar, Ramjay, 94
neo-Hinduism: revivalist movement and, 116–20, 151–54, 170n16; Scientific Spiritualism and, 59–64; Theosophy and, 142–45, 150–54
Nil Darpan (Mitra), 132, 181n5
Noakes, Richard, 63
Nora, Pierre, 128–29
Nuttall, Sarah, 97

occultism: anticolonial internationalism and, 72–73; rise Bhadralok culture of, 12, 55–56; science and, 5–6, 19–21; Theosophy and, 138, 142–45, 147–49
occupied space, work/product distinction in, 90–91
ojhas: magic of, 45–51; training schools for, 48–49
Olaichandi, 40
Olcott, Henry Steel, 137–38, 140–41, 147–49, 152
Oldenburg, Veena, 92
Ollman, Bertell, 103–4
Ong, Walter, 48
"On the Belief in Bhutas" (Walhouse), 45
On the Soul: Its Nature and Development (Mittra), 57
oppressed, Theosophy and, 138–42
oral culture in India: colonialism and, 28–29; community building and, 48–51; listening to literature and, 25
Orientalism: Anglicanism and, 60, 170n14; colonial stereotyping and, 75–77; European scholarship on India and, 24, 28–29, 133–36; Hindu science and, 58; Theosophy and, 138

Pandit, 72, 172n53
Paroloker Katha (Accounts of the Spirit World) (Ghose), 56
Pasha, Damat Ibrahim, 169n7
Pashukanis, Eugene, 124
Peasant Life in Bengal (Temple), 36
Pencho, 40
petni, 32, 34, 156
Petty, William, 99
phantom objectivity, 86, 174n10
phrenology, 143
Phukon, Haliram Dhekial, 42
pir, 38–39
planchettes, 4–6, 56, 72
political sociability, Scientific Spiritualism and, 72–74
poor, images in ghost stories of, 28, 31–35
Prabahini, 80

Prakash, Gyan, 5, 58
Prakrit, literature in, 47
Prakritik Vigyan (Mukhopadhyay), 170n10
precolonial Bengali literature: human-ghost connections in, 32–35, 69–70; multifaith culture and, 39–45
premodern spiritualism, 9
pret, 67, 70
Probasi, 12
Prochar, 59
"Prospectus for a Society for the Promotion of National Feeling among the Educated Natives of Bengal" (Basu), 58, 169n8
Protestantism: capitalism and, 13; decline of magic and, 17
Psychic Society (United Kingdom), 71
Psychological Society of Great Britain (PSGP), 134
public health, ghosts and, 47
public sphere: bereavement in, 125–29; colonialism and, 20, 125–29; Hindu reformism and, 151–54; religion in, 21
Puranic texts, 44–45; death and afterlife in, 68
Puri (pilgrimage city), colonial-Hindu controversy in, 88–89
Putnam, Hilary, 43

Quran, in Indian literature, 49–50

racism: colonialism and, 29; psychic research and, 135–36; Theosophy and, 139–42
Raimangal, 38
Ramos, Imma, 80
Ramtanu Lahiri O Tatkalin Banga Samaj (Shastri), 95, 169n95
Ray, Satyajit, 181n5
reality, enumeration of death and, 103–4
reason: divine and, 58–59; Roy's discussion of, 53–54
rebirth, Hindu idea of, 67–69, 75
religion: Bengali multifaith culture and, 38–45; caste miscegenation and, 37–38; ghosts and, 12; magic and, 17–18; modernity and, 20–21; science and, 59–64; Theosophy and, 142–45; violence and, 21
Religion in the Primitive Culture (Tylor), 12
Ren, Jianto, 40
Richet, Charles, 135
Rig Veda, 68
Risley, Herbert, 39–40, 43–44, 78, 132
Rodenbeck, Max, 97
rojas, 39, 45, 47–51, 69, 78
rope trick, 136
Roy, Bangachandra, 94
Roy, Bharatchandra, 41, 44–45
Roy, Gopaul Chunder, 100
Roy, Kartikeya Chandra, 47, 51–55, 106
Roy, Raja Baroda Kanto, 147–49
Roy, Rammohan, 119, 148, 151–52, 156
Royal Asiatic Society, 125
Royal Society, 13

Sadhana, 105, 113
Sadharani, 72
Sahitya Parishat Patrika, 30
Sahlins, Marshall, 7
Said, Edward, 133
Sakhi Samiti, 141
samaj, 127–29
"Samajik Prabhandha" (Mukhopadhyay), 59
Samajpati, Suresh Kumar, 105
sanitation reform, colonial imposition of, 92–95
Saraswati, Dayanand, 152–53
Sarkar, Akshay Chandra, 69–70, 72, 123
Sarkar, Sumit, 51, 80
sati, abolition of, 149
Satthianadhan, Samuel, 136–37
Satya Pir, 38
Scalmer, Sean, 134
science: campaign for education in, 64–65, 76–77, 170nn9–10; European capitalism and, 13, 132–33; ghosts and, 12, 18–21; Hinduism and, 19–21; modernization and, 5, 12–13, 20–21; Protestantism and, 13; psychic research and, 134–35; supernatural and, 57–64; Tantric traditions and, 145–46, 173n78

Scientific Spiritualism: Bengali culture and, 6; Bhadralok elite and, 70–72, 78–81, 130; business and politics and, 72–73; in children's stories, 111–19; class and caste and, 62–64, 70–71, 74–77; death and afterlife and, 20–21, 68–69; Hinduism and, 80–81; nationalism and, 71–72, 130–31, 147–49, 171n25; neo-Hinduism and, 142; occult practices and, 56–57; old and new ghosts and, 78–81; social networks for, 72–74; Theosophy and, 138, 144–45, 147–50. *See also* spiritualism

séances, 6, 19, 56–58, 71–73, 75, 78–79, 143–46

seclusion, Hindu grief and role of, 125–29

secularism, Theosophy in India and, 152–53

Segal, Robert, 9

"Sekal ar Ekal" (Basu lecture), 51

Sen, Dinesh Chandra, 37, 47, 49, 78–80

Sen, Keshab Chandra, 56, 76, 149

Sen, Krishnabihari, 149–50

Sen, Nabin Chandra, 125–27

Sen, Narendranath, 149–50

Sen, Paritosh, 157

Sen, Ram Kamal, 149

Sen, Ramprasad, 70

sexuality, Tantric traditions and, 80

shankhchunni, 2, 7–8

Shastri, Shibnath, 12, 36–37, 43–44, 84, 94, 95, 169n95

shastric Hindu texts, 69–70, 78–81, 123–24

Shiva, 47; ghosts and, 40–41

Shobha Bazar, 120–21

Singha, Kaliprasanna, 25, 46

Singha, Radhika, 175n21

Sircar, Mahendralal, 76–77

Sircar, Munshi Enayetulla, 47–48, 50–51

Sitala, 40, 41–42, 44

Smith, Adam, 108

sociality: Bengali formation of, 72–74; spatiality and, 90–91, 97–98; *sraddah* (bereavement) ceremonies and, 124–29; Theosophy and, 142–45

social justice campaigns, Bengali advocacy for, 65

Society for Psychical Research (SPR), 131, 134–35

Society for the Acquisition of General Knowledge, 147–48

Somprakash, 77–78, 92–94, 128

sorrow, death and, 119–23

sovereignty, sociality and, 127–29

spatiality: capitalism and, 90; colonialism and, 82–83, 175n31; of death, 89–90; domestic space, hauntings in, 84–88; haunting and, 10; social relations and, 90–91, 97–98; temporality and, 96

spirit photography, 19

spiritualism: after First World War, 6–7; Bengali civil society and, 153; in Calcutta, 4–5; capitalism and, 10–11; Hindu nationalism and, 19–21, 58; indigenous versions of, 9; modern forms of, 18–19; science linked to, 57; Theosophy and, 138, 143–45. *See also* occult practices; Scientific Spiritualism

Spiritual Stray Leaves, 4

sraddha, 67–68, 119–29

Sramanic traditions, *sraddhas* and, 124

state: fear and role of, 156–57; in precolonial India, 127–29

statistics: colonialism and, 99–104; modernity and, 104

Stevenson, Robert Louis, 135

structure of feeling, fear and, 156–57

Subrahmanyam, Sanjay, 162n46

Sugita Genpaku, 169n7

supernatural: Bengali rejection of, 11–12; in children's literature, 111–19; in Europe and North America, 24; European exploration of, 63–64; in literature, 106–11; premodern concepts of, 9; science and, 57–64; in Tagore's short stories, 105–11; validation of, 61–64

superstition: in Bengali culture, 76–77; ghosts and, 12

Swarnamoyee, Maharani, 149

Tagore, Abanindranath, 37, 39, 82, 94
Tagore, Debendranath, 1, 58, 71, 121–23, 127, 151–52
Tagore, Dwarkanath, 1, 121–22
Tagore, Dwijendranath, 104
Tagore, Maharaja Sir Jyotindramohan, 66
Tagore, Rabindranath: anticolonial internationalism and, 72–73; autobiography of, 2–3, 84; *Bharati* family journal and, 30; Brahmadaitya priest and, 2–4; Chattopadhyay and, 125; Dutta and, 146; early life and education, 1–2; family of, 1; ghosts in literature of, 104–6; on kinship of ghosts, 34–35; on modernity and disenchantment, 11–14, 18; on public sphere, 127–28; on *samaj*, 126; on scientific research, 77; stories by, 84–85, 104–11, 155–56, 178n31; on Theosophy, 5; Theosophy and, 141; Visva-Bharati university founded by, 171n25
Tagore family: history of, 1–2; occult practices in, 56; Spiritualism and Theosophy and, 150, 153–54
Tambiah, Stanley J., 43
Tantric traditions: Bhadralok practice of, 38, 78–81; goddesses and, 44–45; magic and, 45–51; science linked to, 173n78; Theosophy and, 145–46
tantrik, 45–51
Tattabodhini Patrika, 58–59
Taussig, Michael, 11, 160n22
Taylor, Charles, 152
technical education, Bengali campaign for, 64–65
Temple, Richard C., 28, 36, 64, 181n3
temporality: British colonialism and, 29; modernity and, 14–15; postcolonial scholarship on, 15–16; spatiality and, 96, 97–98
Tennyson, Alfred (Lord), 135
Thakurani Mai, cult of, 43
Theosophist journal, 139–40, 145
Theosophy: An Appeal to My Countrymen (Satthianadhan), 136–37

Theosophy and the Theosophical Society, 5, 19, 64, 72, 74, 130; Bhadralok elite and, 145–50; bureaucratic practices and, 153–54; colonialism and, 136; founding of, 137–38; in India, 136–38; Mittra and, 145–46; nationalism in India and, 136–37, 146–50; neo-Hinduism and, 142–45, 150–54; social milieu of, 142–45
Thomas, Keith, 17–18
Thompson, Edward, 131
Thompson, E. P., 17–18
Thompson, George, 148
tiger ghosts, 40
traditional (premodern) ghosts: business activities of, 33–35; Mitra's description of, 26–27; mortality rates and, 95–96; Mukhopadhyay's description of, 27–29; multifaith culture of Bengal and, 39–45; worldview of, 30–35
transcendentalism, 7
trees, as ghost domiciles, 84
Trivedi, Ramendrasundar, 76–77
Tylor, Edward, 9, 12

uncanny: in Bengali culture, 3; colonialism and, 159n4; Freudian concept of, 3, 84; modern discourse of, 9–10
United Association of Spiritualists (UAS), 143, 149
United States: Islamophobia in, 153; Theosophy in, 143, 146
universal, capitalism and, 17–18
Upanishads, 68; Hindu reformism and, 151
Uprising of 1857, 28–29, 89, 92, 176n46

Vaishnavism, 71, 150
Vedas/Vedanta: Brahmanism and, 68, 122; death and afterlife and, 68–69, 124; Gupta on, 169n8; Hindu reformism and, 151–52, 185n74; nature and, 59
Vernacular Literature Society, 25–26
Victoria Memorial (Calcutta), 96
Vidyabhushan, Dwarkanath, 77–78
Vidyapati (medieval poet), 127
Vidyaratna, Srish Chandra, 147

INDEX 213

Vidyasagar, Isvar Chandra, 75, 78, 119, 147, 184n56
Vidyasundar, 41
Vietnam: ghosts and, 7, 159n10; religious figures in, 40
violence, capitalism and, 11
Vishwa Hindu Parishad, 152
Visva-Bharati university, Tagore's founding of, 171n25
voluntary organizations, nationalist politics and, 73–74, 147, 184n62
voting rights, women's campaign for, 142

Walhouse, M. J., 45
Wallerstein, Emmanuel, 147
Weatherly, Lionel, 133

Weber, Max, 13, 123
Wellesley, Marquis, 88
white men, ghosts in narratives of, 131
Williams, Monier, 67–68
Williams, Raymond, 156–57
Wimbridge, Edward, 149
Winter, Jay, 6–7
women: in Bengali culture, 11, 51; feminist activist groups and, 72–74, 76–77, 172n64; ghosts as, 119; Theosophy and, 140–42
Women's Home of Service, 141
Women's Indian Association (WIA), 141–42

Yeats, W. B., 72–73, 138, 172n55
Young Bengal student movement, 145

www.ingramcontent.com/pod-product-compliance
Lightning Source LLC
Chambersburg PA
CBHW020837160426
43192CB00007B/692